You're Invited

st. anthony of padua school
east northport, n.y.

There is really no such thing as a book of entirely new and original recipes. Although the recipes in this book may not have all been kitchen tested, their merit has been established by families and friends. St. Anthony of Padua Mother's Guild, nor any contributor, publisher, printer, distributor or seller of this book is responsible for errors or omissions.

Copies of You're Invited may be obtained by addressing:

St. Anthony of Padua School
6 Fifth Avenue
East Northport, New York 11731

For your convenience, order blanks have been. included following the index.

First Edition
First Printing, 5,000 copies

St. Anthony of Padua School
East Northport, New York 11731

ISBN-0-9616243-0-2

Printed in the United States of America

Wimmer Brothers Books
P.O. Box 18408
Memphis, Tennessee 38181-0408

"Cookbooks of Distinction"™

YOU'RE INVITED COMMITTEE

CHAIRPERSONS

Eileen Rathgaber   Judy Hein

EDITORS

Judy Hein   Eileen Rathgaber

TYPISTS
CHAIRPERSONS

Vita Leggio   Diane Darmody

Helen Evancie
Rosemarie DeRosa
Alice Colloton
Carol Lourich
Kathryn Slaska

COVER AND ART WORK
Marguerite Mason

LAYOUT AND DESIGN
Judy Hein
Eileen Rathgaber
Marguerite Mason

A special thanks to Sister Jeannette Tenaglia, C.S.J., Principal, for her continued support and encouragement toward the publication of this book.

YOU'RE INVITED

It is with pleasure, that we dedicate this book to all the children who attend St. Anthony of Padua School. Without our students, the participation and interest of others in this endeavor would not have been possible, nor necessary. We "invite", you, our reader, to join us in thanking our children who have made their school one of which we can all be proud.

Through the interest, and generosity of our contributors; many hours of work, and unending support, we now are able to "invite" our reader to share the fruits of our efforts.

"You're Invited" to peruse these pages of family favorites and, hopefully, be able to expand your own personal kitchen cuisine.

Our families and children, ask you, our reader, to open your hearts, homes and tables, and extend to all the same invitation we give to you . . . . "You're Invited"!

TABLE OF CONTENTS

APPETIZERS 7

SOUPS AND SALADS 27

BREADS 45

VEGETABLES 55

CASSEROLES 71

MEATS 83

POULTRY 103

SEAFOOD 117

CAKES 127

COOKIES 151

DESSERTS 167

ETHNIC COOKING 189

KID'S KORNER 215

BEVERAGES, MICROWAVE, MISCELLANEOUS 229

FOR YOUR INFORMATION 241

INDEX 255

RECIPE FOR A HAPPY HOME

Put together in a house, either old or new, one mother, one father and as many children as Heaven will send. For added spice an animal or two will help. Mix very well with large quantities of love and devotion to God, School, Country, others and each other. Add equal amounts of patience and affection, understanding and kindness, helpfulness and cooperation, obedience and cleanliness, fun and laughter, friendliness and generosity. Slowly stir in just enough outside interests, both individually and collectively so that the major ingredients keep fresh and healthy in mind and body. Sprinkle in a small amount of tears and trials so that blessings will be appreciated.

Frost with joy and contentment. Let stand one lifetime on the good earth. Best results will be noted in family history, but immediate results will be tasted by all who come in contact with such a home from day to day.

Rosanne DeLassio

appetizers

APPETIZERS

ALMOND-PRUNE APPETIZERS
THE LIQUORED UP PRUNE

36 pitted prunes
36 whole almonds
18 slices bacon, halved

2 cups white or red wine or
cognac

Bring wine to boil. Drop prunes into boiling wine. Reduce heat at once and simmer until prunes are barely tender. Remove from heat and drain. Roast almonds in oven until golden brown. Stuff prunes with almonds.

Broil bacon for 5 to 10 minutes. Drain. Wrap bacon slices around prunes. Secure with toothpicks. May be refrigerated. To serve, broil prunes in oven until bacon is crisp. *Yield:* 3 dozen.

Edie Lyons

ARTICHOKE PIE

1 9 ounce package frozen
   artichoke hearts
4 eggs, beaten well
½ cup diced pepperoni
1 cup diced mozzarella

½ teaspoon pepper
½ teaspoon salt
¼ cup grated Romano cheese
1 9 inch frozen pie crust

Defrost pie crust. Pat dry artichokes and cut in half. Blend artichokes with eggs, pepperoni, mozzarella, salt, pepper and Romano cheese. Place in pie crust. Bake 45 minutes at 350 degrees.

Rosanne DeLassio

WRAPPED BREAD STICKS

1 package unseeded bread sticks
1 8 ounce package whipped
   cream cheese

½ pound Genoa salami, sliced

Spread cream cheese on salami and wrap around bread sticks. Chill for a few hours. Serve.

Ann Bardunias

8

EASY BUFFALO WINGS

1 to 2 dozen chicken wings   ½ cup hot sauce
1 cup butter, melted

Cut end tips off of chicken wings. Place in baking dish to fit. Bake chicken wings in 350 degree oven for 30 minutes. Drain and cool. Mix butter and hot sauce. Combine wings and marinade mixture. Refrigerate overnight. Before serving, broil marinated chicken wings for 5 minutes, turning once or twice. *Hot Stuff!*

The Committee

CHEESE BALL

2 8 ounce packages cream   2 or 3 teaspoons minced onion
    cheese, softened   ¼ cup chopped green pepper
1 8 ounce can crushed   1 cup chopped walnuts
    pineapple, drained

Mix cheese, pineapple, onion, green pepper and ½ cup walnuts. Cool overnight. Shape into a ball, and roll in remaining ½ cup of walnuts.

Janice Byrne

CREAM CHEESE BALLS

8 ounces cream cheese, softened   2½ ounce jar chipped beef,
2 tablespoons prepared   shredded fine
    horseradish

With a fork combine cheese with horseradish until blended. Shape into ¾ inch balls. Place chipped beef on waxed paper. Roll cheese balls in chipped beef. Arrange on plate. Cover and refrigerate ½ to 1 hour. Serve with cocktail picks. *Yield:* 2 dozen.

Helen Evancie

DELICIOUS CHOPPED CHICKEN LIVER

3 medium onions, coarsely
  chopped
4 hard boiled eggs
2 teaspoons salt
¼ teaspoon pepper
approximately ¼ cup chicken
  fat or

1 bouillon cube in ¼ cup water
  with melted margarine
1 pound chicken livers

Score chicken livers with sharp knife. Wash, drain and sprinkle lightly with salt. Broil livers for 3 to 5 minutes until cooked. Grind livers finely with onion and eggs. Add salt, pepper and chicken fat. Mix. Chill. Serve with crackers.

Carole Mahoney

BAKED CLAMS

½ cup Parmesan cheese
¼ cup chopped parsley
2 tablespoons oregano
1 tablespoon garlic powder
pepper, to taste

½ cup oil
1 cup flavored bread crumbs
paprika, for garnish
1 dozen clams, shucked, juice
  and shells reserved

Mix clams and juice in a bowl. Add ½ cup bread crumbs to absorb juice. Add ½ cup oil. Add remaining ingredients, except paprika. Stuff clam shells and sprinkle paprika on top. Bake at 375 degrees for 20 minutes.

Maureen Quinan

CLAM DIP

2 7 ounce cans of chopped
clams, reserve juice
1 large onion, chopped
½ cup butter or margarine,
melted

1 cup reserved clam juice
oregano, pinch
24 snack crackers, finely
crushed

Sauté onion in melted margarine. Add onions to clams, clam juice and oregano. Mix crushed crackers into clam mixture. Place in pie pan. Bake at 350 degrees for 30 minutes. Serve on crackers.

Mary Wallin

HOT CLAM DIP

2 7 ounce cans minced clams
and juice
¾ cup margarine
6 ounces crushed snack crackers
2 tablespoons minced onion
2 tablespoons chopped parsley

3 tablespoons lemon juice
1 tablespoon oregano
1 clove garlic, minced, optional
Parmesan cheese, to taste, for
garnish

Melt margarine. Mix with remaining ingredients. Add salt and pepper, if desired. Sprinkle with Parmesan cheese. Bake 20 to 30 minutes in a 350 degree oven. Can be prepared ahead and frozen.

Carol Lowrich

CLAM DIP

1 7 ounce can minced clams
½ cup butter or margarine,
melted
1 cup bread crumbs

1 clove garlic, crushed
½ teaspoon oregano
½ cup Parmesan cheese
1 tablespoon lemon juice

Sauté garlic in melted butter. Remove garlic. Add remaining ingredients to margarine. Stir and add enough water to make a moist mixture. Bake in oven proof dish at 350 degrees until bubbly. Delicious on crackers.

Barbara Butler

APPETIZERS

CLAM PIE

2 7 ounce cans minced clams,
  undrained
2 tablespoons lemon juice
1 cup butter
1 large onion, minced
½ green pepper, chopped
1 tablespoon chopped parsley
1 teaspoon garlic powder

1 teaspoon oregano
4 to 6 drops tabasco sauce
dash cayenne pepper
red pepper flakes, to taste
1 cup bread crumbs
Parmesan cheese, as needed
processed cheese, as needed

Simmer clams and liquid with lemon juice 10 minutes. In a large pan melt butter. Add all other ingredients and simmer until vegetables are soft, about 15 minutes. Add clams, lemon juice combination and bread crumbs. Mix and put in ovenproof serving dish. Top with sprinkle of Parmesan cheese; arrange slices of processed cheese on top. Bake at 400 degrees for 20 minutes. Serve with crackers.

The Committee

CLAM PIE

8 ounces canned clams, with
  liquid
1 onion, minced
1 green pepper, minced
1 clove garlic, minced
celery, minced, to taste

½ cup margarine
1 cup bread crumbs
¼ to ½ cup Parmesan cheese
lemon juice, for garnish
onion crackers, as needed

Simmer can of clams about 10 minutes in liquid. Sauté onions, green pepper, garlic, celery and margarine until brown. Stir clams, bread crumbs, Parmesan cheese and all vegetables together. Mixture should be moist. Line pie plate with ingredients and broil until bubbly. Sprinkle with fresh lemon juice and serve with onion crackers.

Claudia Schappért

BAKED CLAMS

¼ cup plain bread crumbs
1 teaspoon garlic powder
1 tablespoon chopped onion
1 teaspoon chopped parsley
salt and pepper, to taste

2 tablespoons olive oil
grated cheese, to taste
1 7 ounce can minced clams and juice

Sauté garlic, onion, parsley and bread crumbs in oil for 2 minutes. Mix clams, juice, salt and pepper with sautéed mixture. Put into real or store bought shells. Sprinkle cheese on top. Bake at 375 degrees for 25 to 30 minutes. *Yield:* 1 dozen.

Betty Ingalls

CLAM SPREAD

3 6½ ounce cans chopped clams, with juice
1½ cups flavored bread crumbs
1 tablespoon oregano
2 tablespoons chopped parsley

1 tablespoon lemon juice
1 cup chopped onion
½ cup butter
1 cup grated cheese, of choice
2 to 3 cloves garlic, minced

Sauté onion and garlic in butter until soft. Mix first 5 ingredients in bowl. Add sautéed mixture. Mix well by hand. Put in large pie plate. Sprinkle with grated cheese. Serve with crackers.

Marion Guilfoy

CRABMEAT APPETIZER

6 ounces crabmeat
1 jar sharp Cheddar cheese spread
½ cup butter

1½ teaspoons mayonnaise
½ teaspoon garlic
1 package English muffins, halved

Mix cheese, butter, mayonnaise and garlic in processor. Blend in crabmeat with spoon. Mix thoroughly. Spread on English muffin halves, cut into bite size pieces. Place on broiler pan. Broil until bubbly and light brown. *Note:* Not too long, crabmeat dries out!

Angel Byrnes

APPETIZERS

CRABMEAT MOLD

1 10¾ ounce can cream of
   mushroom soup, undiluted
1 8 ounce package cream cheese,
   softened
1 small onion, chopped very fine
½ cup mayonnaise
¼ cup pimento, chopped fine

1 tablespoon sherry or lemon
   juice
2 6½ ounce cans crabmeat
1 envelope unflavored gelatin
   dissolved in ⅛ cup boiled
   water
celery, chopped, to taste

Slowly cook mushroom soup in saucepan. Add cream cheese, onion, celery, mayonnaise, pimento and sherry. Add shredded crabmeat. Finally, add gelatin. Make sure all ingredients are well blended. Pour into greased mold. Chill and set for 1 day.

Pat Whaley

#1 CRABMEAT SPREAD

½ pound flaked crabmeat
1 8 ounce package cream cheese
½ cup mayonnaise
3 tablespoons catsup

1 tablespoon dried onion flakes
¼ cup chopped dill pickle
½ teaspoon Worcestershire
   sauce

Blend and chill. Serve with crackers.

Jerilyn Cancelleire

HOT CRAB SPREAD

8 ounces cream cheese, softened
1 tablespoon milk
6 ounces canned crabmeat
2 tablespoons chopped onion

½ teaspoon horseradish
¼ teaspoon salt
⅓ cup sliced almonds
dash pepper

Blend softened cheese and milk. Add crab and onion, horseradish, salt and pepper. Blend well and spoon into oven proof dish. Sprinkle with almonds and bake at 375 degrees for 15 minutes. Spread on crackers.

Lucille Irving

14

ESCARGOTS

1 dozen snail shells	pinch garlic, minced
1 dozen canned snails	pinch salt
¼ cup butter	pinch shallots, minced
pinch parsley, minced	

Drain snails. Place each snail into its shell. Melt butter and add the remaining ingredients. Fill each snail shell with butter sauce. Place filled snail shells into oven at 350 degrees for 10 minutes. Serve hot.

Marilyn Cozzi

SWEET AND PUNGENT COCKTAIL FRANKS

1 8 ounce jar apricot preserves	2 packages cocktail franks
2 tablespoons prepared mustard	

Mix preserves and mustard to make a thick sauce. Cook franks in boiling water. Drain. Place franks and sauce in chafing dish or fondue pot. Heat and serve.

Rosanne DeLassio

GUAMANIAN CHEESE CANAPES

Note: This recipe is for a canape which I think is a little different. It is fairly simple and very good, but I must admit it doesn't look too appetizing until it is completely finished. Don't give up on it. You'll be pleasantly surprised. A member of my family has fondly nicknamed them "Polish Pizzas".

6 English muffins, split	½ cup mayonnaise
1 6 ounce can pitted, ripe olives	½ teaspoon salt
¼ cup sliced green onions	½ teaspoon curry powder
2 cups grated sharp Cheddar cheese	½ teaspoon chili powder

Heat oven to 325 degrees. Arrange muffin halves on baking sheet. Put drained olives in blender for 1 or 2 seconds then mix with rest of ingredients in a bowl. Spread evenly on muffins and bake for 15 minutes. Then broil until bubbly. To serve, cut each muffin into quarters. May be frozen until ready to serve, and then broiled.

Barbara Brennan

APPETIZERS

GRAPE APPETIZERS

large amount seedless grapes
3 8 ounce packages cream
  cheese, softened

1 to 2 cups slivered almonds,
  toasted

Wash and dry grapes. Split grapes lengthwise and stuff with cream cheese. Dip the stuffed grapes in the slivered almonds. Serve. *Everyone loves them!*

Paula Duggan

GUACOMOLI DIP

2 ripe avocados
1 tablespoon finely chopped
  onion
1 tablespoon lemon juice

1 teaspoon salt
¼ teaspoon chili powder
⅓ cup mayonnaise
nacho chips, for serving

Mix avocados, onion, lemon juice, salt and chili powder in a small bowl. Spread ⅓ cup mayonnaise over the top. Chill. Mix when ready to serve. Serve with nacho chips.

Pat Rayfield

CHOPPED LIVER AND EGGS

½ to 1 pound chicken livers
2 hard cooked eggs, shelled
2 slices bacon, crisply fried,
  optional
1 small onion, chopped fine

curry powder, to taste
celery salt, to taste
pepper and salt, to taste
2 tablespoons mayonnaise,
  mixed with a little milk

Sauté or boil chicken livers in a sauce pan in small amount of water. Mash livers, eggs, bacon together. Add seasonings to taste in small amounts. Add mayonnaise and milk till spreadable. Chill. Serve with crackers.

Kathy Turnbull

HERB DIP

1 cup mayonnaise
½ cup sour cream
1 teaspoon crushed mixed herbs
   of choice
¼ teaspoon salt

½ teaspoon curry powder
2 tablespoons chopped parsley
1½ teaspoons lemon juice
½ teaspoon Worcestershire
   sauce

Blend all ingredients together and chill. Good with raw vegetables.

Jan Guidotti

QUICHE LORRAINE

1 9 inch frozen pie shell
4 eggs
1 pint heavy cream (half and
   half or milk may be used)

1 cup grated Swiss cheese
1 cup shredded ham or bacon
   slices, fried, optional
1 can french fried onions

Beat the eggs and heavy cream together. Place french fried onions in bottom of pie shell. Add grated Swiss cheese, and ham or bacon, if desired. Pour egg mixture over Swiss cheese and poke holes in cheese. Bake 10 minutes at 425 degrees; then lower to 350 degrees. Bake 35 more minutes. Let sit for at least ½ hour before serving. Can be frozen.

Linda J. Candia

STUFFED MUSHROOMS

mushrooms, as needed
1 6½ ounce can minced clams,
   use juice
1 cup bread crumbs
½ tablespoon parsley flakes
1 tablespoon oregano

½ cup butter, melted
Parmesan cheese, as desired
salt, to taste
pepper, to taste
garlic powder, to taste

Preheat oven to 350 degrees. Mix together all ingredients and stuff mushrooms. Bake 15 minutes.

Rose Frey

APPETIZERS

OLIVE CHEESE BALL

1 8 ounce package cream cheese, softened
8 ounces bleu cheese
¼ cup butter

⅓ cup chopped walnuts
⅔ cup well drained, chopped ripe olives
1 tablespoon snipped chives

Blend cream cheese, bleu cheese and butter. Stir in the chopped olives and the snipped chives. Chill slightly; form into a ball. Chill well. Press ⅓ cup chopped walnuts over ball. Serve with assorted crackers. *Yield:* 3 cups.

Terry Laria

TOASTED ONION CANAPES

20 bread rounds or party rye
¾ cup minced onion
½ cup mayonnaise

¼ cup grated Parmesan cheese
bacon bits, optional

Set oven to broil. Place bread rounds on baking sheet and toast one side under broiler until golden brown. Mix onion, mayonnaise, cheese, and bacon bits. Spread on untoasted side of bread. Broil 3 inches from heat for 2 to 3 minutes or until golden brown. *Yield:* 20 canapes.

Carol Gerstheimer

SWEET RED PEPPER RELISH

12 large red peppers
1 teaspoon salt
1 cup cider vinegar

2 cups sugar
8 ounces cream cheese

Grate peppers; mix with salt and let stand 2 hours. Drain water off and press while draining. Mix with vinegar and sugar in pot. Simmer until mixture thickens. Refrigerate and spoon ½ cup chilled relish over an 8 ounce block of cream cheese. Serve with crackers.

Kathy Smith

PICKLED MUSHROOMS

⅔ cup tarragon vinegar
½ cup oil
1 clove garlic, minced
1 tablespoon sugar
2 tablespoons water
dash fresh ground pepper

dash hot pepper sauce
1 medium onion, sliced and
    separated into rings
2 pints fresh mushrooms,
    washed and trimmed

In a bowl combine vinegar, oil, garlic, sugar, water, pepper and pepper sauce. Add onions and mushrooms. Cover and refrigerate at least 8 hours, stirring several times. Dish can be made several days ahead. Drain to serve.

Nancy Besso

PIZZA ROLL

1 package yeast
1 cup warm water
1 teaspoon sugar

½ teaspoon salt
2 cups flour, more or less

Filling:

½ pound slicing pepperoni
1 16 ounce package mozzarella
    cheese, thinly sliced

1 egg, beaten

Dissolve yeast in warm water, then add sugar. Let stand until foamy. Pour yeast mixture into one cup of flour. Gradually add rest of flour, until smooth, non sticky consistency. Put into a greased bowl and cover with plastic wrap. Let rise for 1½ or 2 hours. To fill, roll out dough to a large round. Spread pepperoni over entire round. Spread cheese over pepperoni. Roll dough up and shape in a horseshoe. Brush with beaten egg and bake at 350 degrees for 45 minutes or until golden brown.

Carol Lohmann

APPETIZERS

HOT SAUSAGE AND CHEESE PUFFS

1 pound hot or sweet Italian
sausage
1 pound sharp Cheddar cheese,
shredded

3 cups biscuit baking mix
¾ cup water

Remove sausage from casings. Cook sausage in large skillet, breaking up, until no longer pink. Drain off fat. Place sausage in large bowl and cool completely. Combine sausage, cheese, biscuit mix and water. Mix until blended. Roll into 1 inch balls. Place on cookie sheets 2 inches apart. Bake in 400 degree oven for 12 to 15 minutes or until puffed and browned. Remove and cool completely on wire racks. May be frozen. Reheat at 375 degrees for 10 minutes.

Jan Guidotti

SAUSAGE AND SPINACH PIE

1 deep dish pie shell, plus a top
1 pound sweet sausage
4 eggs
1 10 ounce package frozen
spinach, thawed and well
drained

1 16 ounce package mozzarella
cheese, shredded
1 pound ricotta cheese
½ teaspoon salt
⅛ teaspoon pepper
⅛ teaspoon garlic powder

Remove sausage from casing and cook until well browned. Drain well. Reserve 1 egg yolk. In large bowl combine remaining eggs with the sausage, drained spinach, the two cheeses, salt, pepper and garlic powder. Pour into the pie shell. Flatten and wet the edge of shell. Top with crust. Cut slits in top crust and seal well. Mix a little water with the reserved egg yolk and brush over top crust. Bake at 375 degrees for about 1 hour or until golden.

Gerry Accardo

RUSSIAN PASHKA

12 ounces cream cheese,
  softened
¼ pound margarine
½ cup sugar
½ cup sour cream

1 cup chopped walnuts
1 cup raisins
1 envelope unflavored gelatin
¼ cup cold water

Mash cream cheese. Beat in margarine, sour cream and sugar. Blend till creamy, fold in walnuts and raisins. Soften gelatin in cold water. Dissolve over hot water. Add to cheese mixture and mix well. Oil a 4 cup mold. Pour in mixture and chill overnight. Serve on crackers.

Kathy Erdody

SHRIMP SPREAD

1 8 ounce package cream cheese
⅓ cup mayonnaise
1 teaspoon lemon juice
½ teaspoon minced onion
⅓ cup chili sauce

½ teaspoon salt
2 tablespoons Rhine wine
1 4½ ounce can shrimp, washed
  and chopped

Combine all ingredients, except shrimp and beat well with electric mixer. Blend in chopped shrimp. Serve on crackers or toast cut outs and garnish as desired. *Yield:* 3 dozen snacks.

Maureen Quinan

HOT SPINACH BALLS

4 10 ounce packages frozen
  chopped spinach
1 cup grated Parmesan cheese
1½ cups melted butter or
  margarine
2 cloves of garlic, pressed
2 large onions, diced finely

8 eggs, beaten
1 teaspoon of thyme or poultry
  seasoning
4 to 5 cups packaged herb
  stuffing mix
salt and pepper, to taste

Cook and drain spinach. Mix all ingredients. Chill several hours. Mold into small balls. Place on greased cookie sheet and bake at 325 degrees for about 30 minutes. Serve while still warm. *Yield:* 8 to 12 dozen pieces.

Betty Ingalls

APPETIZERS

SHRIMP DIP FOR VEGETABLES

16 ounces mayonnaise
4 ounce can shrimp, drained and
  crumbled
½ small onion, grated

small clove garlic, grated
1 teaspoon white horseradish
salt and pepper, to taste

Mix all ingredients together. Cover and chill at least 12 hours. Serve with
cut up raw vegetables.

Barbara Romans

SPINACH DIP

16 ounces sour cream
16 ounces mayonnaise
1 small onion, minced
1 8 ounce can water chestnuts,
  chopped
1 package instant vegetable soup
  mix

1 10 ounce package frozen
  chopped spinach, thawed and
  drained
1 pound loaf of bakery rye or
  pumpernickel, unsliced

Combine all ingredients, except bread, in blender or food processor. Scoop
out most of insides of bread and break into pieces to be used for dunking.
Put spinach dip into hollowed out bread shell. Serve cold. Dip may also be
used with raw vegetables.

Betty Ingalls

SPINACH PIE

2 frozen pastry pie crusts,
  thawed
2 10 ounce packages chopped
  spinach, cooked and drained
1 16 ounce package mozzarella
  cheese, diced
1½ pounds ricotta cheese

4 eggs
3 tablespoons grated Parmesan
  cheese
¼ pound provolone cheese,
  shredded, optional
½ pound ham or salami, diced,
  optional

Mix all ingredients together and divide into two pie shells. Cook at 350
degrees for 45 to 55 minutes. May be frozen. *Yield:* 2 pies.

Maureen Tagle

TACO DIP

1 8 ounce package cream cheese
½ cup cottage cheese
8 to 10 ounces sharp Cheddar
  cheese, shredded
1½ tablespoons taco seasoning
  mix

2 medium tomatoes, diced
lettuce, diced
1 small onion, diced
1 8 ounce jar taco sauce

Mix cream cheese, cottage cheese and taco seasoning mix in bowl until smooth. Spread on platter. Spread taco sauce over first layer. Next, layer the tomatoes, onion and lettuce. Top with a thick layer of shredded cheddar cheese. Serve with nacho cheese tortilla chips.

Mary Stylarek

WALKING TACO

1 7 ounce can refried beans
1 7 ounce can picante sauce
8 ounces sour cream
3 to 4 scallions, chopped
1 15 ounce can pitted ripe olives,
  sliced

8 ounces Cheddar cheese,
  shredded
taco chips or corn chips, for
  serving

Layer pie plate with refried beans, sour cream, sliced olives to cover, scallions to cover, picante sauce. Rim the outer edge of plate with remaining scallions and olives. Cover the center of plate with shredded cheese. Chill thoroughly. Serve with taco or corn chips. *Yield:* 6 to 8 servings.

Mary Langhauser

ZUCCHINI APPETIZERS

3 cups sliced zucchini
1 cup buttermilk baking mix
½ teaspoon chopped parsley
½ teaspoon salt
1 clove garlic, chopped

4 eggs, slightly beaten
½ cup grated Parmesan cheese
½ teaspoon oregano
½ cup vegetable oil
dash pepper

Grease a 13x9x2 inch pan. Mix all ingredients and spread in pan. Bake at 350 degrees for 25 to 30 minutes or until golden brown.

Mary Lou Giampietro

APPETIZERS

PARTY MEATBALLS

2 pounds ground beef
1 medium onion, chopped
1 egg
1 8 ounce can tomato sauce with
  onions
1 cup flavored bread crumbs

2 10 ounce cans golden
  mushroom soup
½ can water
2 tablespoons sour cream
salt and pepper, to taste
oil, for frying

Mix all ingredients together, except for soup and water. Make small balls out of mixture and fry in small amount of oil. Drain grease when finished, and put meatballs into saucepot. Add 2 cans of soup and ½ can of water, stirring constantly. When finished serve as an appetizer.

Vita Leggio

ITALIAN GARLIC MOZZARELLA BREAD

1 loaf Italian bread, sliced
  lengthwise
butter, as needed
1 pound mozzarella cheese,
  shredded or sliced

garlic powder, to taste
onion powder, to taste
salt, to taste
parsley, chopped, to taste

Butter both sides of open loaf of bread. Sprinkle to taste with garlic powder, onion powder, salt, mozzarella cheese and parsley. Broil 8 to 10 minutes until bubbly and golden brown on top. Slice and serve.

Mary Gardner

MEAT FILLED MUSHROOM CAPS

2 dozen large mushrooms
½ cup soy sauce
½ pound ground beef
¼ cup minced green pepper
2 tablespoons bread crumbs

1 egg yolk
1 tablespoon minced onion
½ clove garlic, minced
¼ teaspoon salt
¼ teaspoon pepper

Remove stems from mushrooms. Marinate caps for 1 hour in the soy sauce. Finely chop stems and mix with the remaining ingredients. Drain caps. Stuff with meat mixture mounded high. Brush tops with soy sauce. Broil 8 to 10 minutes. Refrigerate or freeze. When ready to serve, bring to room temperature and bake at 350 degrees for 8 to 10 minutes.

Diane Mulhern

MISTO FRITTO
BATTER FRIED VEGETABLES

2 cups flour
1 cup cornstarch
3 heaping tablespoons baking
  powder
salt and pepper, to taste
garlic powder, to taste

cold water
oil, for frying
raw vegetables of choice
  (broccoli, cauliflower, green
  pepper, zucchini).

Mix first 6 ingredients together to make a batter. Dip raw vegetables in batter and deep fry until golden brown.

Mary Lou Giampietro

APPETIZERS

soups and salads

SOUPS

BARLEY SOUP

3 or 4 quarts beef stock
½ to 1 pound chuck, cut into ½
  inch cubes
2 cups pearl barley, washed
2 medium onions, diced
4 celery stalks, sliced

2 leeks, sliced with some of
  green part
6 carrots, diced
2 parsnips, diced, optional
salt and pepper, to taste
parsley, minced

Bring stock to boil. Add meat and barley and simmer 30 to 45 minutes until tender. Add all vegetables. Simmer 10 to 15 minutes until vegetables are tender. Add salt and pepper to taste. Sprinkle minced parsley into soup. Serve hot with buttered rolls. Freezes well.

Helen Evancie

YANKEE BEAN SOUP

1 onion
1 cup water
1 package frankfurters, sliced
1 10 ounce can tomato soup
6 potatoes, peeled and sliced

½ teaspoon thyme
½ teaspoon oregano
1 20 ounce can pork and beans
salt and pepper, to taste

Dice onion and cook in water in large pot until soft. Add sliced frankfurters and sliced potatoes; bring to a boil. Add remaining ingredients; let simmer 30 to 45 minutes. Season to taste. Serve with rolls, or Italian bread and salad.

Barbara Keefe

BROCCOLI SOUP

1 10 ounce package frozen
  chopped broccoli
1 cup chicken broth
1 medium onion, chopped
1 teaspoon nutmeg

1 10¾ ounce can cream of
  mushroom soup
1 tablespoon butter
1 cup sour cream

In saucepan, combine broccoli, broth, onion, nutmeg. Bring to a boil. Cover and simmer 5 minutes. Pour hot mixture into blender; add soup and butter. Cover well and blend until smooth. Add sour cream and blend again. Serve with a dollop of sour cream. May be served hot or cold. *Yield:* 6 servings.

Dolores Gerkin

CREAM OF CELERY SOUP

½ cup butter or margarine
4 cups thinly sliced celery
2 tablespoons finely chopped
  onions
½ cup flour
4 cups chicken stock, or 4
  chicken bouillon cubes
  dissolved in 4 cups hot
  water

4 cups milk
½ cup finely chopped celery
  leaves
1 teaspoon salt
½ teaspoon pepper
pimento strips, for garnish

Melt butter or margarine in a large saucepan. Add celery and onion and sauté 5 minutes or until celery is soft. Remove from heat. Stir in flour. Add stock and milk, stirring constantly. Stir and cook over low heat until soup thickens slightly. Stir in chopped celery leaves. Add salt and pepper. Serve hot, garnished with pimento.

Patricia Farrell

SOUPS

CHICKEN SOUP

3 pounds of chicken
3 large carrots
3 or 4 stalks of celery
1 onion

salt, to taste
3 or 4 peppercorns
3 or 4 chicken bouillon

Place chicken in large pot and cover with water. Bring to boil and skim top. Add vegetables and cook 1½ to 2 hours on low heat. Keep pot half covered. Add bouillion about ½ hour before done.

Sarah and Corinne Rathgaber

CHICK CORN SOUP

3 to 4 quarts chicken broth
1 16 ounce can whole kernel
  corn
1 onion, minced
2 stalks celery, sliced

1 pound thick noodles, such as
  kluskie
leftover chicken, diced
salt and pepper, to taste
parsley, minced

Bring broth to a boil. Simmer onion, celery, corn and noodles according to noodle cooking directions, about 20 minutes. Add chicken, and salt and pepper to taste. Sprinkle parsley into soup. Serve hot with buttered rolls.

Helen Evancie

FISH CHOWDER

2 pieces bacon
¼ cup chopped onion
1 clove garlic, crushed
1 stalk celery, sliced
½ cup chopped green pepper
1 28 ounce can crushed tomatoes
1 8 ounce can tomato sauce
1½ cups water

4 large potatoes, peeled and
  cubed
¼ teaspoon salt
¼ teaspoon pepper
1 bay leaf
1 teaspoon oregano
2 pounds assorted fish

Brown bacon in large pot and crumble. Sauté onion and garlic. Add all other ingredients and cook over medium heat about two hours.

Carol Lohmann

EASY CLAM BISQUE

1 10¾ ounce can cream of potato soup	half-n-half or light cream
1 7 ounce can minced clams	2 tablespoons butter
	dash garlic powder

Empty potato soup into blender. Drain clams, reserving juice. Place clam juice into soup can and fill to top with half-n-half or light cream. Add to soup. Blend several minutes. Place in saucepan adding 2 tablespoons butter, garlic powder and clams, heat through, do not boil.

Eileen Rathgaber

BLENDER GAZPACHO

2 10½ ounce cans tomato soup	1 medium onion, chopped
1½ cups water	2 cloves garlic
½ cup white vinegar	1 beef bouillon cube
½ cup dry red wine	salt and pepper to taste
1 cucumber, cubed	
1 green pepper, seeded and cut in chunks	

Combine all ingredients gradually in blender, taking care to blend and purée in stages, if necessary. Pour soup into large bowl and chill several hours. Serve cold with crackers or breadsticks.

Judy Hein

LENTIL SOUP

2 cups dried lentils, washed	2 or 3 cloves garlic, minced
2 medium onions, sliced	1 bay leaf
2 carrots, chopped	2 tablespoons basil
3 or 4 ribs celery with tops, chopped	1 teaspoon pepper
1 or 2 small potatoes, diced	7 to 8 cups vegetable stock
	2 or 3 sprigs parsley, minced

Combine all ingredients in a large pot. Bring to a boil. Cover and simmer for 2½ to 3 hours. Add pepper to taste. *Yield:* 8 servings.

Eleanor McCann

MUSHROOM BARLEY SOUP

3 quarts beef stock
¾ to 1 pound mushrooms, sliced
2 cups pearl barley, washed

salt and pepper, to taste
parsley, minced

Sauté mushrooms about 3 minutes, stirring, until tender but firm. Set aside. Bring beef stock to a boil. Add barley and simmer, about 45 minutes, until tender. Add cooked mushrooms and simmer a few minutes. Salt and pepper to taste. Sprinkle with parsley. Serve hot. Freezes well.

Helen Evancie

MINESTRONE SOUP

1 large onion, chopped
2 stalks celery, chopped
1 clove garlic, minced
2 tablespoons olive or cooking
 oil
4 tomatoes, finely chopped or
 one 15 ounce can tomatoes,
 cut up
2 tablespoons snipped parsley
1½ teaspoons dried basil,
 crushed
½ teaspoon dried oregano,
 crushed

⅛ teaspoon pepper
1 bay leaf
2½ to 3 cups vegetable or beef
 broth
2 cups desired vegetables
½ cup thin spaghetti, broken
¾ cup cooked or canned kidney
 beans
grated romano or Parmesan
 cheese, for garnish

In a large dutch oven, cook onion, celery, and garlic in hot oil until onion is tender. Add tomatoes, parsley, basil, oregano, pepper, and bay leaf. Add vegetable broth. Bring to boiling; reduce heat. Cover and simmer 50 minutes. Add desired vegetables. Simmer, covered 15 minutes more or until the vegetables are just tender. Add spaghetti and cooked beans. Cook 15 minutes more or until the spaghetti is done. Remove bay leaf. Sprinkle 1 tablespoon grated cheese over each serving of soup. *Yield:* 6 to 8 servings.

Vita Leggio

FRENCH ONION SOUP

5 cups thinly sliced onions
3 tablespoons butter
1 tablespoon olive oil
1 teaspoon salt
¼ teaspoon sugar
3 tablespoons flour
2 cups boiling beef stock or
    bouillon, not comsommé

1 cup dry red wine
salt and pepper, to taste
rounds of hard toasted french
    bread
1 to 2 cups shredded Swiss
    cheese

Cook onions slowly with butter and oil in heavy saucepan, covered, for 15 minutes. Uncover. Raise heat. Stir in sugar and salt. Cook 40 minutes, stirring frequently until onions have turned golden brown. Sprinkle in flour and stir 3 minutes. Remove from heat and blend in boiling liquid. Add wine and season to taste. Simmer, partially covered, for 30 to 40 minutes more. Just before serving, pour into soup tureen. Float bread rounds on top and spread on grated cheese. Bake 20 minutes in oven at 325 degrees. Serve immediately.

Marge Deegan

PEA SOUP

1 pound split green peas
1 clove garlic, crushed
1 large carrot, chopped
1 pound bacon
3 tablespoons egg barley

½ teaspoon oregano
1 large onion, diced
1 stalk celery, diced
1 cup grated romano cheese
salt and pepper, to taste

Fry bacon until crisp. Remove from pan. Add onion and garlic to bacon drippings and fry until transparent. Wash peas and place in a large soup pot. Add onions and 2 or 3 quarts water to pot. Bring to boil. Skim film off top of pot. When clear, add remaining ingredients. Simmer over low heat for 4 hours, stirring frequently.

Jerilyn Cancelleire

SOUPS

SPLIT PEA SOUP

1 ham hock
3 quarts water
1 pound green split peas, washed

1 medium onion, minced
salt and pepper, to taste
croutons, optional

Bring water and ham hock to boil. Skim if needed. Add split peas and onion. Simmer about 3 hours until mixture is thick. Add salt and pepper to taste. Pick meat off ham hock and dice. Add meat to soup. Serve hot with croutons or buttered rolls. Soup may be diluted with milk or cream when served. Better the second day.

Helen Evancie

CREAMED POTATO SOUP

5 to 6 medium potatoes peeled
    and diced
salt and pepper, to taste
1 to 2 tablespoons flour

5 ounces sour cream
onion chopped, to taste
paprika, to taste
vinegar, to taste

Place potatoes in large soup pot. Add enough water to cover potatoes. Season with salt and pepper to taste. Cook until potatoes are done. In mixing cup, blend 1 to 2 tablespoons flour, 2 tablespoons sour cream and ⅓ cup water. Gradually add 4 ounces of sour cream to above mixture, stirring until smooth. Add to soup. Sauté chopped onion in small amount of water and add to soup. Add 1 to 2 tablespoons vinegar and cook 5 minutes longer. Sprinkle with paprika, if desired.

Diane Mulhern

ONION SOUP

6 cups sliced yellow onions	½ teaspoon dry mustard powder
6 tablespoons butter	3 tablespoons flour
2 tablespoons oil	8 cups beef consommé
1 teaspoon salt	1 cup dry white wine
¼ teaspoon sugar	salt and pepper, to taste

Garnish:
grated Parmesan cheese   sliced mozzarella cheese
toasted bread rounds

Heat the butter and oil in a 4 quart pot with cover. Add onions, cover and cook slowly for 20 minutes. Uncover. Add salt, sugar and mustard powder and cook on medium heat for about 40 minutes, until onions are deep brown. Remove from heat, add flour and blend well. Return to heat and bring to a boil. Add consommé, then wine. Simmer, covered, 30 minutes. Adjust seasonings and pour into individual bowls. Top with bread rounds, mozzarella slices and Parmesan cheese, if desired. Bake in oven until cheese melts.

Maire Kane

THREE BEAN SALAD, ITALIAN STYLE

1 20 ounce can cannellini beans, drained	½ cup garlic flavored wine vinegar
1 20 ounce can red kidney beans, drained	1¾ teaspoons Italian seasoning
1 20 ounce can chick peas, drained	1 teaspoon salt
1 scallion or green onion, sliced	1 teaspoon sugar
	lettuce leaves

In medium sized bowl, combine all ingredients. Cover and chill for 6 to 8 hours. Serve on lettuce leaves garnished with sliced scallions, if desired. *Yield:* 6 cups.

Eleanor McCann

SALADS

BROCCOLI SALAD

1 can condensed milk
1 egg
½ cup white vinegar
3 teaspoons mustard
salt, to taste
celery seed, to taste

onion, to taste, chopped and
 fried
¼ pound bacon, fried and
 chopped
1 bunch fresh broccoli, chopped

Combine first four ingredients to make dressing. Mix thoroughly. Add salt
and celery seed to taste. Pour over chopped broccoli. Add bacon and onion.
Toss and serve.

Patricia Amen

LOW CALORIE CARROT SALAD

3 carrots, grated
4 teaspoons low calorie
 mayonnaise
2 teaspoons vinegar

1 ounce skim milk
1 package low calorie sweetener
2 tablespoons raisins

Blend mayonnaise, vinegar, sugar together. Mix milk, carrots and raisins.
Pour mayonnaise mixture over carrots and raisins. Mix well. Chill and
serve. *Yield:* 1 to 2 servings.

Jackie Greene

COLE SLAW

1 head of cabbage, shredded
2 tablespoons sugar
3 tablespoons white vinegar

4 heaping tablespoons
 mayonnaise

Mix all ingredients and refrigerate.

Linda J. Candia

CALIFORNIA CHICKEN SALAD

2½ to 3 cups cooked chicken
1 cup sliced celery
2 tablespoons chopped green
  onion
2 tablespoons capers
1 teaspoon salt
1 11 ounce can mandarin
  oranges, drained

1 9 ounce can pineapple chunks,
  drained
½ cup slivered almonds, toasted
½ teaspoon grated lemon peel
lettuce greens
mayonnaise, to taste

Use leftover cooked chicken or cook 2 whole chicken breasts in water with 1 teaspoon salt, pepper, and small onion for 30 minutes. Cool. Combine chicken with celery, green onions, salt and capers. Cover and chill. Before serving add oranges, pineapple and almonds. Combine mayonnaise and lemon peel. Mix carefully and spoon into a bowl lined with greens. *Yield:* 6 servings.

Angel Byrnes

COLD CHICKEN AND PASTA

¾ cup mayonnaise
¾ cup buttermilk
¼ cup grated Parmesan cheese
2 teaspoons basil leaves
3 cups diced cooked chicken
8 ounces cooked corkscrew
  pasta
4 ounces sliced cooked zucchini,
  cooled

4 ounces sliced cooked carrots,
  cooled
4 ounces sliced cooked beans,
  cooled
4 ounces cooked cauliflower
  flowerettes, cooled
1½ teaspoons oregano

In large bowl, mix mayonnaise, buttermilk, cheese and basil. Mix in chicken, pasta, and vegetables. Chill at least 1 hour before serving.

Adriana Algieri

SALADS

COLE SLAW

8 cups shredded cabbage
10 cups cold water

1 cup shredded carrots
½ cup finely chopped onion

Dressing:
1 cup mayonnaise
3 tablespoons sugar
3 tablespoons cider vinegar

2 teaspoons prepared mustard
¾ teaspoon salt
⅛ teaspoon pepper

In large bowl, soak shredded cabbage in cold water mixed with salt at least 1 hour, or up to 8 hours refrigerated. Drain well; set aside.

In large bowl, combine dressing ingredients and stir until smooth. Add cabbage, carrots and onion to dressing. Toss until well coated. Serve at once or refrigerate covered up to 2 days. *Yield:* 8 servings.

Marie Sluka

CRANBERRY GELATIN SALAD

1 3 ounce package red gelatin
1 16 ounce can whole cranberry
  sauce
1 11 ounce can mandarin
  oranges, drained

1 tablespoon lemon juice
1 8 ounce can crushed
  pineapple, undrained
½ cup chopped walnuts

Make jello with 1 cup boiling water. Add remaining ingredients. Put into a 6 cup mold. Chill overnight. *Note:* Delicious with poultry, ham or other pork dishes. *Yield:* 10 servings.

Dolores Murphy

CUCUMBER ASPIC

1 3 ounce box of lime gelatin
1 3 ounce box of lemon gelatin
2 cucumbers, peeled and sliced
  thin

1 can crushed pineapple, drained
1 pint sour cream
1 tablespoon mayonnaise

Mix the lime and lemon gelatin into 1½ cups of boiling water. When cool add the cucumbers and crushed pineapple. Then add the sour cream with the mayonnaise. Mix thoroughly and put into a mold overnight. Chill.

Mary Primiani

CREAMY CRANBERRY MOLD

1 20 ounce can crushed
  pineapple
1 6 ounce package strawberry
  gelatin
1 cup water
1 16 ounce can whole cranberry
  sauce

3 tablespoons lemon juice
1 teaspoon grated lemon peel
¼ teaspoon nutmeg
2 cups sour cream
½ cup chopped walnuts

Drain pineapple and reserve juice. Combine juice and gelatin in large saucepan. Add water and heat to boiling until gelatin dissolves. Remove from heat and add cranberry sauce, lemon juice, lemon peel and nutmeg. Chill until slightly thickened. Blend sour cream into gelatin mixture. Fold in crushed pineapple and nuts. Pour into a 2 quart mold and chill. Unmold at serving time. *Yield:* 8 servings.

Judy Hein

MARINATED CUCUMBER SALAD

3 or 4 cucumbers
½ cup vinegar
¼ cup water
3 tablespoons sugar

salt, to taste
pepper, to taste
parsley, for garnish

Peel cucumbers. Slice very thinly. Combine other ingredients, except parsley. Stir in sugar. Pour over cucumbers, covering them with marinade. Chill several hours or overnight, covered. Garnish with chopped parsley before serving.

Helen Evancie

FIVE CUP SALAD

1 cup sour cream
1 cup crushed pineapple
1 cup mandarin oranges

1 cup coconut flakes
1 cup miniature marshmallows

Drain all juice from oranges and pineapple. Mix together all ingredients. Put into suitable serving dish or mold and chill in refrigerator at least four hours. *Yield:* 8 to 10 servings.

Marge Weir

MACARONI SALAD

1 pound elbow macaroni, cooked
   and drained well
½ onion, diced
2 stalks celery, diced

3 heaping tablespoons
   mayonnaise
½ tomato, diced, optional
½ green pepper, diced, optional

Add onion and celery to cooked macaroni and chill 2 hours or overnight. Add mayonnaise. Mix. Add diced tomatoes or green pepper. *Note:* Same ingredients may be used for potato salad.

Linda J. Candia

ORZO SALAD

1 pound box orzo
1 10 ounce package chopped
   spinach, drained
1 medium red onion, chopped
1 medium tomato, seeded and
   chopped

1 slice or small package feta
   cheese, crumbled
olive oil, as needed
salt and pepper, to taste

Cook orzo according to directions. Drain well. Defrost spinach, wring out and flake. Combine all ingredients. Add enough olive oil to moisten. Add salt and pepper to taste. *Note:* Remember that the cheese is salty, so go easy!

JoAnne Halloran

COLD PASTA SALAD

1 cup each chopped red and
   green pepper
1 small red onion, cut in rings
½ cup grated Parmesan cheese

black pitted olives, optional
1 8 ounce bottle Italian dressing
1 pound pasta, (twists or small
   shells), cooked

Combine all ingredients and mix with pasta. Chill well before serving.

Betty Ingalls

ROTELLI SALAD

1 pound rotelli macaroni,
  cooked
2 cloves garlic
1 cup olive oil
1 bunch broccoli
chopped scallion, to taste

shredded carrots, to taste
radishes, to taste
raw string beans, as desired
cauliflower, as desired
packages garlic and cheese salad
  dressing

Drain rotelli and put in large bowl. Sauté fresh cloves of garlic in 1 cup olive oil in saucepan. Cut up head of broccoli. Add to oil and garlic. Cover and simmer 15 minutes. Add to rotelli and mix well. Cut up fresh cauliflower into bite size pieces and add to rotelli. Add scallions, carrots, radishes, cut up string beans and toss well. Mix 2 packages of garlic and cheese dressing. Add to salad and toss well. Serve warm or cold.

The Committee

SPINACH SALAD

2 pounds spinach, stems
  discarded, washed and dried
3 cups shredded Swiss cheese
¾ pound mushrooms, sliced

½ pound bacon, crisply cooked,
  drained and chopped
3 hard cooked eggs, chopped
tomato wedges, for garnish

Dressing:
2 tablespoons sherry wine
  vinegar
2 egg yolks
2 teaspoons dijon mustard

2 teaspoons chopped tarragon
¼ teaspoon salt
pinch of freshly ground pepper
2 cups oil

Combine first six dressing ingredients in medium bowl and blend well with a whisk. Slowly add oil in steady stream, whisking constantly. Store in tightly covered container. Can be refrigerated up to one week. Place spinach in large salad bowl. Add cheese, mushrooms, bacon and eggs and toss with just enough dressing to coat lightly. Arrange on chilled individual plates and garnish with tomatoes. Serve with additional dressing. *Yield:* 6 servings.

Sister Jeannette Tenaglia

SALADS

MEXICAN PINEAPPLE CABBAGE SALAD

1 cup mayonnaise
juice of 2 limes
1 teaspoon celery salt
¼ teaspoon salt
⅛ teaspoon pepper

½ large cabbage, about 1 pound,
  shredded
2 medium carrots, shredded
1 20 ounce can crushed
  pineapple, drained

In large bowl combine mayonnaise, lime juice, celery salt, salt, and pepper. Combine cabbage, carrots and dressing with drained pineapple. Mix until well coated. Refrigerate until ready to serve.

Carol Lohmann

PISTACHIO COCONUT SURPRISE

2 cups sour cream
1 3 ounce package pistachio
  instant pudding and pie filling

1⅓ cups coconut
1 8¼ ounce can crushed
  pineapple

Combine sour cream and pudding mix. Add coconut and pineapple and stir until blended. Spoon into 8x4 or 9x5 inch loaf pan and freeze until firm, at least 3 hours. Dip pan in warm water and unmold onto serving plate. *Yield:* 6 servings.

Irene Francis

TACO SALAD

1 head lettuce, shredded
2 tomatoes, cut up
2 green peppers, cut up

8 ounces Cheddar cheese,
  shredded
1 onion, chopped, if desired

Mix all ingredients in a large bowl. Top with crushed nacho cheese chips and mild taco sauce or French dressing.

Marge Weir

BASIC POTATO SALAD

6 medium potatoes, diced:
  cooked about 25 minutes
½ cup diced celery
2 tablespoons minced parsley

1 medium to large onion, finely
  chopped
green pepper, for garnish

Dressing:
1 cup mayonnaise
¼ cup white vinegar
1 teaspoon salt

dash paprika
dash pepper

Toss salad ingredients with dressing until well mixed. Cover and chill.
Garnish with green pepper slices.

Annabelle Pilkington

SPINACH SALAD

½ pound fresh spinach, washed
1 pound fresh mushrooms
½ pound bacon, fried crisply
garlic, to taste
2 hard boiled eggs, chopped
bleu cheese salad dressing, to
  taste

vinegar, to taste
oil, to taste
salt and pepper, to taste
salad croutons, to taste

Fry bacon, adding garlic for flavor. Slice mushrooms and brown in
drippings from bacon. Sprinkle salt, pepper, oil and vinegar over cleaned
spinach leaves. Add mushrooms, bacon bits and chopped eggs to spinach.
Toss with bleu cheese dressing.

Regina Whitaker

TOMATO MOZZARELLA SALAD

2 firm, ripe, medium tomatoes   fresh basil, chopped, to taste
1 pound mozzarella cheese

Slice tomatoes about ¼ inch thick. Slice mozzarella cheese ¼ inch thick. Arrange tomatoes and cheese alternately around a large round serving plate. Sprinkle with fresh basil. Cover and chill 1 hour. Serve cold. If desired, vinegarette dressing may be sprinkled over all. *Yield:* 6 servings.

Helen Evancie

VINEGARETTE DRESSING

3 cups oil   1½ teaspoons salt
1 cup vinegar   ½ teaspoon pepper
3 tablespoons sugar

Blend all ingredients in a jar. Shake vigorously before serving. *Yield:* 1 quart.

Helen Evancie

breads

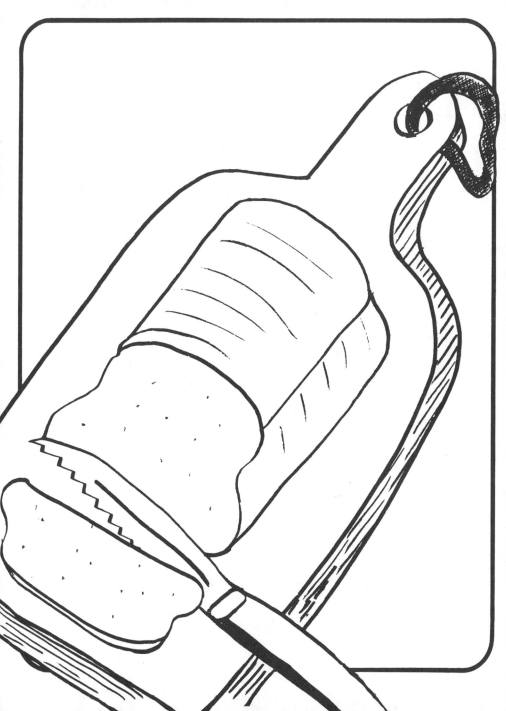

BREADS

APPLE MUFFINS

3 cups pared apples, chopped
3½ cups flour
2 cups sugar
1 teaspoon salt

1 teaspoon baking soda
12 ounces oil
1 teaspoon vanilla; 4 ounces
   chopped nuts, optional

Combine all dry ingredients thoroughly. Add oil. Spray and flour muffin
tins. Fill almost to the top. Bake in 350 degree oven 15 minutes for small
muffins; 30 minutes for large.

Rosalie Bradley

BANANA BREAD

2 ripe, peeled bananas
¾ cup packed brown sugar
½ cup of softened butter
1 egg
¼ cup sour cream
1 teaspoon vanilla

2¼ cups flour
1 teaspoon baking powder
½ teaspoon baking soda
½ teaspoon salt
½ teaspoon ground cinnamon
1 cup chopped walnuts

Slice bananas into blender; purée. Beat sugar and butter until light and
fluffy. Beat in egg. Beat in banana, sour cream, vanilla until blended.
Combine flour, baking powder, baking soda, salt and cinnamon. Add to
banana mixture. Beat until blended. Stir in walnuts. Pour into 9x5x2 inch
loaf pan. Bake in 350 degree oven 65 to 70 minutes until toothpick inserted
comes out clean. Cool in pan 10 minutes. *Yield:* 1 loaf.

Ray O'Connor

BLUEBERRY MUFFINS

1½ cups flour
½ cup sugar
2 teaspoons baking powder
½ teaspoon salt

¼ cup softened butter
1 egg
½ cup milk
1 cup blueberries

Mix first seven ingredients well. Fold in blueberries. Grease muffin tins
and fill ⅔ full with batter. Bake at 400 degrees for 20-25 minutes.
Yield: 1 dozen.

Pat Whaley

BEER BREAD

3 cups self-rising flour
2 tablespoons sugar

12 ounce can or bottle of beer,
at room temperature

Put flour and sugar in a bowl. Pour in beer, stirring into a ball, until smooth. Grease a 9x5 loaf pan. Put dough in pan. Brush with melted butter. Let rise one hour. Bake at 350 degrees for 50 to 60 minutes. Take out of oven. Brush again with melted butter while hot. Cool before slicing. Can be doubled to make two loaves.

Helen Evancie

3 C BREAD

3 eggs, beaten
½ cup vegetable oil
½ cup milk
2½ cups flour
1 cup sugar
1 teaspoon baking powder

1 teaspoon baking soda
1 teaspoon ground cinnamon
½ teaspoon salt
2 cups shredded carrots
1⅓ cups flaked coconut
½ cup snipped cherries

Combine beaten eggs, oil and milk. In large bowl sift together flour, sugar, baking powder, baking soda, cinnamon and salt. Add egg mixture. Mix just until thoroughly combined. Stir in carrot, coconut and cherries. Turn into four well greased and floured 16 ounce fruit or vegetable cans. Bake in 350 degree oven for 45 to 50 minutes. Remove from cans and cool thoroughly. Wrap and refrigerate overnight or till used.

Barbara Murphy

CORN STICKS

¾ cup cornmeal
1 cup flour
⅓ cup sugar
3 tablespoons baking powder

¾ teaspoon salt
1 cup milk
1 egg, beaten
2 tablespoons butter, melted

Mix first five ingredients well. Add last three ingredients. Beat together until well mixed. Pour mixture into well greased cast iron corn stick mold. Bake at 425 degrees for 15 minutes. *Yield:* 14 sticks.

Frank DePasquale

BREADS

CRANBERRY NUT BREAD

2 cups flour
1 cup sugar
1½ teaspoons baking powder
½ teaspoon baking soda
1 teaspoon salt
¼ cup margarine or butter
¾ cup orange juice

1 tablespoon grated orange or
  lemon rind
1 egg, beaten
½ cup chopped walnuts
1 to 2 cups coarsely chopped
  cranberries

Note: A blender is helpful, especially if berries are frozen. Do not purée berries. Combine first 9 ingredients to make batter. Fold cranberries and nuts into batter mixture. Grease a 9x5x3 inch loaf pan. Spoon batter into pan. Bake at 350 degrees for 1 hour, or until center is done. Remove from pan. Cool on rack, wrap and refrigerate. Delicious when sliced and rewarmed. *Yield:* 1 large loaf.

Judy Hein

IRISH SODA BREAD

4 cups flour
½ teaspoon salt
½ teaspoon baking soda
2 teaspoons baking powder

¾ cup sugar
½ pint sour cream
3 eggs
raisins or caraway seeds, to
  taste

Sift all dry ingredients. After sifting, mix dry ingredients well. Fold in raisins or caraway seeds. Stir. In separate bowl beat eggs and sour cream together. Mix well with dry mixture. If dough is too dry add milk. When dough is mixed well, roll in flour. Put into round glass pie plate. Bake at 325 degrees for about 1 hour or until done.

Pat Schmitt

PUMPKIN NUT BREAD

2 cups sifted flour
2 teaspoons baking powder
½ teaspoon baking soda
1 teaspoon cinnamon
¼ cup softened butter or
  margarine
½ cup chopped walnuts or
  pecans

1 cup solid pack pumpkin
1 cup sugar
½ cup milk
½ teaspoon nutmeg
2 eggs
½ cup dark raisins
1 teaspoon salt

Sift together flour, baking powder, baking soda, salt and spices. Combine pumpkin, sugar, milk and eggs in mixing bowl. Add dry ingredients and softened butter; mix until well blended. Stir in nuts and raisins. Spread in well greased standard 9x5x3 inch loaf pan. Bake in 350 degree oven for 45 to 55 minutes or until toothpick inserted in center comes out clean. Bread may be frozen. *Note:* Fresh pumpkin cooked and finely sieved may be substituted. *Yield:* 1 loaf.

Marie Sluka

SIMPLE IRISH SODA BREAD

2½ cups flour
⅔ cup sugar
3 teaspoons baking powder
1 large teaspoon shortening
1 teaspoon butter

2 beaten eggs
1 cup milk
raisins, to taste
1 tablespoon caraway seeds,
  optional

Mix all ingredients together, except eggs, milk and raisins, in large bowl. Mix eggs and milk together and then add to rest of ingredients. Mix all together with wooden spoon until mixture is very thick and bulky. Add raisins and spoon through mixture. Also add caraway seeds (optional). Bake in round black iron frying pan or 9 inch round cake pan. Bake at 350 degrees for 1 hour or until top is golden. Serve plain or with butter.

Diane Bass

BREADS

PEPPERONI BREAD

1 frozen pizza dough, defrosted
¼ pound sliced pepperoni

8 ounces ricotta cheese
8 ounces mozzarella cheese

Preheat oven to 350 degrees. Spread two to three tablespoons of oil on cookie sheet. Roll pizza dough out to form long oblong shape, approximately 10 inch x 18 inch. In middle of dough, layer pepperoni slices so that they overlap. Then spread a ½ inch thick layer of ricotta. Slice mozzarella and place over ricotta and pepperoni. Fold one side of dough over pepperoni and cheese; then fold other side over to form a roll. Make sure to pinch around edge of dough and on ends. Rub top with oil and bake at 350 degrees for 30 minutes or until top is nicely browned. Serve hot. *Yield:* 1 loaf.

Pat Rayfield

CANDLELIGHT POPOVERS

1 cup sifted flour
1 cup milk
2 eggs

¼ teaspoon salt
1 tablespoon butter, melted
butter for greasing muffin pans

Put ⅓ teaspoon butter in each muffin pan and place in warm oven for 5 minutes, while making batter. Sift flour and salt together in bowl. Beat eggs and milk, and 1 tablespoon butter. Add sifted flour, beating only until smooth. Fill hot muffin pans ⅓ full of the mixture. Bake at 450 degrees for 30 minutes. Reduce heat to 350 degrees for 15 minutes more or until firm, brown and popped. *Yield:* 6 large or 9 small.

Stephanie Rabuse

STRAWBERRY BREAD

2 cups flour	1 cup sugar
1 teaspoon baking powder	1 teaspoon vanilla
1 teaspoon baking soda	2 eggs, separated
1 teaspoon salt	1 cup crushed strawberries,
½ cup margarine, softened	fresh or frozen

Sift together flour, baking powder, baking soda, and salt. Set aside. In a large bowl, cream margarine, sugar and vanilla. Add egg yolks, one at a time, beating after each addition. Alternately, add flour mixture and strawberries, mixing well with each addition. Set aside. In a separate bowl, beat egg whites until peaks form. Fold in strawberry batter mixture. Line a 9 inch loaf pan with greased waxed paper. Spoon batter into prepared pan. Bake at 325 degrees for 65 minutes or until center is firm. Cool in pan 20 minutes. Remove from pan. Remove waxed paper. Cool on rack. May be frozen in plastic wrap. *Yield:* 1 loaf.

Judy Hein

SWISS ONION SPIRAL BREAD

½ cup chopped onion	1 cup shredded Swiss cheese
2 tablespoons butter or	2 tablespoons crisp, cooked and
margarine	crumbled bacon or canned
16 ounce loaf frozen white bread	bacon bits
dough, thawed	1 egg, beaten
poppyseed or dillseed, to taste	

In a small skillet, cook onion in butter or margarine until tender. On floured surface, roll out bread dough to a 17x7 inch rectangle; spread cooked onion evenly over dough. Sprinkle cheese and bacon on top. Roll up jelly roll fashion from the long side, pinching edges to seal. Place roll, seam side down, on a greased cookie sheet. Score top of loaf crosswise, making cuts ¼ inch deep. Cover; let rise in a warm place for 30 to 45 minutes or till almost double. Brush top of bread with egg; sprinkle with poppyseed or dillseed. Bake in 350 degree oven for 25 to 30 minutes. Serve warm. To reheat, wrap in foil, heat in 400 degree oven for 15 to 20 minutes.

Gail Seale

SOUR CREAM MUFFINS

1⅓ cups flour	1 cup sour cream
1 teaspoon baking powder	1 egg
½ teaspoon salt	2 tablespoons sugar
½ teaspoon baking soda	1 tablespoon margarine, softened

Beat one egg, lightly. Beat in 2 tablespoons sugar, 1 tablespoon soft margarine, 1 cup sour cream. In a separate bowl sift together 1⅓ cups flour, 1 teaspoon baking powder, ½ teaspoon baking soda, ½ teaspoon salt. Combine all ingredients. Bake in greased muffin tins at 400 degrees for 20 to 30 minutes.

Marianne Penfied

YOGURT BREAD BAKED IN A CAN!

2 cups whole wheat flour	1 cup raisins
½ cup flour	½ cup molasses
2 teaspoons baking soda	2 29 ounce fruit juice cans, one
1 teaspoon salt	end removed
2 cups plain nonfat yogurt	

In a large bowl, combine flours, baking soda, and salt. Stir in yogurt, raisins, molasses and blend well. Lightly grease fruit juice cans. Divide batter evenly into the cans. Bake at 350 degrees for 45 minutes or until center is done. Cool for 10 minutes. Turn out upright onto racks to cool completely. Refrigerate. Use within 5 days. *Yield:* 16 servings.

The Committee

ZUCCHINI BREAD

4 eggs
2 cups sugar
1 cup oil
3½ cups flour
1½ teaspoons baking soda
1½ teaspoons salt

1 teaspoon cinnamon
¾ teaspoon baking powder
2 cups grated, unpeeled zucchini
1 cup chopped walnuts
1 teaspoon vanilla

Beat eggs; gradually add sugar and oil. Combine dry ingredients and add to egg mixture, alternating with zucchini. Stir in nuts and vanilla; beat well. Bake in a 350 degree oven for 55 to 60 minutes in two greased and floured loaf pans. *Yield:* 2 loaves.

Joan Duffy

ZUCCHINI CHEDDAR BREAD

1 cup chopped onion
¼ cup margarine
2½ cups buttermilk baking mix
1 tablespoon chopped parsley
½ teaspoon dried basil

½ teaspoon dried thyme
¼ cup milk
3 eggs
1½ cups shredded zucchini
1 cup shredded Cheddar cheese

Melt margarine in skillet and sauté onion until tender. Combine onion, baking mix, parsley, basil, thyme, milk and eggs. Beat one minute until smooth. Stir in zucchini and cheese. Grease and flour a 9 inch pie pan. Spread batter in pan. Bake at 400 degrees approximately 40 minutes until center is done. Cool slightly and remove from pan. *Yield:* 1 loaf.

Judy Hein

ZUCCHINI NUT LOAF

2½ cups flour
2 teaspoons baking powder
1 teaspoon baking soda
¾ teaspoon salt
½ teaspoon cinnamon
¼ teaspoon ginger

2 eggs
1¼ cups sugar
½ cup oil
2 cups chopped zucchini
1 cup chopped walnuts

In large bowl stir together flour, baking powder, baking soda, salt, cinnamon and ginger. Add remaining ingredients. Pour into buttered loaf pan. Bake in 350 degree oven for 50 to 60 minutes.

Mary Innace

BREADS

vegetables

VEGETABLES

ARTICHOKE PIE

1 8 ounce can or 1 package
frozen artichoke hearts
1 package pie crust
1 8 ounce package mozzarella
cheese, shredded

5 eggs
3 large cloves garlic, or 6 small
cloves
½ cup grated cheese

Fry artichokes in a small amount of oil with cloves of garlic. Fry until soft and mash artichokes and garlic with a fork. Beat 5 eggs and add mozzarella into the beaten eggs. Add smashed artichokes and garlic to eggs. Then add ½ cup of grated cheese and mix. Prepare pie crust as directed on box. Place in a pie dish, add mixture to pie crust and bake in a 350 degree oven for 30 minutes. When finished slice like pie and serve.

Vita Leggio

ARTICHOKE RICE SALAD

1 cup rice
2½ cups chicken broth
4 green scallions, chopped
2 6 ounce jars artichoke hearts

¾ teaspoon curry powder
⅓ cup mayonnaise
½ green pepper, chopped
12 pimento stuffed olives, sliced

Cook rice as directed, using chicken broth instead of water. Let cool in a large bowl. Add scallions, green pepper, olives. Drain artichokes, reserving marinade. Slice artichoke pieces into thirds. Add to bowl. Separately, combine marinade with curry and mayonnaise. Pour over mixture. Toss and chill. May be made one day in advance. *Yield:* 4 to 6 servings.

Mary Langhauser

SWEET N' SOUR RED CABBAGE

16 ounce jar red cabbage
1 tablespoon butter

1 tablespoon flour
1 teaspoon sugar

Melt butter in small pot and brown slightly. Stir flour into butter and make a paste. Place red cabbage in a pot and blend in flour paste. Add sugar. Mix together and heat on low.

Annabelle Pilkington

GREEN BEANS CAESAR

1½ pounds fresh green beans
2 tablespoons oil
1 tablespoon vinegar
1 tablespoon instant minced
  onion
¼ teaspoon salt
1 clove garlic, crushed

⅛ teaspoon pepper
2 tablespoons bread crumbs
2 tablespoons grated Parmesan
  cheese
1 tablespoon butter or
  margarine, melted
paprika, for garnish

Steam green beans until still slightly crisp. Heat oven to 350 degrees. Toss beans with oil, vinegar, onion, salt, garlic and pepper. Pour into ungreased 1 quart casserole. Stir together bread crumbs, cheese and butter; sprinkle over beans. Sprinkle with paprika. Bake uncovered 15 to 20 minutes or until heated through. *Yield:* 6 servings.

Diane Darmody

BAKED BROCCOLI

1 cup mayonnaise
1 cup grated Cheddar cheese
1 10¾ ounce can cream of
  mushroom soup

3 eggs, slightly beaten
2 10 ounce packages frozen
  chopped broccoli

Heat oven to 325 degrees. Cook broccoli first. Drain. Grease a 2 quart casserole dish. Combine all ingredients and pour into casserole dish. Bake for 1 hour. Cool for 10 to 15 minutes.

Rose Frey

VEGETABLES

CAROL'S BROCCOLI CASSEROLE

1 onion, minced
6 tablespoons butter
4 tablespoons flour
2 cups milk
½ teaspoon salt

⅛ teaspoon pepper
1 egg yolk
1 cup Parmesan cheese
1 bunch broccoli, cooked
½ cup bread crumbs

Cook onion in butter until tender. Stir in flour. Add milk slowly and cook until thick. Add salt, pepper, egg yolk and cheese. Pour half of sauce into greased baking dish. Add broccoli and remaining sauce. Sprinkle with bread crumbs and dot with butter. Bake in a 400 degree oven for approximately 20 minutes.

Carol Lohmann

BROCCOLI AND CHEESE PUFF

2 10 ounce packages frozen
  chopped broccoli
1 cup buttermilk baking mix
1 cup milk

2 eggs
½ teaspoon salt
1 cup shredded Cheddar cheese

Cook broccoli and drain. Mix together buttermilk baking mix, milk, eggs and salt. Stir in broccoli and cheese. Pour mixture into a buttered 10 inch pan. Bake for 1 hour in a 325 degree oven.

Mary Innace

RICE AND CHEESE BROCCOLI CASSEROLE

1 10 ounce package frozen
  chopped broccoli
½ cup butter
1 medium onion, chopped
1 cup instant rice, uncooked

1 10¾ ounce can cream of
  mushroom soup
10 ounces Cheddar cheese,
  shredded

Place frozen broccoli and butter in medium saucepan without water. Cover and simmer approximately 20 to 30 minutes, until soft. Add onion, rice, soup and cheese. Mix well and put in casserole. Bake at 300 degrees for 30 minutes. If desired, add topping of buttered croutons or buttered bread crumbs. Garnish with paprika.

Arlene Geraghty

BROCCOLI CHEESE QUICHE

1 cup milk
3 eggs
¼ cup flour
1 teaspoon salt
¼ teaspoon pepper
¼ teaspoon nutmeg

1 medium onion, chopped
1 10 ounce frozen chopped
    broccoli, uncooked and
    drained
1 cup shredded Cheddar cheese
1 9 or 10 inch unbaked pie shell

Preheat oven to 350 degrees. In a bowl combine all ingredients except onion, cheese and broccoli. Mix well. Now add onion, cheese and broccoli and hand mix until well blended. Pour into pie shell. Bake 50 to 60 minutes. Let stand 10 minutes before serving.

Maria Lombardo

BROCCOLI, MUSHROOM AND SWISS QUICHE

4 eggs
2 cups heavy cream
¼ teaspoon salt
½ cup frozen chopped broccoli,
    thawed and drained

¼ cup canned sliced
    mushrooms, well drained
1 cup shredded Swiss cheese

Beat eggs. Add cream and salt; mix well. Place broccoli and mushrooms in a pie crust. Top with Swiss cheese. Pour in egg mixture. Bake at 450 degrees for 15 minutes. Reduce temperature to 350 degrees and bake an additional 45 to 60 minutes; or until a knife inserted in center comes out clean.

Pat Sullivan

FRIED EGGPLANT

1 large eggplant
¾ cup flour
2 eggs, beaten

1½ cups seasoned bread crumbs
oil, for frying

Pare eggplant and cut into slices or sticks. Dip in flour, then eggs and then into bread crumbs. Fry in oil, turning until all sides are golden brown. *Note:* Freezes well in plastic bags. Reheat in 300 degree oven for 20 to 25 minutes.

Judy Hein

CREAMED CARROTS

2 pounds carrots, cut in 1 inch
  long chunks
2 tablespoons margarine, melted
1 onion, chopped
3 tablespoons flour

1¼ cups water
3 chicken bouillon cubes
1 tablespoon sugar
parsley, for garnish

Sauté carrots and onion in melted margarine for 5 minutes. Add flour to carrots. Set aside. Dissolve bouillon in 1¼ cups boiling water. Add bouillon and sugar to carrots. Bring to full boil. Reduce heat and simmer until carrots are tender. Garnish with fresh parsley.

Marilyn Tuohy

CURRIED CAULIFLOWER CASSEROLE

1 large cauliflower, broken into
  flowerettes
1 10¾ ounce can cream of
  mushroom soup
1 cup shredded Cheddar cheese

⅓ cup mayonnaise
1 teaspoon curry powder
¼ cup bread crumbs
2 tablespoons sweet butter or
  margarine

Cook cauliflower and drain well. Place in a 2 quart casserole. Blend soup, cheese, mayonnaise and curry powder. Pour over cauliflower. Toss lightly to coat. Combine bread crumbs with butter and sprinkle over top. Bake at 350 degrees for 30 minutes or until bubbly.

Rosalie Bradley

GOLDEN CHEESE BAKE

3 cups shredded carrots
2 cups long grain rice, cooked
2 cups shredded American
  cheese
1 cup milk

2 eggs, beaten
2 tablespoons instant minced
  onion
1 teaspoon salt
¼ teaspoon pepper

Cook carrots in 1 cup water for 10 minutes. Drain. Combine carrots with rice, 1½ cups cheese, milk, eggs, onion, salt and pepper. Turn into 1½ quart casserole. Top with remaining ½ cup cheese. Bake uncovered at 350 degrees for 1 hour. *Yield:* 6 servings.

Terry Laria

CORN FRITTERS

1 16 ounce can kernel corn,
   drained
2 cups buttermilk baking mix
1⅓ cups milk

1 egg
salt and pepper, to taste
garlic or onion powder, to taste
oil, for frying

Combine baking mix, milk and egg. Beat until smooth. Fold in drained corn and seasonings. Make fritters by pouring ¼ cup batter into oiled frypan. Fry until golden on both sides. Delicious with roast meats accompanied with gravy. *Yield:* 2 dozen.

Judy Hein

CORN FRITTERS

1 egg
½ cup milk
1 cup pancake mix

1 12 ounce can whole kernel
   corn, drained
oil to depth of 1 inch in skillet

Blend egg and milk. Add pancake mix, stirring until smooth. Fold in corn. To insure lightness, do not overbeat. Drop by teaspoonfuls into heated oil. Fry in 325 degree oil until golden brown, about 4 minutes. Serve as a vegetable or with applesauce. *Yield:* 20 to 24 fritters.

Geri Wheeler

STUFFED EGGPLANT ROLLS

2 medium eggplants
flour, for dredging
2 eggs, beaten
oil, for frying
1 pound ricotta

1 tablespoon finely chopped
   parsley
½ pound mozzarella
16 ounces marinara sauce

Wash eggplant, remove stems and skin and slice lengthwise. Dredge eggplant in flour. Dip into beaten eggs. Fry until golden. Drain on paper towel. Combine ricotta and parsley. Place a scoop of this mixture in the middle of each eggplant slice. Top with a slice of mozzarella. Roll eggplant and secure with toothpick. Place eggplant rolls in a greased shallow baking pan and top with marinara sauce. Bake in 350 degree oven for 15 to 30 minutes. If desired, garnish with chopped parsley. *Yield:* 8 to 10 servings.

Rosanne DeLassio

VEGETABLES

LIMA BEANS WITH BACON

4 slices bacon
1 10 ounce package frozen lima
  beans
½ cup water
¼ teaspoon salt

⅛ teaspoon pepper
⅛ teaspoon leaf rosemary,
  crumbled
2 tablespoons chopped parsley

Cook bacon in a medium size saucepan until crisp; drain on paper toweling; crumble; reserve. Add lima beans, water, salt, pepper and rosemary to fat remaining in pan. Bring to boiling; lower heat slightly; cover. Cook until beans are tender, about 8 minutes. Uncover; cook beans over high heat, shaking pan frequently, until almost all the liquid has evaporated. Sprinkle with reserved bacon and parsley. *Yield:* 4 servings.

Sister Jeannette Tenaglia

MUSHROOMS BORDELAISE

1¼ pounds fresh mushrooms
⅓ cup peanut or vegetable oil
½ teaspoon freshly ground
  pepper
1½ tablespoons unsalted butter
  or margarine

⅓ cup fresh, unsalted bread
  crumbs
3 tablespoons finely chopped
  shallots
3 tablespoons finely chopped
  parsley

Rinse the mushrooms in cold water and drain well. Cut each mushroom into quarters. Heat oil in 1 or 2 heavy skillets and when hot and almost smoking, add the mushrooms and pepper. Cook, stirring and shaking the skillet, over high heat. The mushrooms will give up a good deal of liquid. Continue cooking until this liquid evaporates, stirring often. Cook until the mushrooms are slightly crisp and brown. The total cooking time will be about 15 minutes. Drain oil from mushrooms through a colander. Return the skillet to the heat and add the butter. When it is foaming, return the mushrooms to the skillet. Cook, shaking the skillet and stirring, about 3 minutes. Add the bread crumbs and stir. Add shallots and continue cooking, shaking the skillet and stirring, about 45 seconds. Add the parsley and stir. Spoon mixture into a serving dish. Serve while crisp.

Sister Jeannette Tenaglia

MISTO FRITTO

2 cups flour
1 cup cornstarch
3 heaping tablespoons baking powder
salt, to taste
pepper, to taste
garlic powder, to taste
water, as needed
raw vegetables, of choice

Combine ingredients and mix together. Dip vegetables into mixture and then deep fry. Drain and serve warm.

Mary Lou Giampietro

STUFFED MUSHROOMS

large mushrooms for stuffing
flavored bread crumbs, as needed
grated cheese, to taste
garlic powder, to taste
fresh parsley, chopped
oil, as needed

Judge amount of ingredients according to how many mushrooms you will be stuffing. Wash and dry mushrooms and remove the stems. Mix together bread crumbs, grated cheese, garlic powder, chopped parsley and oil. Use only a small amount of oil, enough to keep the bread crumbs moist. Stuff the mushrooms with the bread crumb mixture. Place in a shallow pan. Bake at 350 degrees until mushrooms are tender. Serve warm.

Vita Leggio

POTATOES AU GRATIN

2 quarts cooked potatoes
1 10 ounce cream of chicken soup
1 pint sour cream
½ cup shredded, mild Cheddar cheese
½ cup chopped onions
½ cup butter

Topping:
¼ cup melted butter
1½ cups crushed cornflakes

Melt butter and mix in soup and sour cream. Fold in potatoes, cheese and onion. Put mixture in a greased pan and add topping. Bake at 350 degrees for 45 minutes. *Yield:* 6 to 8 servings.

Diane Darmody

VEGETABLES

BEER BATTER ONION RINGS

1 cup buttermilk baking mix
2 large Spanish or Bermuda
  onions
2 cups buttermilk baking mix

2 eggs
1 teaspoon salt
1 cup beer
oil, for frying

Peel onions and cut into ¼ inch slices. Separate into rings and place in a bowl. Lightly coat rings with first cup of baking mix. In separate bowl, blend 2 cups baking mix, eggs, salt and beer to a smooth batter. Dip onion rings into batter and fry several at a time, turning when golden. Remove from pan and drain on paper toweling or brown paper bags. Continue frying rings until all are done. *Note:* Thin batter if necessary with additional beer, while frying onions. When cooled, these may be bagged and frozen. Reheat in 300 degree oven for 20 to 30 minutes. Season as desired.

Judy Hein

POTATOES OREGANATO

4 baking potatoes, unpeeled,
  scrubbed and sliced
1 teaspoon salt
2 teaspoons oregano

2 tablespoons minced parsley
2 tablespoons minced garlic
⅓ cup oil

Mix all ingredients together. Place in casserole and put into a preheated 350 to 375 degree oven for 1 hour.

Mary Primiani

POTATO PUDDING

10 large potatoes, peeled and
  finely grated
1 medium onion, finely chopped
5 slices bacon, cut narrowly,
  crosswise

3 eggs, beaten
½ cup hot milk or heavy cream
2 teaspoons salt
¼ teaspoon pepper

Fry bacon until crisp. Sauté onion with bacon. Add milk to bacon and onion and heat. Combine bacon mixture and grated potatoes. Add salt, pepper and beaten eggs. Mix well. Pour into greased 9x12 inch pan. Bake 400 degrees for 15 minutes. Reduce oven to 375 degrees for 45 minutes.

Aldona Vainius

POTATO SOUFFLÉ

1 cup milk
¼ cup margarine
3 cups mashed potatoes
1 teaspoon salt
½ cup shredded American
  cheese

1 teaspoon dry mustard
2 egg yolks
2 egg whites

Beat milk and margarine together in a saucepan. Stir in mashed potatoes. Beat until fluffy. Beat in American cheese, salt and dry mustard. Beat egg yolks until thick. Fold into potato mixture. Beat egg whites until stiff. Fold into potato mixture. Turn mixture into greased 1½ quart casserole dish. Bake in oven at 350 degrees for 45 to 50 minutes. Serve immediately. *Yield:* 6 to 8 servings.

Geri Wheeler

RICE PILAF

½ cup butter, melted
1 large onion, sliced thin
1 6 ounce can mushrooms,
  drained
¼ cup finely chopped green
  pepper

1 cup raw rice
dash dried thyme
2 cups water or bouillon

Preheat oven to 350 degrees. Cook onion in ¼ cup butter. Add mushrooms and green pepper. Cook until tender. Remove vegetables and set aside. In same pan, heat rest of butter. Add rice and brown slightly, stirring over low heat. Stir in vegetables and thyme. Heat chicken broth to boiling point. Stir in rice and vegetables. Bake 30 to 40 minutes, until liquid is absorbed and rice is tender.

Rosalie Toja

RICE PILAF

1 cup rice
½ cup orzo macaroni

¼ pound butter or margarine
2 13¾ ounce cans chicken broth

Melt butter in 3 quart casserole. Lightly brown orzos, being careful not to burn them. Add chicken broth and cover until boiling. Stir in rice; cover, and simmer for 20 minutes.

Janice Byrne

SPINACH PIE

1 10½ ounce package frozen,
  chopped spinach
5 ounces of ricotta cheese
3 eggs

½ cup Parmesan cheese
salt and pepper, to taste
1 frozen 9 inch deep dish pie
  crust

Cook spinach in boiling water for one minute. Drain spinach well. Press out excess moisture, if necessary. Mix eggs, ricotta cheese, Parmesan cheese, salt and pepper in a bowl. Add cooked spinach and mix well. Fold into unbaked pie crust and bake at 350 degrees for 45 minutes, or until golden brown.

Cecilia Lupis

SAVORY SPINACH

½ cup sour cream
1 package cheese garlic salad
  dressing mix

1 10 ounce package frozen
  chopped spinach

Heat oven to 350 degrees. Combine sour cream and salad dressing mix; fold into spinach. Pour into a 3 cup casserole. Bake for 20 minutes. *Yield:* 4 servings.

Anne Carey

SPINACH QUICHE

2 10½ ounce packages frozen
  chopped spinach
3 tablespoons butter
3 tablespoons flour
1½ cups milk
6 eggs
8 ounces grated mozzarella or
  Swiss cheese

2 tomatoes
garlic powder
salt
nutmeg
1 can of onion rings
2 pie shells

Cook spinach and drain. Melt butter and mix with spinach. Stir in milk. Add garlic powder, salt and nutmeg. Beat eggs. Add eggs and cheese to spinach. Fold in onion rings. Pour mixture into pie shells and top with sliced tomatoes. Bake at 350 degrees for 40 to 45 minutes. *Yield:* 2.

Kathy Kit

POTATO PANCAKES

7 to 8 potatoes	1 teaspoon salt
2 eggs	⅛ teaspoon pepper
3 tablespoons flour	oil, for frying

Peel and grate potatoes. Mix remaining ingredients into potatoes. Heat 2 tablespoons oil in frying pan. Drop large spoonfuls of potato batter into hot oil. Flip pancake when edges are brown and crusty. Fry until golden brown. Serve with sour cream or applesauce.

Aldona Vainius

SPINACH PIE

½ package fillo dough - 16 sheets	3 eggs
¼ cup butter or margarine	15 ounces whole milk ricotta
½ cup finely chopped onion	¾ cup butter or margarine, melted
3 10 ounce packages chopped spinach, thawed and drained	salt and pepper, to taste

Preheat oven to 350 degrees. Let pastry leaves sit at room temperature. In ¼ cup melted butter, sauté onion. Stir in spinach and remove from heat. In large bowl, beat eggs. Stir in cheese, salt, pepper and spinach-onion mixture. Mix well. Brush a 13x9x2 inch baking pan with melted butter. In bottom of baking pan layer 8 pastry leaves, brushing top of each with melted butter. Spread spinach mixture evenly over leaves. Repeat layer. Use scissors to trim off any uneven edges of pastry. Cut through top pastry layer on diagonal; then again in opposite direction, to form 3 inch diamonds. Bake 30 to 35 minutes, or until top crust is puffy and golden. *Note:* Keep unused pastry leaves covered with damp paper towels, to prevent drying.

Marie Beyer

BAKED ZUCCHINI

4 medium zucchini
1 pound mozzarella cheese
1 small onion, chopped
4 pieces fresh garlic, minced

olive oil, as needed
salt, to taste
pepper, to taste

Wash and slice zucchini. In a small pan sauté onion and garlic. Using a 4 quart saucepan, bring zucchini to boil, then simmer until tender. Drizzle olive oil into 9x13x2 inch baking pan. Arrange zucchini slices in pan. Put onion and garlic on zucchini. Slice mozzarella into large, thin slices and place on top. Sprinkle salt and pepper to taste. Drizzle olive oil on top, to taste. Bake in a 325 degree oven for 40 minutes.

Cheryl McGivney

ZUCCHINI

2 slices bacon fried, drippings
  reserved
1 onion, sliced
3 medium zucchini, sliced
½ cup chicken broth

2 teaspoons soy sauce
1 teaspoon cornstarch
½ teaspoon salt
2 teaspoons water

Fry bacon until crisp; put aside. Use 3 tablespoons of bacon drippings in fry pan. Add onion and zucchini; toss. Pour in broth, cover and steam for 3 minutes. Mix together remaining ingredients. Add to zucchini mixture. Bring to a boil. Put in serving dish and crumble bacon on top.

Patricia Seibert

FRIED ZUCCHINI

2 large zucchini
1 egg

1 cup flavored bread crumbs
1 cup oil, or more, if needed

Peel zucchini and slice into sticks or round slices. Beat egg in bowl. Dip zucchini in egg, then in bread crumbs. Fry in oil in a skillet. When golden brown, remove and drain on paper towels to absorb extra oil. Enjoy!

Vita Leggio

ITALIAN ZUCCHINI QUICHE

2 tablespoons olive oil
1 cup sliced small zucchini
½ cup thinly sliced onion
2 cloves garlic, crushed
2 fresh tomatoes, sliced
3 eggs

1 cup milk
4 tablespoons grated Parmesan
  cheese
4 ounces mozzarella cheese,
  shredded
1 unbaked 9 inch pie shell

In a medium skillet, heat olive oil and sauté zucchini, onion and garlic for 5 minutes. Cool slightly and place in unbaked pie shell. Cover with tomato slices. Beat eggs, milk, Parmesan cheese and half of the mozzarella. Pour over mixture. Bake in a 400 degree oven for 10 minutes. Lower heat to 350 degrees and bake until set, about 25 minutes. Remove from oven and sprinkle with remaining mozzarella cheese. Allow to cool for 10 minutes before serving. *Yield:* 6 servings.

Eleanor McCann

ZUCCHINI PIE

3 cups zucchini, thinly sliced
4 eggs
1 cup buttermilk baking mix
¼ cup grated Parmesan cheese

1 onion, chopped
salt and pepper, to taste
basil, to taste

Combine all ingredients in one large bowl. Pour into a greased 9 inch pie plate. Top with bread crumbs. Bake at 350 degrees for 45 minutes.

Diane Darmody

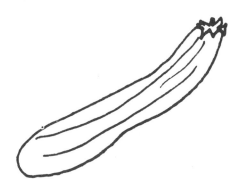

ZUCCHINI LASAGNA
LOW CALORIE

1 pound ground veal	¼ cup minced parsley
1 small onion, diced	¼ teaspoon thyme
2 cloves garlic, slivered	¼ teaspoon basil
1 16 ounce can crushed tomatoes	2 bay leaves
1 ounce part skim mozzarella	3 to 4 zucchini
cheese, shredded	salt and pepper, to taste
1 8 ounce can tomato sauce	

Brown veal, onion and garlic in hot skillet. Add all other seasonings, tomatoes and tomato sauce. Simmer uncovered for 30 minutes. Remove bay leaves. Slice zucchini lengthwise in ¼ inch slices. Line bottom of non stick baking pan with ½ the zucchini slices. Cover with ½ the veal sauce. Sprinkle ½ the cheese on top. Repeat the three layers. Bake uncovered in preheated 350 degree oven for 45 minutes.

Mary Ellen Kaufold

casseroles

CHICKEN AND BROCCOLI

1½ pounds of chicken cutlets
1 10¾ ounce can cream of
  mushroom soup

pepper and salt, to taste
1 bunch broccoli
½ cup fresh mushrooms, sliced

Cube chicken and brown in oil in frying pan and set aside. Parboil broccoli, cut up into short strips. Parboil mushrooms. Place chicken cutlets, mushrooms and broccoli in layers in 10x14 pan or baking dish. Add pepper and salt. Mix mushroom soup with ½ water, pour this mixture on top of casserole. Bake at 350 degrees for ½ hour in the oven or 10 minutes on high in microwave.

Ellen Kelly

BEEF CHOW MEIN CASSEROLE

1 tablespoon butter
1 green pepper, finely chopped
1 small onion, chopped
½ cup tomato juice
6 ounce can of Chinese noodles

1 pound ground beef
1 cup chopped celery
1 teaspoon salt
1 10¾ ounce can cream of
  mushroom soup

Preheat oven to 350 degrees. Grease 2 quart casserole. Melt butter in frying pan. Brown beef over medium heat. Add pepper, onion, celery, salt. Cook over low heat until tender. Add the water, soup, juice, and half of the Chinese noodles. Stir to blend; pour into casserole. Sprinkle with remaining noodles. Bake 30 minutes.

Diane Castagna

BROCCOLI QUICHE

1 pound broccoli, chopped
2 tablespoons butter
1 tablespoon oil
1 9 inch frozen pie shell
3 tablespoons Parmesan cheese

3 eggs, beaten
¼ cup heavy cream
⅛ teaspoon nutmeg
4 ounces Muenster cheese
salt and pepper, to taste

Sauté broccoli in butter and oil until crisp tender. Add salt and pepper. Bake pie shell according to package directions for 5 minutes. Place broccoli in shell. Combine eggs, heavy cream and nutmeg. Pour over broccoli, sprinkle Parmesan cheese on top. Lay slices of Muenster cheese on top to cover. Bake at 350 degrees for 40 minutes or until golden brown.

Cira Whittle

TEXAS CHILI

2 tablespoons oil
2 pounds chuck, cubed
1 cup chopped onion
1 green pepper, seeded and
  chopped
1 clove garlic, minced
1 12 ounce can tomato paste
2½ cups water
2 pickled jalapeno peppers,
  chopped

1½ tablespoons chili powder
½ teaspoon crushed red pepper
  flakes
½ teaspoon salt
½ teaspoon oregano
½ teaspoon cumin
1 16 ounce can pinto beans,
  drained

In a large heavy pot or dutch oven, heat oil and brown beef on all sides. Add onions, green pepper and garlic and cook with beef for about 5 minutes. Add all remaining ingredients except beans, and simmer for 1½ hours or until meat is tender. Add beans and simmer ½ hour longer.

Judy Hein

CHINESE BEEF CASSEROLE

1½ pounds shoulder London
  broil
salt and pepper, to taste
2 tablespoons oil
3 teaspoons soy sauce
1 green pepper, sliced
1 10 ounce can tomatoes,
  drained

2 tablespoons flour
1 clove garlic, minced
1 10 ounce can beef gravy, or 2
  beef bouillon cubes dissolved
  in 10 ounces water

Slice meat into ½ inch thick slices about 5 inches long. Put flour, salt and pepper into plastic bag and dredge meat. Brown meat and garlic in oil. Add gravy, soy sauce and green pepper. Bake in 350 degree oven for 45 minutes. Add tomatoes and bake for additional ½ hour. Serve over rice or thin noodles. *Yield:* 5 to 6 servings.

Jean Ciano

CASSEROLES

BAKED CHICK PEAS

3 1 pound cans chick peas,
  drained, reserve liquid
4 slices bacon, fried crisply
3 teaspoons dry mustard powder

¼ cup brown sugar
¼ cup dark molasses
salt and pepper, to taste
garlic salt, to taste

Mix half of reserved liquid from peas, with equal amount of water. Mix in dry mustard, brown sugar, molasses, salt, pepper and garlic salt. Combine with chick peas. Place in casserole. Bake at 350 degrees for one hour. Add remaining half of reserved chick pea liquid if casserole becomes dry during baking time. Garnish with crisply broiled bacon strips before serving.

Kathy Turnbull

CHICKEN CASSEROLE

½ cup butter
½ teaspoon basil
2 cups ricotta
½ cup Parmesan cheese
1 egg
1 10 ounce package chopped
  broccoli

½ cup flour
5 cups diced cooked chicken
8 ounces egg noodles, cooked
3½ cups chicken broth
4 ounces mozzarella, shredded

Melt butter. Blend in flour and basil. Beat in chicken broth. Stir until thick. Add chicken, set aside. Mix ricotta and eggs. Grease a 3 quart casserole. Place ⅓ chicken, ½ of the noodles, ½ the cheese, ½ the broccoli, ½ mozzarella in layers. Repeat and end with cheese spread on top. Sprinkle Parmesan cheese. Bake covered at 350 degrees for 40 minutes.

Annette Laino

HOT CHICKEN SALAD

6 cups cooked chicken (leftovers
  are fine)
2 10 ounce cans cream of
  chicken soup
1 cup chopped walnuts

salt and pepper, to taste
½ cup chopped onion
2 cups chopped celery
1 cup mayonnaise
potato chips, crushed

Line baking dish with crushed potato chips. Combine ingredients. Top with crushed chips. Bake at 325 degrees for 30 minutes.

Ellen Fusaro

CHICKEN DIVAN

2 10 ounce packages frozen
  broccoli
¼ cup flour
½ cup heavy cream
3 teaspoons white wine
2 pounds chicken cutlets or
  boned breasts

¼ cup butter
2 cups chicken broth or reserved
  liquid from poaching
¼ cup grated Parmesan cheese

Cook broccoli and drain. Set aside. Poach chicken in water and reserve liquid if not using broth. Slice into strips and set aside. In skillet, melt butter and add flour. Add liquid or broth and thicken; add cream and wine. Place broccoli and chicken in baking dish, add ½ sauce to chicken. Mix cheese with remaining sauce and pour over chicken. Bake at 350 degrees for 20 minutes. Serve over noodles or rice.

Cathy Manfredonia

HAMBURGER CORN BREAD PIE

1 tablespoon shortening
1½ pounds ground beef
1 cup chopped onions
2 teaspoons chili powder (more
  if desired)
2 8 ounce cans of tomato sauce

¾ teaspoon salt
1 teaspoon Worcestershire
  sauce, optional
1 16 ounce can red kidney beans
1 package of corn bread mix

Put shortening in skillet and heat, then add ground beef and onions. Brown meat until it is no longer pink in color. Add salt, chili powder and Worcestershire sauce, and simmer for 10 minutes. Drain red kidney beans and add kidney beans and tomato sauce to the meat mixture. Simmer another 5 minutes. Mix corn bread as directed on box. Put meat mixture into a casserole dish, and pour the corn bread mixture over the top. Bake at 450 degrees for 20 to 25 minutes.

Vita Leggio

CASSEROLES

SAUCY CHEESY BAKE

8 ounces egg noodles
2 15 ounce cans tomato sauce
1 tablespoon chopped parsley
¼ teaspoon garlic powder
3 cups shredded Cheddar or
    mozzarella cheese, about 12
    ounces

1 pound ground beef
½ cup chopped onion
¼ teaspoon basil
¼ teaspoon oregano

Preheat oven 350 degrees. Cook noodles according to package directions. In medium skillet, brown ground beef; drain. Stir in tomato sauce, onion, parsley, basil, garlic powder and oregano; simmer, stirring occasionally, 15 minutes. In 3 quart oblong baking dish, layer ½ sauce, noodles and cheese; repeat ending with cheese. Bake 25 minutes or until heated through. Makes about four servings.

Judy Flinn

BEEF AND MACARONI CASSEROLE

¼ cup olive oil
2 cloves garlic, finely minced
1½ pounds ground beef, chuck
½ cup beef broth or canned beef
    bouillon
2 teaspoons salt
½ teaspoon freshly ground black
    pepper
1 8 ounce package elbow
    macaroni, cooked and drained
⅓ cup freshly grated Parmesan
    cheese

⅓ cup finely chopped onion
1½ cups diced celery
1 pound fresh mushrooms, sliced
1 6 ounce can of tomato paste
1 19 ounce can of Italian style
    tomatoes
½ teaspoon oregano
1 10 ounce package frozen
    spinach, cooked and drained
½ cup buttered bread crumbs
basil, to taste

Heat oil in a large heavy skillet and sauté the onion and garlic until tender. Add the celery and meat; cook until the meat loses its red color. Add the mushrooms, beef broth, tomato paste, tomatoes, salt and pepper. Bring mixture to a boil and simmer 1 to 1½ hours, stirring occasionally. Add more beef broth if the mixture becomes too thick. Preheat oven to 350 degrees. Mix the sauce with the oregano, basil, macaroni and spinach and pour into a buttered 3 quart casserole. Top with the bread crumbs mixed with the cheese. Bake 30 minutes or until bubbly hot and lightly browned. *Yield:* 8 servings.

Colleen Maguire

76

CHEESE CASSEROLE

10 slices stale bread
3 cups milk
½ to 1 pound Cheddar cheese, shredded

6 eggs
1 teaspoon dry mustard
paprika

Preheat oven to 350 degrees. Cut bread into large cubes. Alternate bread and cheese in layers in greased baking pan, ending with cheese layer. Combine beaten eggs, milk, mustard, paprika and pour over cheese. Sprinkle with paprika. Let stand in refrigerator 1 hour. Bake in 350 degree oven about 1 hour, until a knife comes out of center clean. Serve at once with green vegetable or salad.

Helen Evancie

SPAGHETTI PIE

6 ounces spaghetti
2 tablespoons butter or margarine
⅓ cup grated Parmesan cheese
2 well-beaten eggs
1 cup cottage cheese
1 pound ground beef or bulk pork sausage
½ cup chopped onion

¼ cup chopped green pepper
1 8 ounce can tomatoes, cut up
1 6 ounce can tomato paste
1 teaspoon sugar
1 teaspoon crushed dried oregano
½ teaspoon garlic salt
½ cup shredded mozzarella cheese

Cook the spaghetti according to package directions; drain. Stir butter or margarine into hot spaghetti. Stir in Parmesan cheese and eggs. Form spaghetti mixture into a crust in a buttered 10 inch pie plate. Spread cottage cheese over bottom of spaghetti crust. In skillet cook ground beef or pork sausage, onion, and green pepper till vegetables are tender and meat is browned. Drain off excess fat. Stir in undrained tomatoes, tomato paste, sugar, oregano, and garlic salt; heat through. Turn meat mixture into spaghetti crust. Bake, uncovered, in 350 degree oven for 20 minutes. Sprinkle the mozzarella cheese on top. Bake 5 minutes longer or until cheese melts. *Yield:* 6 servings.

The Committee

CASSEROLES

HAMBURGER PIE

1½ pounds chuck, chopped
chopped onion, to taste
salt and pepper, to taste
1 10 ounce can tomato soup

2½ cups cooked green beans
4-5 medium potatoes
1 egg, beaten

Peel, cook and mash potatoes. Set aside. Brown beef and onion. Drain. Add salt and pepper. Place in 2 quart greased casserole. Add undiluted tomato soup. Spread green beans over top of meat. Mound mashed potatoes to cover entire top of casserole. Brush top of potatoes with beaten egg. Bake 30 minutes at 350 degrees uncovered.

Diane Mulhern

MACARONI CHEESE AND TUNA

1 pound macaroni
14 ounces extra sharp Cheddar
  cheese, shredded
1 28 ounce can peeled tomatoes

1 16 ounce can peeled tomatoes
1 13 ounce can solid white tuna,
  drained
4 cups water

Purée all tomatoes in blender or processor. Place tomato purée and water in 5-6 quart pot and bring to boil. Add macaroni and boil 10 minutes, stirring frequently. Add cheese and stir until melted. Add tuna and stir. Pour into large casserole, top with additional cheese, to taste. Bake at 350 degrees for 15 minutes. Delicious leftovers, fried in generous amount of margarine until brown and crispy.

Ellen Dougherty

OLD FASHIONED MACARONI AND CHEESE

¼ cup margarine
¼ cup flour
2 cups, 8 ounces, shredded sharp
  Cheddar cheese

2 cups of milk
1 teaspoon salt
1 7 ounce package of elbow
  macaroni

Cook and drain macaroni. Heat oven to 350 degrees. Make white sauce with margarine, flour, milk and salt. Add cheese, reserving ½ cup; stir until melted. Layer half of macaroni and cheese sauce in 1½ quart casserole; repeat layers. Top with remaining cheese. Bake at 350 degrees 20 to 25 minutes. *Yield:* 6 to 7 servings.

Paula Duggan

LOW CALORIE RATTATOUILLE

1½ cups tomato juice
1½ cups diced eggplant
1½ cups diced zucchini
1 cup fresh sliced mushrooms
1 medium green pepper, diced
1 medium tomato, diced
4 ounces sliced onions
½ cup chicken bouillon

½ bay leaf
dash garlic powder
dash basil leaves
8 ounces cubed cooked chicken
  or fish
1 teaspoon salt or to taste
½ teaspoon pepper or to taste
1 teaspoon chopped parsley

Combine tomato juice, eggplant, zucchini, mushrooms, green pepper, tomato, onion, bouillon, bay leaf, garlic powder and basil in a flameproof casserole. Simmer covered for 30 minutes. Uncover. Add chicken or fish and heat through. Add salt and pepper, sprinkle with parsley. Serve right from casserole. *Yield:* 2 servings.

Mary Langhauser

ITALIAN SAUSAGE AND LENTIL SKILLET

¾ pound sweet Italian sausage
¼ pound hot Italian sausage
2 onions, chopped
1 bay leaf
3 cups chicken broth
2 cups sliced zucchini
salt and pepper, to taste

parsley, for garnish
1 clove garlic, minced
½ teaspoon oregano
1¼ cups lentils, washed
3 tomatoes, peeled and sliced in
  strips
3 cups hot cooked brown rice

Remove sausage from casings. In a large skillet, sauté sausage until browned. Drain and set aside. Reserve fat. In remaining fat, sauté onion and garlic. Add bay leaf and oregano. Stir in chicken broth and lentils. Bring to a boil; cover and simmer 15 minutes. Add zucchini, tomato, salt and pepper. Cover and cook until lentils and zucchini are tender, about 15 minutes. Add cooked sausage and simmer until heated through. Sprinkle with chopped parsley. Serve over hot rice. *Yield:* 8 servings.

Eleanor McCann

CASSEROLES

PORK CHOP, ONION, RICE BAKE

6 pork chops
1 tablespoon margarine
2 tablespoons chopped red
   peppers

1 4 ounce can mushrooms
1 envelope dry onion soup mix
1 cup uncooked rice

Brown chops in margarine. Spread uncooked rice in bottom of a 9x13 baking pan. Reserve 1 tablespoon of onion soup mix. Sprinkle remaining mix over rice. Drain mushrooms, reserving liquid. Place mushrooms on top of rice and add enough water to reserved mushroom liquid to make 3 cups. Pour over rice and add peppers. Arrange pork chops over rice. Sprinkle with reserved onion soup mix. Cover and bake at 350 degrees for ¾-1 hour. Uncover, continue to bake 10 minutes, until all excess liquid evaporates.

Diana Piagentini

QUICK ITALIAN CASSEROLE

1½ pounds chop meat
1 8 ounce can stewed tomatoes
1 clove garlic, crushed
5 ounces cooked noodles or
   spaghetti

¼ to ½ cup chopped onion
1 10 ounce can tomato soup
1 cup sour cream
3 ounces cream cheese, softened

Brown chop meat, onion and garlic for 5 minutes. Add stewed tomatoes and tomato soup and continue to simmer for 10 minutes. Cook noodles or spaghetti, drain and set aside. When meat mixture has simmered, add the sour cream and cream cheese and mix thoroughly and evenly. Add the noodles and mix so that the sauce is distributed evenly. Pour into a 2 quart covered baking dish. Cook in a 350 degree oven for 30 to 35 minutes or until top is just beginning to brown.

Dianna Ebe

CHEESE SAUSAGE CASSEROLE

2 pounds sausage
½ pound mozzarella cheese,
   cubed
1 package crescent rolls

½ pound Muenster cheese,
   cubed
6 eggs

Remove sausage from casing, crumble and fry. Grease and flour a rectangular oven proof pan. Mix all ingredients except rolls together. Place on bottom of pan and cover with layer of rolls. Bake for 40 minutes at 350 degrees.

Mary Ellen Giuliani

PORK CHOPS AND POTATOES

6 pork chops
1 tablespoon margarine
6 medium potatoes, sliced thin
6 slices of American cheese

½ cup chopped onion
1 10¾ ounce can cream of
   mushroom soup
1¼ cups milk

Brown pork chops in margarine. In a large baking dish put half of the potatoes, then add the 6 slices of cheese, then the pork chops. Then layer again with the other half of potatoes. Sauté onions, then add cream of mushroom soup and milk, slowly. When heated, pour over the potatoes and meat. Bake 20 minutes, covered, then remove the cover and cook 45 minutes longer in a 350 degree oven.

Vita Leggio

TUNA CASSEROLE

1 13 ounce can tuna, drained
   and flaked
1 celery stalk, diced
1 carrot, diced
1 small onion, diced
8 ounces peas, canned or frozen

4 ounces elbow macaroni, or
   thin noodles, cooked
2 10 ounce cans cream of
   mushroom or chicken soup
1 tablespoon bread crumbs

Mix carrot, celery, onion and peas with uncooked soup. Add macaroni and tuna. Pour into 9x12 baking pan. Sprinkle with bread crumbs. Bake at 350 degrees for 25-30 minutes.

Lu Ann Clemente

CASSEROLES

ELEPHANT STEW

1 elephant   pepper
2 rabbits (optional)   brown gravy
salt

Cut elephant into small bite-size pieces. This should take about two months. Add enough brown gravy to cover. Cook over kerosene fire for about four weeks at 465 degrees. This will serve 3,000 people. If more are expected, add the two rabbits, but, do this only if necessary, as most people do not like to find HARE in their stew. *Happy Hunting!*

meats

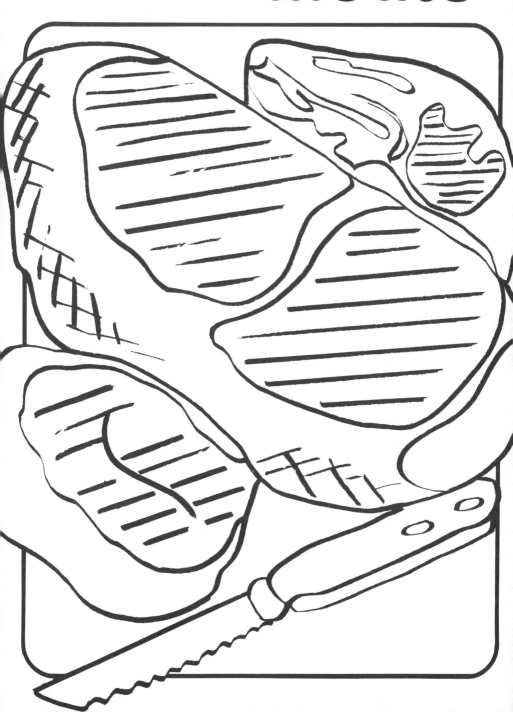

MEATS

BEEF PAPRIKA

¼ cup shortening
2 pounds beef chuck or round,
  cut into one inch cubes
1 cup sliced onion
1 small clove garlic, minced or
  ⅛ teaspoon garlic powder
¾ cup catsup
2 tablespoons Worcestershire
  sauce

1 tablespoon brown sugar
2 teaspoons salt
2 teaspoons paprika
½ teaspoon dry mustard
dash cayenne red pepper
1½ cups water
2 tablespoons flour
¼ cup water
3 cups noodles, cooked

Melt shortening in large skillet. Add meat, onion, and garlic. Cook and stir until meat is brown and onion is tender. Stir in catsup, Worcestershire sauce, sugar, salt, paprika, mustard, cayenne and 1½ cups water. Cover; simmer 2 to 2½ hours. Blend flour and ¼ cup water; stir gradually into meat mixture. Heat to boiling, stirring constantly. Boil and stir one minute. Serve over noodles. *Yield:* 6 to 8 servings.

Marie Domenici

MEATBALLS IN BUTTERMILK

1 pound ground beef
½ cup breadcrumbs
¼ cup chopped onion
½ cup milk

1 teaspoon salt
⅛ teaspoon pepper
3 tablespoons butter

Combine ingredients, except butter and shape into balls. Brown meatballs in butter. Remove from skillet. Keep warm. Pour most of drippings from skillet.

Sauce:
¼ cup butter
¼ cup flour
2¼ cups buttermilk
¼ teaspoon salt

2 tablespoons sugar
1½ teaspoons dry mustard
1 egg, beaten
1 teaspoon pepper

In skillet, combine remaining drippings and sauce ingredients. When thickened, add meat balls and simmer until flavors are blended.

Mrs. Nygaard

GOOD BEEF STEW

2 pounds beef stew meat, cut into one inch pieces
⅓ cup flour
¼ cup oil
½ cup snipped parsley
3 tablespoons packed brown sugar
1 tablespoon salt
½ teaspoon dried rosemary leaves

1 10½ ounce can condensed beef broth
¼ cup vinegar
1 12 ounce can beer
1 large onion, sliced
1 small clove garlic, crushed
6 large potatoes

Heat oven to 325 degrees. Coat beef pieces with flour. Brown beef in oil in dutch oven over medium heat; drain. Remove beef.

Mix parsley, brown sugar, salt and rosemary in Dutch oven. Stir in broth and vinegar gradually, scraping bottom of pan, until gravy is smooth. Heat to boiling, stirring constantly. Stir in beer, onion, garlic and beef. Add potatoes. Cover and bake until beef and potatoes are tender, about 3 hours. *Yield:* 6 servings.

Marie Domenici

FRENCH BEEF STEW

¼ pound cooked bacon, reserve drippings
2 pounds top round or sirloin, cubed
1½ teaspoons salt
1½ teaspoons pepper
1½ cups dry red wine
1½ cups water

1 carrot, sliced
½ teaspoon chopped parsley
½ teaspoon thyme
1 clove garlic, crushed
1 bay leaf
1 pound small white onions, peeled
½ pound fresh mushrooms

Brown beef slowly in 2 tablespoons bacon drippings. Sprinkle with salt pepper and flour to coat evenly. In a skillet boil wine, water, carrot, garlic, parsley, thyme and bay leaf. Pour over meat, in ovenproof casserole. Cook in a 350 degree oven for 2 hours, covered. Sauté onion and mushrooms in oil. Add to beef and cook for an additional 30 minutes.

Kathy Kit

WINTER BARBECUED ROAST BEEF DINNER

4½ pounds eye round   salt and pepper, as needed

Gravy:
2 cups cold water   4 tablespoons catsup
1 tablespoon vinegar   3 large onions, diced
1 teaspoon sugar
3 tablespoons Worcestershire
   sauce

Vegetable:
potatoes, amount desired, peeled

Preheat oven to 450 degrees. Wash and season meat generously with salt and pepper. Place meat upside down in roasting pan and brown in oven for 10 minutes. Reduce heat to 425 degrees.

For gravy, mix all ingredients in saucepan. Stir and heat to boiling. Pour into roasting pan. Roast meat 2 to 2½ hours. Quarter potatoes and add to pan 1½ hours before meat is cooked. Add extra cup boiling water if needed up to ½ hour before done. *Yield:* 4 to 6 servings.

Linda J. Candia

THREE HOUR BEEF STEW

2 pounds chuck, cubed   1 pound green beans
2 medium onions, sliced   2 beef boullion cubes
8 carrots, peeled   pepper to taste
8 potatoes, peeled

Place meat and onions in a Dutch oven. Stir. Add enough water to cover meat. Add boullion cubes. Cover and bake in a 350 degree oven for two hours.

Cut carrots and beans into one inch lengths. Quarter potatoes.

When meat has cooked two hours, add all vegetables and return to oven for one hour or until meat is tender. Add pepper. Stew may be thickened with cornstarch or flour.

Helen Evancie

GLAZED CORNED BEEF WITH VEGETABLES

4 to 5 pounds lean corned beef brisket
1 medium onion
6 to 8 whole cloves
2 bay leaves
1 clove garlic
½ teaspoon whole peppercorns
2 stalks celery with leaves, cut in chunks
8 to 10 medium potatoes, peeled and quartered
1 bunch carrots, peeled and chunked
½ cup catsup
2 tablespoons vinegar
2 tablespoons prepared mustard
1 medium head cabbage
chopped parsley, for garnish
spicy hot mustard
½ cup honey

Put brisket in large kettle and cover with water. Peel onion, stud with cloves, then add studded onion, bay leaves, garlic, peppercorns and celery to kettle. Bring to a full boil, then lower heat. Cover and simmer for 2½ hours or until meat is fork tender. Remove meat from liquid and place on rack in a shallow roasting pan. Reserve broth. *Note:* At this point, you may refrigerate meat and broth overnight or for several hours.

One hour before serving: Preheat oven to 350 degrees. Return broth to kettle and bring to full boil on top of stove. Add potatoes and carrots to broth. Reduce heat. Cover and cook gently for about 30 minutes.

While broth is cooking, make meat glaze, by combining catsup, vinegar, honey and prepared mustard in small saucepan. Cook for a few minutes over medium heat, stirring constantly until smooth. Spoon or brush glaze evenly over meat. Bake meat in shallow roasting pan for 30 to 40 minutes; basting occasionally with glaze. *Note:* Foil under meat will make clean up easier! About 15 minutes before meat is done, core cabbage and cut into eight wedges; add to simmering broth and continue to simmer until all vegetables are tender to taste.

To serve, remove meat from oven, cut in slices across the grain, arrange slices on large platter. Scoop vegetables from broth with slotted spoon and arrange, surrounding brisket on platter with vegetables.

Patricia Farrell

MEATS

QUICK FRANKFURTER AND POTATO SKILLET

4 medium potatoes, peeled and
  sliced
2 onions, sliced thin
2 tablespoons oil
1 pound frankfurters, cut in
  chunks

1 cup beef broth
1 tablespoon prepared mustard
½ teaspoon salt
¼ teaspoon pepper

In a large skillet, sauté potatoes and onions in hot oil until vegetables begin to brown. Add remaining ingredients. Bring to a boil; cover; simmer 10 minutes or until potatoes are tender. *Yield:* 4 servings.

Kathy Henry

HAMBURGER STROGANOFF

½ cup chopped onion
½ cup margarine or butter,
  melted
1 pound ground beef
1 pound sliced mushrooms
2 tablespoons flour
1 clove garlic, minced

¼ teaspoon pepper
½ teaspoon paprika
1 10¾ ounce can condensed
  cream of mushroom soup
1 cup sour cream
1 pound cooked noodles
chopped chives, for garnish

Sauté onion in melted butter until soft. Add beef, mushrooms, flour, garlic, pepper and paprika. Stir and sauté until beef is cooked. Add soup and simmer for 10 minutes. Stir in sour cream. Serve over noodles and top with chopped chives.

Nancy Besso

BARBECUED BEEF

2 pounds chuck, cubed
1 cup catsup
4 teaspoons brown sugar
1 tablespoon cider vinegar

½ teaspoon salt
1 medium onion, minced
pepper, to taste
¾ cup water

Place all ingredients in covered dutch oven. Stir. Cover and simmer 1½ to 2 hours, until tender. Serve over rice.

Helen Evancie

HAM HAWAIIAN

¼ cup chopped green pepper	2 tablespoons brown sugar
¼ cup chopped onion	½ teaspoon dry mustard
1 cup chopped ham	2 tablespoons vinegar
1 16 ounce can pineapple chunks, juice reserved	⅔ cup instant rice dash salt and pepper
2 tablespoons cornstarch	

Brown green pepper and onion in oil over low heat; add ham. Drain pineapple. Add water to reserved juice, to equal one cup liquid. Mix in cornstarch and add to ham in skillet. Dissolve brown sugar and mustard in vinegar; add to skillet. Stir constantly until thickened. Season to taste. Add pineapple chunks and rice. Cover and simmer 5 to 10 minutes. *Yield:* 4 servings.

Kathy O'Rourke

BARBECUED LAMB

3 to 4 cloves garlic	¼ cup lemon juice
2 cups white wine	1 leg of lamb, boned and
¼ cup oil	butterflied

Marinate lamb in first 4 ingredients for at least 6 hours, turning once. Place liquid marinade into aluminum or stainless steel roasting pan. Brown lamb on hot grill.

Place lamb in roasting pan, cover with foil. Place pan on grill for 45 to 60 minutes over medium, hot coals.

Cathy Manfredonia

POLISH KIELBASA AND SAUERKRAUT

2 pounds country style spareribs	pigs feet, optional
3 pounds kielbasa, smoked or fresh	caraway seeds, pinch fresh ham drippings, if available
1 pound beef ribs	

Put all ingredients in a large 8 quart pot. Cook over low flame 2 to 3 hours. *Serve! Yield:* 8 serving.

Gloria La Mura

MEATS

SWEET AND SOUR MEATBALLS

1 pound ground beef
1 egg, beaten
1 tablespoon cornstarch
1 teaspoon salt
2 tablespoons chopped onion
pepper, to taste
1 tablespoon oil
1 can pineapple chunks, reserve
   liquid

3 tablespoons cornstarch
1 tablespoon soy sauce
3 tablespoons vinegar
6 tablespoons water
½ cup sugar
3 large green peppers, seeded,
   cut into strips

Mix beef, egg, 1 tablespoon of cornstarch, salt, chopped onion and pepper. Form into balls and brown in a small amount of oil.

In a Dutch oven, combine oil and 1 cup of pineapple juice. Cook over a low heat for a few minutes. Mix 3 tablespoons cornstarch, soy sauce, vinegar, water and sugar. Add to Dutch oven. Cook until thickened, stirring constantly.

Add meatballs, pineapple chunks and green peppers. Heat thoroughly. *Note:* Serve as an hors d'oeuvre or over rice for a meal.

Diane Darmody

STUFFED PEPPERS
Low Calorie

6 green peppers
6 tablespoons chopped onion
4 tablespoons chopped celery
2 cloves garlic, minced
2 tablespoons oil
½ pound ground beef

4 ounces tomato paste
½ teaspoon salt
¼ teaspoon pepper
2 tablespoons grated Parmesan
   cheese

Slice tops from peppers and reserve. Core and seed peppers. Chop remainder of tops. Sauté chopped pepper tops, onion, celery and garlic in oil. Add meat and cook until browned. Drain excess fat. Add tomato paste, salt and pepper to meat mixture. Stuff pepper shells with mixture. Sprinkle each pepper with cheese. Place in baking pan. Bake, covered, in 350 degree oven for 35 to 45 minutes. *Yield:* 6 servings.

The Committee

GRANNY'S MEATBALLS

2 pounds ground round
4 thick, or 6 thin slices bread,
   broken into small pieces
tomato juice, enough to
   thoroughly moisten the bread

2 eggs
1 tablespoon soy sauce
1 teaspoon salt
pepper, to taste
2 large onions, sliced

Soak the bread in tomato juice, add eggs and salt. Mix ingredients together, except onions and shape into balls. Fry in hot oil until brown. Remove the meatballs from pan and fry two large onions in the pan. Return meatballs and cook until done.

Katherine Mikolivich

ITALIAN MEATLOAF

2 pounds ground beef
2 cups soft breadcrumbs
½ cup chopped onion
¼ cup grated Parmesan cheese
2 eggs, slightly beaten
1 teaspoon salt

⅓ teaspoon pepper
1 8 ounce can tomato sauce
½ teaspoon oregano
4 ounces part skim mozzarella
   cheese, shredded

Combine meat, breadcrumbs, onion, Parmesan cheese, eggs, salt and pepper; mix lightly. Press mixture into a 13x9 inch baking pan. Bake at 350 degrees for 30 minutes. Pour off drippings. Combine tomato sauce and oregano. Pour mixture over meatloaf. Top meatloaf with 1 cup mozzarella cheese and continue baking for 30 minutes. *Yield:* 8 to 10 servings.

Eileen Dunne

FIREHOUSE POT ROAST

3 pounds boneless rump roast
2 10¾ ounce cans golden
   mushroom soup

1 package dry onion soup mix

Preheat oven to 325 degrees. Place roast on double thickness of aluminum foil. Pour mushroom soup over meat and sprinkle onion soup mix on top. Enclose meat entirely in foil. Place in shallow pan. Cook 2½ hours or until tender. *Note:* The juices from the meat will blend with the soups and produce a thick, smooth gravy that can be served on the side.

Mary McGuire

COUNTRY STYLE POT ROAST

4 pounds brisket
1 envelope dry onion soup mix
1 12 ounce can beer
½ can whole cranberry sauce

½ cup catsup
salt and pepper, to taste
garlic powder, to taste

Place meat in a Dutch oven or covered roasting pan. Mix remaining ingredients together and pour over meat. Bake at 350 degrees for about 2 hours, or until tender. Remove from pan and allow to cool. Slice meat and return to pan with gravy from which all the fat has been removed.

To serve, heat in a 350 degree oven, covered for about 30 minutes or until heated. Do not allow meat to sit in gravy overnight. *Note:* This dish can be made a day ahead and reheated.

Carole DeCillia

MUSHROOM POT ROAST

3 to 4 pounds boneless beef pot
  roast
1 10¾ ounce can cream of
  mushroom soup

¾ cup water
2 to 4 tablespoons flour

In large pot, brown meat, using some shortening if necessary. Pour off fat. Stir in soup and ½ cup water. Cover and simmer 2½ to 3 hours or until tender. Gradually blend ¼ cup water into flour; slowly stir into sauce. Cook, stirring until thickened. *Yield:* 6 to 8 servings.

Eileen Dunne

SAVORY POT ROAST

1 tablespoon oil
¼ cup red wine vinegar
¼ cup catsup
2 tablespoons soy sauce
2 tablespoons Worcestershire
  sauce

1 teaspoon rosemary leaves
½ teaspoon garlic powder
½ teaspoon dry mustard
3 to 4 pounds pot roast

Brown meat in oil. Drain off fat. Sprinkle roast with salt. Combine other ingredients; pour over roast. Cover tightly and simmer 1½ to 1¾ hours.

Susan Jencen

BARBECUED RIBS

2 pounds pork spareribs
1 cup water
2 teaspoons salt
2½ tablespoons chili sauce
2 tablespoons finely chopped
  onion
1½ cups maple syrup

1 tablespoon Worcestershire
  sauce
2 teaspoons salt
½ teaspoon dry mustard
¼ teaspoon chili powder
⅛ teaspoon pepper
vegetable spray

In a medium bowl, combine 1 cup water and 2 teaspoons salt to make salt water mixture. In a separate bowl, combine remaining ingredients, except spareribs. Mix well.

Place spareribs on grill, coated with vegetable spray, about 5 to 7 inches above low temperature coals. Cook spareribs about 45 minutes, turning and brushing frequently with salt water mixture. Continue cooking 15 minutes or until done, turning and brushing frequently with maple syrup sauce. *Yield:* 3 to 4 servings.

Sister Jeannette Tenaglia

CHINESE SPARERIBS

½ cup brown sugar
½ teaspoon garlic powder
¼ teaspoon ginger
2 tablespoons soy sauce

¾ cup boiling water
1 beef bouillon
spareribs

Dissolve bouillon in boiling water. Add remaining ingredients and stir until well blended. Arrange spareribs in 13x9x2 inch pan and pour mixture over. Let stand covered about 1 hour. Bake at 350 degrees for 1½ hours.

Eileen Rathgaber

FAVORITE PORK CHOPS

6 to 8 pork chops
1 16 ounce can sauerkraut
2 apples, sliced
2 onions, sliced

caraway seeds, pinch
pepper, to taste
¼ cup water

Place chops in ovenproof casserole. Cover chops with sauerkraut. Add remaining ingredients to casserole. Cover and bake at 300 degrees for 2½ hours or until chops are done and tender. *Yield:* 6 to 8 servings.

Sister Eleanor McDonnell

OVEN BAKED PORK CHOPS

¼ cup oil
½ cup brown sugar
¼ cup chili sauce
¼ cup catsup
½ cup cider vinegar

1 medium onion, thinly sliced
1 teaspoon mustard
1 teaspoon Worcestershire sauce
6 pork chops

Mix first 8 ingredients. Arrange chops in shallow dish. Pour marinade over. Cover and refrigerate for two hours. Bake in a 325 degree oven for 1½ hours.

Mary Ellen Giuliani

POLYNESIAN SWEET AND SOUR PORK

2¾ pounds pork, cut into ½ inch
   cubes

Marinade:
½ cup sherry
3 to 4 tablespoons soy sauce

¼ teaspoon black pepper

Polynesian Mixture:
1¼ cups sugar
1 16 ounce can pineapple
   chunks, reserve juice
1 cup apple cider vinegar
½ cup finely chopped candied
   ginger
3 tablespoons cornstarch

1 tablespoon soy sauce
2 large green peppers, sliced
   into strips
2 large carrots, sliced and
   cooked
flour, as needed
oil, as needed

Marinate chops in sherry, soy sauce and pepper for at least ½ hour. Drain, reserving marinade. Mix sugar and cornstarch, add vinegar and reserved juice from pineapple. Add chopped ginger and soy sauce and any drained marinade. Stir well until sauce has thickened. Coat pork with flour and fry in hot oil until well browned. Add pork, green pepper, carrots and pineapple chunks to sauce. Stir gently until well coated with sauce. Serve on white rice.

Paula B. Fisher

CHOPS AND STUFFING

4 to 6 pork chops
3 cups soft bread cubes
2 tablespoons chopped onion
¼ cup margarine, melted
¼ cup water

¼ teaspoon poultry seasoning
¼ teaspoon parsley
1 10¾ ounce can cream of
   mushroom soup
⅓ cup water

Brown pork chops on both sides in skillet. Place in shallow oven proof casserole dish. Lightly mix together bread cubes, onion, margarine, ¼ cup water, poultry seasoning and parsley. Place a mound or overly generous tablespoonful of stuffing on top of each chop. Blend soup and ⅓ cup of water until smooth. Pour over chops and stuffing. Bake at 350 degrees for approximately 1 hour. *Yield:* 4 to 6 servings.

Judy Hein

PORK ROAST

3 to 4 pounds pork loin roast
salt and pepper, to taste
1 tablespoon flour

pinch of rosemary
1 pound can sauerkraut, drained
1 pound jar chunky applesauce

Rub roast with mixture of salt, pepper, flour and rosemary. Brown roast in 450 degree oven for 15 to 20 minutes. Place in Dutch oven. Add sauerkraut over meat and cover with applesauce. Cover tightly and simmer slowly about four hours.

Carol Lohmann

SAUSAGE AND PEPPERS

5 pounds Italian sweet sausage
5 pounds green peppers, sliced
3 tablespoons corn oil

8 large onions, sliced
1 large can Italian tomatoes
salt and pepper, to taste

Cut up sausage and place in large roasting pan with oil, salt and pepper, and sliced onions. Bake at high temperature of 400 degrees for 45 minutes, turning often. Lower temperature to 350 degrees and add peppers. Cook for 10 minutes; add tomatoes. Bake for an additional 40 minutes, turning occasionally. Turn oven off. Leave sausage and peppers in oven for 30 to 45 minutes. Serve, or freeze for future use.

Marie Sluka

MEATS

ROSY RIBS

4 pounds spareribs
salt and pepper, to taste

paprika, to taste

Sauce:
3 to 4 tablespoons oil
1 pound onions, chopped
2 cloves garlic, crushed
½ cup catsup
9 tablespoons Worcestershire
  sauce

½ cup lemon juice
1½ cups water
5 tablespoons sugar

Cut spareribs into serving size pieces. Place in roasting pan and sprinkle with salt, pepper and paprika. Place in oven and bake at 350 degrees for 1½ hours, turning ribs and draining fat when necessary. Meanwhile prepare sauce. Blend sauce ingredients together and simmer 10 to 15 minutes. When ribs are cooked, drain all fat and pour sauce over ribs. Let stand for ½ hour. Return to oven for ½ hour, bake at 350 degrees, turning occasionally.

Kathy Kiley

PEPPER STEAK

1½ pounds sirloin steak, ½ inch
  thick
3 tablespoons soy sauce
2 green peppers, cut into 1 inch
  pieces
2 tomatoes, peeled and cut into
  eighths

2 medium onions, chopped
1 cup beef broth
1 clove garlic, minced
2 tablespoons cornstarch
¼ cup cold water
3 to 4 cups hot, cooked rice

Trim fat and bone from meat. Cut meat into 4 to 6 pieces. Grease large skillet lightly with fat from meat. Brown meat on one side; turn and season with ¼ teaspoon salt. Brown other side of meat; turn and season with remaining ¼ teaspoon salt. Push meat to one section. Add onion, cook and stir until tender. Stir in broth, soy sauce and garlic. Cover; simmer 10 minutes or until meat is tender. Add green peppers. Cover and simmer 5 minutes. Blend cornstarch and water; stir gently into meat mixture. Cook, stirring constantly, until mixture thickens and boils. Boil and stir 1 minute, add tomatoes; heat through. Serve over rice. *Yield:* 4 to 6 servings.

Maria Lombardo

SAUSAGE AND SPINACH PIE

1 deep dish pie shell and top
  crust
4 eggs
1 16 ounce package mozzarella
  cheese, shredded
½ teaspoon salt

⅛ teaspoon garlic powder
1 pound sweet Italian sausage
1 10 ounce package frozen
  spinach, thawed and drained
1 pound ricotta cheese
⅛ teaspoon pepper

Remove sausage from casings and cook until well browned. Drain well. Reserve 1 egg yolk. In a large bowl combine the remaining eggs with the sausage, drained spinach, the two cheeses, salt, pepper and garlic powder. Pour into the pie shell. Flatten and wet the edge of the shell. Top pie with crust. Cut slits in the top crust. Seal it well. Mix a little water with the reserved egg yolk and brush it over the top crust. Bake pie at 375 degrees for about one hour or until golden.

Gerry Accardo

SHORTCUT CUBE STEAK STEW

3 tablespoons flour
1½ teaspoons salt
¼ teaspoon pepper
4 cube steaks, cut into 2x½ inch
  strips
3 tablespoons shortening
1 large onion, sliced
1 clove garlic, minced
4 medium potatoes, pared, cut
  into cubes

2 16 ounce cans stewed tomatoes
1 8 ounce can tomato sauce
1 teaspoon salt
1 10 ounce package frozen peas
½ medium green pepper, cut
  into strips
½ pound fresh mushrooms,
  sliced

Mix flour, salt and pepper. Coat meat with mixture. Melt shortening in Dutch oven; brown meat. Add onion, garlic, potatoes, tomatoes, tomato sauce; heat to boiling. Reduce heat. Simmer, uncovered, stirring occasionally, about 30 minutes or until meat and potatoes are almost tender.

Add peas, pepper, mushrooms. Heat to boil. Reduce heat and simmer 10 minutes longer or until peas are tender and peppers are tender-crisp. *Note:* For thicker stew, shake ⅓ cup water and 2 tablespoons flour in a jar. Stir into stew, until thickened. *Yield:* 6 servings.

Jean Betette

MEATS

PEPPER STEAK

1 pound round steak, cut into
strips
2 tablespoons oil
4 peppers, cut up
½ cup chopped onions
1½ cups sliced celery
2 cloves garlic, crushed
1 teaspoon salt

½ teaspoon pepper
½ teaspoon sugar
2 cups beef bouillon
1 8 ounce can water chestnuts
1 4 ounce can mushrooms
2 tablespoons cornstarch
1 tablespoon soy sauce
¼ cup water

Brown meat in hot oil in a skillet. Add peppers, onion, celery, garlic, salt, pepper, sugar and bouillon. Simmer, covered 40 minutes or until meat is tender. Add water chestnuts and mushrooms. Mix cornstarch with soy sauce and water. Stir into hot mixture. Bring to a boil and cook until thickened. Serve over rice.

Carol Lohmann

MINUTE STEAK STEW

4 minute steaks
2 tablespoons flour, seasoned
with salt and pepper, to taste
2 tablespoons butter
1 small onion, finely diced

1 cup peas and carrots
½ cup water
6 to 8 small round potatoes
1 8 ounce can of tomato sauce

Cut steaks into one inch strips. Roll steak strips in flour. In skillet, heat butter until it begins to bubble; add meat. Brown well and add remaining ingredients. Cover skillet and simmer 10 minutes.

Ann Marcic

STEAK TERIYAKI

¼ cup light brown sugar, packed
¼ cup soy sauce
1 tablespoon oil
¼ teaspoon ginger

1 clove garlic
2 pounds flank steak or London
broil

Combine first 5 ingredients. Add steak to marinade. Marinate overnight. Next day turn steak over until ready to cook. Broil steak and serve. Marinade may be heated and served over steak.

Terry Howley

RICE BALLS

1 large onion, diced	1 pound cooked rice
1 pound chopped beef	½ cup margarine or butter,
¼ cup oil	melted
1 6 ounce can of tomato paste,	¾ cup grated Parmesan cheese
plus one 6 ounce can of water	2 eggs
salt and pepper, to taste	bread crumbs, as needed

Sauté onion and chopped beef in ¼ cup oil. Add tomato paste, water and salt and pepper to taste. Cook to make a moist mixture, about ½ hour. In a large bowl mix, rice, margarine, eggs, and grated cheese. Put a small scoop of rice in palm of hand. Place one teaspoon or more of meat mixture in center and add more rice to form a ball. Roll in bread crumbs. Deep fry the rice balls until golden brown. Drain. *Yield:* 24 rice balls.

Mary Primiani

VEAL CORDON BLEU

4 boneless veal cutlets, or 1	¼ teaspoon pepper
pound veal round steak	¼ teaspoon allspice
4 thin slices boiled or cooked	1 egg, slightly beaten
ham	½ cup bread crumbs
4 thin slices Swiss cheese	3 tablespoons shortening
2 tablespoons flour	2 tablespoons water
½ teaspoon salt	

If using veal round steak, cut into 4 serving pieces. Pound meat to ¼ inch thickness. Place a slice of ham and cheese on each piece of meat. Roll up carefully, beginning at narrow end; secure rolls with wooden picks. Mix flour salt, pepper and allspice; coat rolls with flour mixture. Dip rolls into egg, then roll in bread crumbs. Melt shortening in large skillet; brown rolls about 5 minutes. Reduce heat and add water. Cover; simmer 45 minutes or until tender. Remove cover last 2 to 3 minutes to crisp rolls slightly. *Yield: 4 servings.*

Diane Darmody

MEATS

VEAL STEW ITALIAN STYLE

1½ pounds boneless veal
  shoulder,
  cut into 1 inch cubes
¼ cup flour
2 teaspoons salt
¼ teaspoon pepper
3 tablespoons butter or
  margarine
8 ounces marinara sauce
1 teaspoon dried basil leaves
3 parsley sprigs
1 bay leaf
2 tablespoons chopped parsley
1 tablespoon grated lemon peel

3 tablespoons olive oil
1 cup coarsely chopped onion
3 pared large carrots, cut into 2
  inch pieces
½ cup diced celery
2 cloves garlic, crushed
½ cup dry white wine
1 teaspoon dried thyme leaves
2 medium size zucchini, cut into
  1 inch pieces
linguini, cooked and buttered,
  amount desired

Wipe veal with damp paper towels. On sheet of waxed paper combine flour, salt and pepper; roll veal cubes in mixture, coating them well on all sides.

In hot butter and oil, in 5 quart Dutch oven, over medium heat, brown veal, turning to brown well on all sides for 30 minutes. Remove as browned; set aside.

To drippings in Dutch oven, add onion, carrot, celery and garlic; sauté, stirring until onion is tender, about 5 minutes. Add marinara sauce, wine, ¾ cup water, basil, thyme, parsley and bay leaf. Bring mixture to boiling. Reduce heat; add browned veal. Simmer, covered for 30 minutes. Add zucchini; cook 30 minutes longer or until veal is very tender.

Meanwhile, in small bowl combine chopped parsley and grated lemon peel; mix well. Place veal on warm serving dish. Sprinkle with remaining parsley mixture. Serve with linguini, tossed with butter.

Kathryn Slaska

VEAL SCALLOPINI MARSALA

1 pound veal cutlets, or chicken
    cutlets
1 egg, slightly beaten
flavored breadcrumbs, as needed
2 cups water

2 packages brown gravy mix
4 ounces fresh or canned
    mushrooms, sliced
1 cup Marsala wine
parsley, for garnish

Flatten cutlets with meat mallet. Dip cutlets in egg and flavored breadcrumbs; brown in oil. Remove meat, scrape sides and bottom of pan. Mix water and brown gravy mix in pan. Add mushrooms. Place meat back in pan. Add 1 cup of Marsala wine. Simmer 45 minutes. Sprinkle with parsley.

Linda J. Candia

VENISON STEAK PROVIDENCE STYLE

1 onion, chopped
2 tablespoons butter
2 pounds venison, sliced
flour
2 cups water

1 teaspoon dry mustard
1 tablespoon vinegar
1 teaspoon salt
1 teaspoon paprika
¼ teaspoon cayenne pepper

Sauté onions in butter, until translucent. Dredge meat in flour and fry quickly in same skillet with onions. Remove meat and set aside.

Add 1 tablespoon flour, mustard, vinegar, salt, paprika and cayenne pepper to skillet. Stir; add water, stir again. Add meat; cover and simmer 15 minutes.

Frank DePasquale

MEATS

poultry

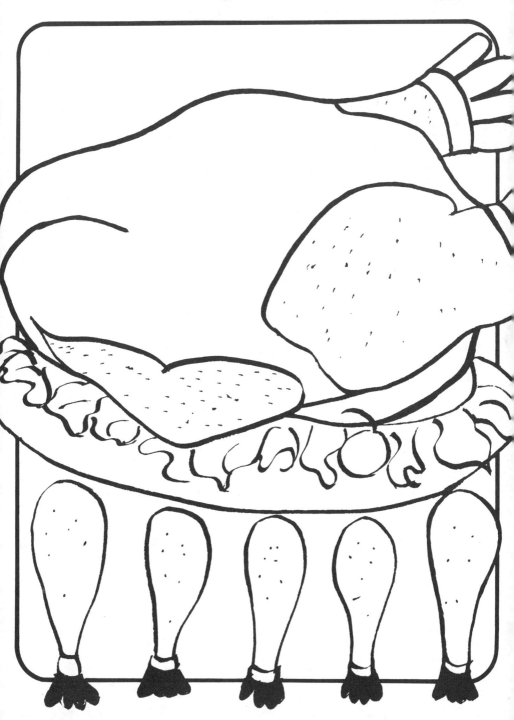

POULTRY

ALMOND CHICKEN

1 pound chicken, cubed
3 tablespoons soy sauce
1 cup celery, sliced
1 cup bamboo shoots
8 water chestnuts
½ cup almonds, lightly toasted

¾ teaspoon salt
1 teaspoon sugar
1 tablespoon cornstarch
2 tablespoons sherry
¼ cup chicken broth
peanut oil, as needed

Sprinkle soy sauce over chicken and let dry a little. Make sauce of salt, sugar, cornstarch, sherry, and chicken broth. Sauté chicken until tender in small amount of peanut oil. Remove from pan. Stir fry vegetables, stir sauce and add chicken. Garnish with almonds which have been lightly toasted. Serve with rice and fresh fruit.

Susan Jensen

BAKED CHICKEN

1 12 ounce jar apricot preserves
1 envelope onion soup mix
2 chickens, cut into pieces

¾ tablespoon Worcestershire
   sauce

Combine apricot preserves, onion soup mix and Worcestershire sauce. Place chicken in baking dish and spoon sauce over chicken. Bake uncovered 1 hour in 350 degree preheated oven. Increase temperature to 450 degrees and bake 10 minutes more. *Yield:* 8 servings.

Mary McGuire

BARBECUED CHICKEN

1 chicken, quartered
½ cup vinegar
¼ cup catsup
¼ cup cooking oil
1 teaspoon pepper

2 tablespoons salt
1 tablespoon Worcestershire
   sauce
1 tablespoon prepared mustard
1 teaspoon onion salt

Combine all ingredients, except chicken. Pour mixture over chicken and let stand 1 hour. Cook on outdoor grill or broil in oven, turning and basting frequently with remaining marinade about 1 hour or until tender. If chicken tends to scorch under broiler, place foil loosely over top of chicken after browning. *Yield:* 4 servings.

Mrs. Blanco

SHERRIED ARTICHOKE CHICKEN

1 frying chicken, approximately
  3 pounds, cut up
salt, pepper and paprika, to
  taste
6 tablespoons butter or
  margarine
1 can artichoke hearts, drained

¼ to ½ pound mushrooms
2 tablespoons flour
⅔ cup chicken broth
¼ cup sherry
rosemary, to taste

Sprinkle chicken generously with salt, pepper and paprika. Brown chicken on all sides. Place in an oven proof dish. Arrange artichoke hearts between chicken pieces. Add remaining butter to the drippings. Add mushrooms and sauté just until tender. Sprinkle flour over mushrooms. Stir in chicken broth, sherry and rosemary. Cook, stirring a few minutes. Pour over chicken. Cover and bake at 375 degrees for 40 minutes.

Sister Jeannette Tenaglia

JANET'S CHICKEN KIEV

¾ cup butter, softened
1 tablespoon green onion,
  shallots or chives, finely
  minced
salt and pepper, to taste
flour, as needed
1 tablespoon chopped parsley

½ teaspoon salt
⅛ teaspoon pepper
6 chicken cutlets
1 egg plus 1 tablespoon cold
  water
¾ cup bread crumbs

Mix softened butter, chives, shallots or green onions, salt and pepper. Shape into 6 sticks. Chill or freeze. Place chicken cutlets between two pieces of waxed paper. Pound with mallet. Repeat with other breasts. Place butter on each breast. Roll breast so butter is completely encased. Close with toothpicks. Sprinkle lightly with salt and pepper. Heat oven to 400 degrees. Dredge chicken in flour. Dip in egg and water mixture and roll in bread crumbs. Brown in ¼ cup butter or margarine in skillet until golden brown on all sides. Place chicken in shallow baking pan. Bake 15 to 20 minutes or until tender. *Hint:* For company, do everything except bake. Place in refrigerator before company comes. When ready to serve dinner, remove from refrigerator and turn oven to 400 degrees and then bake 20 minutes or until tender.

Joanne Halloran

POULTRY

CHEESE-FILLED CHICKEN BREASTS

3 large chicken breasts, split,
skinned and boned
2 tablespoons finely chopped
ripe olives
6 large fresh mushroom caps
1 tablespoon water
2 tablespoons snipped parsley

3 tablespoons flour
3 ounces cream cheese, softened
⅛ teaspoon thread saffron,
crushed
1 egg, beaten
½ cup seasoned bread crumbs

Place each piece of chicken between 2 pieces of clear plastic wrap. With a meat mallet pound chicken breast halves to ¼ inch thickness; remove plastic wrap. Sprinkle with salt. In a bowl stir together cream cheese, olives and saffron. Spread on one side of each breast half. Center one mushroom cap atop each breast half. Fold in edges of chicken envelope-style. Mix egg and water. Combine breadcrumbs and snipped parsley. Dip chicken rolls in flour, then dip them in the egg mixture. Roll in crumb mixture on all sides. Place in a 10x6x2 inch baking dish. Bake in a 350 degree oven for 45 to 50 minutes or till done. Drain on paper toweling. Cool. Cover and chill. *Yield:* 6 servings.

Vivian G. Guffin

SHELLS WITH CHICKEN AND BROCCOLI

1 pound small macaroni shells
1 cup broccoli flowerettes
2 scallions, chopped
1 cup heavy cream
salt and freshly ground pepper,
to taste

4 tablespoons butter
1 cup mushrooms, sliced
8 ounces chicken breast, cut
into narrow strips
grated Parmesan cheese,
optional

Cook shells according to package directions. In a medium skillet, melt 3 tablespoons butter and sauté broccoli for 3 to 4 minutes. Add mushrooms and scallions and cook 2 minutes longer. Remove from pan and set aside. Add remaining tablespoon of butter and quickly sauté chicken strips. Return vegetables to pan and add heavy cream, salt and pepper. Bring to a boil, lower heat and simmer 2 minutes. Pour over cooked pasta and toss lightly. Sprinkle with cheese.

Pauline Comando

CHICKEN IN BROWN GRAVY

8 chicken breasts or parts
flour, enough to coat chicken
1 onion, sliced
1 cup flour
2 tablespoons liquid gravy
  browning product

butter, as necessary
salt and pepper, to taste
12 small potatoes, peeled

Lightly grease a large roasting pan. Dredge chicken in flour and place in pan. Dot each piece with a pat of butter. Season with salt and pepper. Mix 1 cup flour with enough water to thin. Add flour mixture and liquid gravy browning product, with onion to chicken. Cut potatoes in small chunks and add to chicken. Bake for 1½ hours or until chicken and potatoes are done, in a 350 degree oven. *Yield:* 6 to 8 servings.

Isabella Love

BARBECUED CHICKEN

1 frying chicken, cut up
3 ounces horseradish mustard
4 ounces butter
1 teaspoon Worcestershire sauce

3 teaspoons catsup
2 teaspoon vinegar
½ cup hot water

Brown chicken in frying pan and set aside in an oven proof dish. Combine and simmer remaining ingredients for 25 minutes and pour over chicken. Bake 1 hour at 350 degrees.

Geri Wheeler

CHICKEN CORDON BLEU

8 chicken cutlets
8 thin slices Swiss cheese
1½ teaspoons paprika
¼ cup butter
1½ to 2 cups chicken broth

8 thin slices boiled ham
3 tablespoons flour
⅛ teaspoon pepper
⅓ cup sherry

Flatten chicken breast with spatula; on one half of breast place folded slice of ham and cheese. Fold over to cover and secure with toothpicks. Combine flour, paprika and pepper and coat chicken. In hot butter, sauté on both sides until golden. Add sherry and broth and simmer covered 30 minutes, turning once.

Mary Deveau

CHICKEN CACCIATORE
(Spanish Style)

1 3 pound chicken, cut up
¼ cup shortening
2 cups thinly sliced onion rings
½ cup chopped green pepper
2 cloves garlic, crushed

½ 3 ounce can tomato paste
4 large potatoes, pared
1 teaspoon salt
¼ teaspoon oregano
4 cups water

Wash chicken and pat dry. In large skillet put in chicken, onion rings, pepper, garlic, salt, oregano, tomato paste and water. Cook chicken with ingredients over medium heat 15 to 20 minutes. Heat to boiling, stirring occasionally. Reduce heat. Add potatoes to skillet and cover. Simmer 30 to 40 minutes or until thickest pieces are tender.

Steven Gonzalez

CHICKEN CORDON BLEU

3 chicken breasts, about 2½
  pounds
3 slices Swiss cheese, cut in half
3 slices boiled ham, cut in half
2 tablespoons butter or
  margarine

1 10 ounce can cream of chicken
  soup
¼ cup milk
parsley, chopped

Flatten chicken breasts. Top each with ½ slice cheese, then ham. Secure with toothpicks. In skillet, brown chicken-side down in butter. Stir in soup and milk. Cover, cook over low heat 20 minutes or until tender. Stir occasionally. Garnish with parsley.

Ray O'Connor

LUCIE'S CHICKEN

1½ pounds chicken cutlets
1 cup chicken bouillon
⅛ teaspoon mace
¼ cup butter

½ teaspoon lemon rind
1 cup mushrooms
pepper, to taste

Coat chicken with flour. Melt ¼ cup butter. Sauté floured chicken cutlets. Add all ingredients. Cover. Simmer 30-40 minutes. Serve on rice. *Yield:* 4 to 5 servings.

Lucille Irving

CHICKEN CONFETTI

4 to 5 pound broiler-fryer, cut up
1 teaspoon salt
⅛ teaspoon pepper
¼ cup salad oil
½ cup chopped onion
1 clove garlic, minced
2 16 ounce cans tomatoes
1 8 ounce can tomato sauce

1 6 ounce can tomato paste
2 tablespoons minced parsley
1 tablespoon basil
¼ teaspoon pepper
7 or 8 ounces spaghetti cooked
  and drained
grated Parmesan cheese

Wash chicken pieces and pat dry. Season with 1 teaspoon salt and ⅛ teaspoon pepper. In large skillet or dutch oven, brown chicken in oil; remove chicken. Pour off all but 3 tablespoons fat. Add onion and garlic; cook and stir until onion is tender. Stir in chicken and remaining ingredients, except spaghetti and cheese. Cover tightly, cook chicken slowly 1 to 1½ hours or until tender, stirring occasionally and adding water if necessary. Skim off excess fat. Serve on spaghetti; sprinkle with Parmesan cheese. *Yield:* 4 to 6 servings.

Antonia De Lisi

CHICKEN - BOB

1 pound boneless chicken
  breasts, cut in bite size
  pieces
½ onion, thickly cubed
1 green pepper, cut in large
  julienne pieces

1 tomato, thickly cubed
fresh mushrooms, sliced, to
  taste
feta cheese, to taste

Marinade:
¼ teaspoon garlic powder
¼ teaspoon salt
3 tablespoons oil

½ teaspoon oregano
⅛ teaspoon pepper
½ freshly squeezed lemon

Blend all marinade ingredients and let vegetables and chicken marinate for 24 hours in refrigerator. Remove, and sprinkle with crumbled feta cheese and place under the broiler for 10-12 minutes turning twice. Serve on rice pilaf. *Yield:* 2 to 3 servings.

Sister Jeannette Tenaglia

CHICKEN DELICIOUS

1 chicken, cut up
6 medium potatoes, peeled and
  quartered
2 pounds sweet sausage
⅓ cup oil

1 teaspoon paprika
1 teaspoon oregano
1½ teaspoons salt
½ teaspoon garlic powder
½ teaspoon black pepper

Mix oregano, paprika, garlic powder, salt and black pepper together. Cut sausage links into thirds. Put potatoes into a 3 quart casserole and sprinkle half the seasoning on them. Put chicken and sausage on top of potatoes and pour oil on chicken and sausage. Sprinkle rest of seasoning on top. Cook 1 hour at 425 degrees in covered pan. Reduce heat to 375 degrees and take cover off. Cook another 30 minutes or until browned. If 3 quart casserole is unavailable, you may use a roasting pan and cover it with aluminum foil.

Deborah Zito

FOOLPROOF FRIED CHICKEN

1 fryer chicken, 2½ to 3 pounds,
  cut up
½ cup flour
1 teaspoon salt

pepper, to taste
2 eggs, beaten
2 cups cornflake crumbs
oil, as needed

Par-boil chicken and drain. Dredge chicken in flour, salt and pepper. Dip coated chicken in eggs and then in cornflake crumbs. Chicken can be fried in skillet or deep fryer. If using skillet, fry until chicken is golden brown and crispy. In deep fryer, chicken is done when it floats to top. *Yield:* 4 to 6 servings.

Diane Darmody

CHICKEN MARINARA

3 to 4 chicken breasts, boned
  and skinned
6 tablespoons fresh parsley or 2
  tablespoons dry parsley
4 cloves of garlic, diced finely

1 teaspoon oregano
1 teaspoon sweet basil
2 28 ounce cans crushed
  tomatoes

Combine all the ingredients in a large saucepan, bring to a boil; then simmer 40 minutes. Serve with spaghetti. *Yield:* 4 servings.

Eileen Czarniecki

CHICKEN DIVAN

2 pounds chicken cutlets	2 10 ounce cans cream of
1 cup mayonnaise	chicken soup
1 teaspoon lemon juice	½ cup shredded Cheddar cheese
2 packages frozen broccoli,	½ cup butter, melted
preferably flowerettes	½ cup bread crumbs

Layer broccoli flowerettes in 13x9x2 inch baking pan. Then layer chicken cutlets on broccoli. Mix chicken soup, mayonnaise, lemon juice, and Cheddar cheese. Pour this mixture over chicken and broccoli. Sprinkle breadcrumbs over this. Drizzle butter over bread crumbs. Bake at 350 degrees for 30 to 35 minutes. Sauce should bubble and be lightly brown on top.

Marie Beyer

CHICKEN MARSALA

1 chicken, quartered	¼ cup chicken broth
2 tablespoons butter	¼ pound mushrooms, sliced
1 tablespoon oil	1 tablespoon cornstarch
½ cup Marsala wine	1 tablespoon chopped parsley

Heat butter and oil in large skillet. Brown chicken on both sides. Add wine and broth. Cook 15 minutes. Turn chicken over and cook 15 minutes with mushrooms. Remove chicken. Mix cornstarch in a little water. Stir into gravy until thick. Pour over chicken. Serve with rice. *Yield:* 4 servings.

Janet Reynolds

CHICKEN AND PEPPERS

1 chicken, cut in pieces	½ teaspoon pepper
3 to 4 large green peppers	½ teaspoon garlic salt
1 large onion	1 teaspoon oregano
¼ pound mushrooms	1 8 ounce can tomato sauce
½ pound sausage	¼ cup oil
½ teaspoon salt	½ cup vinegar

Cut up and combine chicken, peppers, onion, mushrooms, sausage. Mix in all other ingredients. Bake 1½ hours at 350 degrees. Mix every ½ hour.

Carole Lohmann

POULTRY

CHICKEN CUTLETS ALLA PIZZAIOLA

6 chicken cutlets	½ cup dry red wine
¼ teaspoon salt	⅓ cup sliced mushrooms
1 32 ounce can crushed tomatoes	1 teaspoon oregano
1 clove garlic	oil, as needed
½ cup flour	

Mix flour with salt. Flour chicken cutlets and place in skillet with oil. Allow to brown, two minutes on each side. Remove from skillet. Brown clove of garlic and add crushed tomatoes and dry red wine. Simmer 15 minutes, then add mushrooms, salt and pepper and oregano; and simmer another 10 minutes. Then place chicken cutlets in sauce. Heat over low flame for 10 minutes. *Yield:* 3 to 4 servings.

Rosanne DeLassio

CHICKEN BREAST PIQUANT

3 chicken breasts, split in half to make 6 breasts	¾ cup Rosé wine
¼ cup oil	¼ cup soy sauce
1 clove garlic, diced	2 tablespoons water
½ teaspoon oregano	1 teaspoon ginger
	1 tablespoon brown sugar

Combine wine with soy sauce, oil, water, garlic, ginger, oregano and brown sugar. Arrange chicken breasts in baking dish, pour wine mixture over breasts. Cover. Bake at 375 degrees for 1½ hours. *Yield:* 6 servings.

Mrs. O'Rourke

CHICKEN IN A POT

1 frying chicken, about 2½ pounds	1 teaspoon salt
½ cup olive oil	¾ teaspoon pepper
1 onion, minced	1 tomato, chopped
1 garlic clove, minced	½ cup dry white wine

In Dutch oven, brown chicken in olive oil until golden brown. Sprinkle with onion, garlic, salt and pepper. Cover and simmer 30 minutes. Add tomato and wine and simmer 30 minutes longer, or until chicken is tender. Serve with brown rice.

Eileen DeNapoli

112

COQ AU VIN

2 pounds chicken parts
¼ cup flour
¼ teaspoon salt
dash paprika
¼ cup shortening
10 small white onions
½ cup chopped celery
1 clove garlic, minced

⅛ teaspoon leaf thyme
dash rosemary
1 crushed bay leaf
1 10 ounce can beef consommé
¼ cup Burgundy
mushrooms, to taste
2 tablespoons parsley, chopped

Coat chicken with flour, salt and paprika. Brown in Dutch oven and pour off all but 1 tablespoon of drippings. Add onions, celery, garlic, thyme, rosemary and bay leaf. Cook a few minutes. Stir in any remaining flour.

Gradually blend in soup and wine. Add chicken. Cover and cook for 45 minutes over low heat, stirring occasionally. Add mushrooms and parsley. Cover and cook 15 minutes longer. Remove cover and cook until sauce is desired consistency. *Yield:* 5 to 6 servings.

Diane Darmody

CHICKEN AND RICE DINNER

1 chicken, cut up
1 10¾ ounce can cream of
  mushroom soup

1 cup uncooked rice
2 cups water
1 envelope dry onion soup mix

Spread rice over bottom of greased baking dish. Top with chicken pieces. Mix together soup and water; pour over chicken. Sprinkle with onion soup mix. Cover and bake for 1 hour at 350 degrees; remove cover and bake 30 minutes longer or until chicken is tender and lightly browned. *Yield:* 4 to 6 servings.

Regina Whitaker

CHICKEN ROLL UP

1½ pounds chicken cutlets
1 pound mozzarella cheese,
  sliced

bread crumbs, as needed
Italian dressing, as needed

Dip chicken in Italian dressing, then into bread crumbs. Put a slice of cheese on the chicken and roll chicken around the cheese. Bake at 350 degrees for 45 minutes.

Gina Leveque

ROAST CHICKEN WITH VEGETABLES

1 chicken, cut up
4 medium potatoes, pared and
  quartered
⅓ cup vegetable or olive oil
1½ teapoons salt
½ teaspoon paprika

1 large green pepper, cut into
  strips
1 clove garlic, crushed
1 teaspoon dried oregano
½ teaspoon pepper

Arrange chicken, pepper and potatoes in single layer in roasting pan. Combine garlic, oil, oregano. Mix well. Drizzle over chicken and vegetables. Sprinkle with salt, pepper and paprika. Bake uncovered 1 hour in 350 degree oven. Baste frequently with pan juices. Increase oven to 400 degrees. Bake another 15 minutes.

Eileen DeNapoli

SWEET-AND-SOUR CHICKEN

1 15¼ ounce can pineapple
  chunks
4 chicken breasts, skinned and
  boned
2 tablespoons oil
¼ cup light corn syrup
¼ cup red wine vinegar

2 tablespoons catsup
2 tablespoons soy sauce
1 tablespoon cornstarch
2 tablespoons water
1 large green pepper, cut into 1
  inch pieces
hot cooked rice

Drain pineapple, reserving juice. Set aside. Cut chicken into pieces. In skillet, over medium heat, cook in oil about 5 minutes, stirring until fork-tender. Add reserved juice, corn syrup, vinegar, catsup and soy sauce. Heat to boiling. Reduce heat to low and simmer 10 minutes. In small cup, mix water and cornstarch. Add this to pineapple mixture until thick. Add pineapple and green pepper. Cook until pepper is soft. Serve over rice. *Yield:* 4 servings.

Janet Reynolds

CHICKEN CUTLETS IN WINE

6 large chicken cutlets
4 eggs, beaten
1½ cups bread crumbs seasoned
   with salt and pepper, to taste
1 cup vegetable oil

1½ cups chicken broth or
   chicken bouillon made
   with 2 cubes
1½ cups dry white wine
1 pound fresh mushrooms, sliced

Dip chicken cutlets into bread crumbs, then into egg, then into bread crumbs again. Heat oil over a medium flame in a 12 inch skillet. Sauté chicken on both sides, until brown. Lift out onto paper towels to drain. In the same skillet, sauté mushrooms for 5 to 10 minutes. Do not over cook, especially if you plan to freeze and reheat the dish. Arrange chicken cutlets in 9x11 inch baking dish. Add broth and white wine to the mushrooms, and pour over chicken. Bake, covered, for 20 minutes in a 350 degree oven, then uncover for 30 minutes, basting frequently with the liquid. This dish reheats or freezes beautifully. *Yield:* 6 servings.

Eileen Rathgaber

CHICKEN BREAST IN WINE

2 lemons, sliced
1½ to 2 cups white wine

rosemary, to taste
2 pounds chicken cutlets

Pour wine into roasting pan. Add chicken. Do not layer. Bake at 350 to 400 degree oven for 5 minutes and turn. Add lemon slice on top of each piece of chicken. Sprinkle with rosemary. Bake for additional 10 to 15 minutes, until cooked. Serve with low calorie vegetables such as broccoli, cauliflower, brussel sprouts, spinach.

Cathy Manfredonia

GOLDEN CHICKEN WINGS

3 tablespoons sugar
4 tablespoons soy sauce
1 teaspoon salt

1 heaping tablespoon honey
4 pounds chicken wings

Combine all the ingredients and rub into the chicken wings. Let stand at room temperature for two hours. Turn the chicken wings in the marinade occasionally. Bake for 20 minutes in a 350 degree preheated oven, then turn and bake for another 20 minutes or until golden.

Kathy Henry

TURKEY CROQUETTES

5 cups ground cooked turkey
½ teaspoon salt
¼ teaspoon pepper
1 tablespoon parsley

2 eggs, lightly beaten
bread crumbs, as needed
oil for frying

White Sauce:
4 tablespoons margarine
1½ cups milk

4 tablespoons flour

Mix the turkey, salt, pepper and parsley until well blended. Set aside. Melt the margarine in a heavy bottomed saucepan over low heat. Stir in the flour and cook, stirring constantly, until the paste cooks and bubbles a bit, but do not let it brown, about 2 minutes. Gradually add the white sauce to meat mixture until well blended. Cover with foil and refrigerate until chilled, about 1 hour. Form small cones about 2 inches at base and 2½ inches high. Roll cones in the bread crumbs, then dip into the lightly beaten eggs, then into the bread crumbs again. Set them to dry on piece of wax paper. Refrigerate if you are not going to fry them immediately. Brown croquettes in oil in electric frying pan, turning to brown evenly. Drain on paper towels. Place on warm platter and serve with gravy, white sauce, or canned creamed soup. *Yield:* 10 servings.

Marie Sluka

seafood

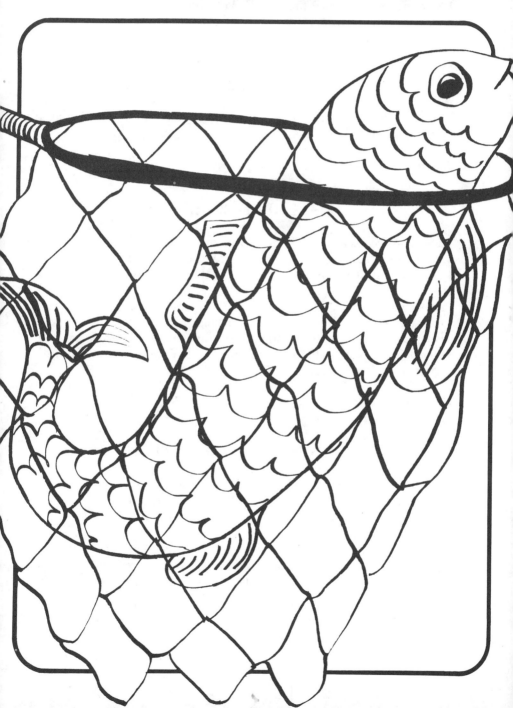

MUSSELS WITH RICE

4 to 6 dozen fresh mussels, washed
1 32 ounce can crushed tomatoes
2 cloves garlic, crushed
½ teaspoon salt
½ teaspoon oregano
½ teaspoon sugar
¼ teaspoon crushed red pepper
½ cup raw rice

Mix salt, oregano, sugar and red pepper with tomatoes. Place mussels, tomato mixture, rice and crushed garlic in large pot. Cover and cook on medium heat. Bring to a boil, then lower heat to simmer until mussels are open and rice is tender. Serve. *Variation:* Substitute 1 pound cooked linguine for rice. Place mussels over drained linguine.

Jackie Greene

SCALLOPED SCALLOPS

1½ pounds sea scallops
4 cups breadcrumbs
1 teaspoon minced parsley
¼ cup butter
1 teaspoon grated onion
1 tablespoon lemon juice

Slice large scallops. Melt butter, add all other ingredients and toss together. Arrange in well buttered baking dish in alternate layers of scallops and crumb mixture, ending with crumb mixture. Bake in hot oven of 400 degrees about 20 to 30 minutes until lightly browned. Serve hot with vegetable and/or green salad. *Yield:* 6 servings.

Helen Evancie

BARBECUED SHARK STEAK

2 pounds Mako shark steak, 1 inch thick
¼ cup bourbon
¼ cup corn oil
2 cloves garlic, crushed

Marinate steaks in mixture of oil, bourbon and garlic for one hour, turning once. Place steaks on well greased grill. Cook over hot coals 5 minutes on each side; or until fish flakes at touch. Baste with marinade frequently while grilling.

Bridget DePasquale

LOBSTER SHELL STOCK

all leftover remains from
  approximately 4 lobsters,
  shells, meat, etc.
1 cup butter
1 to 2 teaspoons chopped
  shallots
1 to 2 garlic cloves, crushed
¼ cup cognac

4 tablespoons tomato paste
1 tablespoon dried or fresh
  chopped tarragon
pinch of thyme
white pepper, to taste
chicken stock, or water, or ½
  and ½ to cover

Put shells into deep pot and crush in bottom with potato masher. In small pan, cook shallot and garlic in butter a few minutes. Remove from heat. Add tomato paste and herbs to butter and mix well. Add to lobster shells, stir and increase heat. Add cognac and flame it. Add chicken stock or water to barely cover. Bring to a boil, cover and simmer 30 minutes. Strain and taste; should have good lobster flavor, if not, recrush lobster and simmer again 15 to 20 minutes. Strain well and discard shells. Can be put into containers and frozen at this point for later use. *OR:*

Use your recipe for white sauce but add stock instead of milk. Steam some mussels. Add mussels with or without shells to sauce and serve over pasta. *OR:*

Add shrimp and serve over any baked fish. *OR:*

Add ½ cup white wine to sauce and ½ cup heavy cream and 2 tablespoons of tomato paste, sprinkle with tarragon and you have lobster soup. Remember to taste till you're happy. *Note:* Don't be shy about asking for a doggy bag of your lobster shells when eating out. This stock makes great inexpensive gourmet meals to make up for that dinner out.

Edie Lyons

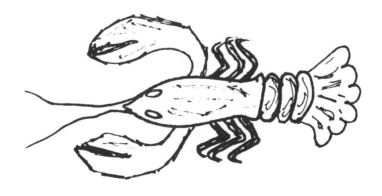

SEAFOOD

CIOPINO FISH STEW

¼ cup olive oil
3 large cloves garlic, finely
  chopped
1 32 ounce can tomatoes
3 cups water
1 teaspoon salt
2 whitings, approximately 3
  pounds, cleaned and filleted
18 littleneck clams, scrubbed
  well
4 cups cooked rice

2 medium onions, chopped
1 cup dry white vermouth
1 teaspoon fennel seed
2 cups fish stock or bottled clam
  juice
¼ teaspoon freshly ground
  pepper
1 pound medium or large
  shrimp, shelled and
  deveined
⅓ cup chopped parsley

In a large pot, heat oil and sauté onions until golden. Add garlic and sauté 1 to 2 minutes. Add vermouth and stir over high heat 1 minute. Add fennel and cook for a few seconds more. Add tomatoes. Break them up with wooden spoon. Add clam juice, water, salt and pepper. Simmer gently, uncovered for 20 minutes. Cut fish fillets into serving pieces. Add fish, shrimp and clams. Simmer, covered, for 15 minutes or until clams open. Stir in chopped parsley. Serve over rice. *Yield:* 8 servings.

Rosalie Toja

SHRIMP DE JONGHE

1 cup sweet butter, and ½ cup
  stick margarine and ½ cup
  butter
pinch pepper
1½ cups crushed, thin bacon
  flavored crackers

2 tablespoons chopped chives
½ teaspoon garlic powder
2 pounds shrimp, cleaned

Preheat oven to 350 degrees. In saucepan melt butter. Add chives, garlic powder and pepper. Stir to blend. Dip shrimp into melted butter. Roll shrimp in cracker crumbs to coat. Layer shrimp in 2 quart baking dish. Add remaining crumbs to remaining butter. Stir to blend. Sprinkle over shrimp. Bake for 25 to 30 minutes, until shrimp are tender. Serve with rice and green vegetable or salad. *Yield:* 4 servings.

Jane Frances Evancie

120

SHRIMP CURRY

1 10 ounce can cream of shrimp
  soup
1 pint sour cream
1 pound shrimp

½ tablespoon curry powder, or
  to taste
1 large onion, sliced

Cook shrimp for 3 minutes. Warm soup; add shrimp. Fry onion in butter. Add curry powder. Mix all ingredients except sour cream; cook for 5 minutes. Before serving, blend in sour cream. Serve over rice.

Mary Ann Eckel

SHRIMP IN GARLIC BUTTER

½ cup butter
3 cloves garlic, minced
1 tablespoon minced parsley
2 tablespoons lemon juice

¼ teaspoon salt
1½ to 2 pounds fresh shrimp,
  shelled and deveined

Melt butter, add garlic, parsley, lemon juice and salt. Set aside. Place shrimp under broiler in individual serving dishes or 1 large platter. Grill 15 to 20 minutes turning and brushing occasionally with garlic butter. *Note:* Two 12 ounce packages of frozen large shrimp, thawed, can be used in place of fresh shrimp.

Patrick Keefe

SEAFOOD SCAMPI

1 pound shrimp, medium size
1½ pounds small scallops
1½ pounds sea legs or crabmeat
½ cup butter

3 cloves garlic
¼ cup chopped parsley
½ cup dry white wine

Sauté garlic, butter, white wine and parsley until all blended, about 5 minutes. Add all seafood at same time. Sauté, mixing about every minute, for about 10 minutes. Serve in a casserole dish as is, or over wild or white rice. *Yield:* 4 to 6 servings.

Gloria LaMura

SEAFOOD

ALASKAN CRAB CAKES

2 tablespoons butter	½ teaspoon salt
3 tablespoons flour	⅛ teaspoon nutmeg
1 cup milk	½ cup soft white bread cubes
2 egg yolks, slightly beaten	¾ cup bread crumbs
2 6½ ounce cans crab meat	2 tablespoons chopped parsley
oil, as needed	dash of cayenne pepper

Melt butter in saucepan; remove from heat. Stir in flour to make smooth mixture, gradually stir in milk. Bring to boil over medium heat, stirring. Reduce heat and simmer 1 minute. Beat some of hot mixture into egg yolks; return to rest of mixture in saucepan. Cook, stirring several minutes until thickened; remove from heat.

Drain crab meat; remove any cartilage. To mixture in saucepan, add crab, parsley, salt, nutmeg, cayenne, bread cubes, ¼ cup breadcrumbs; mix well. Refrigerate, covered, 1 hour. Heat oil ¼ inch deep in large skillet. Shape crab mixture into 8 cakes, about 2½ inches in diameter. Roll in rest of bread crumbs, coating completely. Sauté crab cakes in oil, turning until golden brown on both sides. Drain on paper towels. Serve hot with tartar sauce or lemon. *Yield:* 4 servings.

Jean Sweeney

SHRIMP MILANESE

2 pounds shrimp, peeled and deveined	½ cup fresh lemon juice
1 tablespoon finely chopped onion	1 cup dry sherry
1 tablespoon finely chopped carrots	½ cup dry vermouth
1 tablespoon finely chopped celery	1 cup consommé
1 teaspoon chopped garlic	salt and pepper, to taste
½ cup butter	1 egg, beaten
	bread crumbs
	oil for frying

Dip shrimp in egg and bread crumbs, and fry in hot oil. Remove and drain. Melt butter in saucepan and add all vegetables. Cook 10 minutes and add sherry and vermouth. Add shrimp, consommé, salt and pepper. Simmer to desired thickness. Serve. *Note:* This recipe can also be made with chicken or veal.

Pat Whaley

MUSSELS PIQUANT

2 bay leaves
½ teaspoon oregano
½ teaspoon salt
½ teaspoon white pepper
½ teaspoon cayenne pepper

½ teaspoon paprika
½ teaspoon black pepper
½ teaspoon thyme
½ teaspoon basil

Note: Combine seasoning ingredients and set aside.

4 tablespoons olive oil
1 cup chopped fresh tomatoes
1 cup chopped scallions
1 cup chopped celery
1 tablespoon sugar
1 cup chopped green pepper

2 crushed garlic cloves
1 cup tomato sauce
2 teaspoons hot pepper sauce
5 to 6 pounds mussels
¼ cup cornmeal

Scrub mussels and remove beards, set aside in bowl of cold water to which cornmeal has been added. Place oil in large pot and heat over medium heat. Stir in tomato, scallions, celery, peppers. Stir in garlic and seasoning ingredients. Cook until onion is translucent. Add tomato sauce, sugar and hot sauce. Simmer until vegetables are tender. Add mussels, cover and cook until mussels open.

Bridget DePasquale

SHRIMP SCAMPI

1 pound large raw shrimp
½ cup butter or margarine
½ teaspoon salt
6 cloves garlic, crushed

2 tablespoons chopped parsley
1 teaspoon grated lemon peel
1 tablespoon lemon juice
lemon wedges

Preheat oven to 400 degrees. Shell shrimp; leave on tails with their shells. Devein; wash under running water. Drain on paper towels. Melt butter in a 13x9x2 inch baking dish, in oven. Add salt, garlic, and 1 tablespoon parsley. Mix well. Arrange shrimp in single layer in baking dish. Bake uncovered 5 minutes. Turn shrimp, sprinkle with lemon peel, lemon juice, and remaining parsley. Bake 8 to 10 minutes longer, or just until tender. Arrange shrimp on heated serving platter. Pour garlic butter drippings over all. Garnish with lemon. *Note:* The best shrimp to use are the largest available. *Yield:* 4 servings.

Christopher Dillon

SEAFOOD

SCAMPI ALLA LIVRONESE

2 pounds jumbo shrimp
1 cup flour
6 shallots, minced
½ cup sweet butter
3 bay leaves
dash red pepper
oil, as needed

½ gallon sauterne or chenin
blanc wine
1 clove garlic, minced
salt and pepper, to taste
1 teaspoon oregano
1 teaspoon fresh parsley

In a bowl mix flour, 1 teaspoon salt and 1 teaspoon pepper. Add shrimp one at a time, flouring each one completely. Sauté shrimp in a frying pan with oil for 3 minutes or until lightly brown. DO NOT OVER COOK! Set aside shrimp in a dish lined with paper towel to catch the excess oils.

In another frying pan add ½ gallon of wine, shallots, garlic, bay leaves, oregano, red pepper, parsley and a dash of salt and pepper. Allow to boil until half the original volume is achieved, uncovered. Just before you are ready to serve, add shrimp to the wine mixture and bring to a boil allowing shrimp to heat thoroughly. Add butter and allow to melt. Once all the butter is melted, stir mixture until uniform and serve over bed of boiled rice.

Mrs. Basilice

SHRIMP SCAMPI

2 pounds shrimp cleaned and
deveined
2 cups butter or margarine
2 to 3 cloves garlic, minced
1 tablespoon chopped fresh
parsley

1 cup white cooking wine
1 tablespoon oregano
1 tablespoon breadcrumbs

In a sauce pan, melt butter or margarine. Add all other ingredients, except bread crumbs. Place shrimp in medium size baking pan. Pour butter sauce over shrimp. Sprinkle bread crumbs over. Place in oven temperature 350 degrees. Cook 20 minutes or until shrimp turns pinkish color. Serve over rice or alone.

LuAnn Clemente

SALMON LOAF

1 15 ounce can salmon	3 tablespoons butter
1 cup milk	1 tablespoon lemon juice
1 cup bread crumbs	2 eggs, separated

Heat milk just to boiling. Add bread crumbs and butter. Mix. Add to salmon. Add lemon juice, onion and egg yolks. Beat egg whites until stiff. Fold whites into mixture. Butter baking dish or loaf pan. Shake breadcrumbs on sides and bottom of dish. Add salmon mixture. Bake for 45 minutes at 350 degrees.

Diane Mulhern

SHRIMP SCAMPI

¼ cup butter or margarine	½ teaspoon salt
1 tablespoon garlic powder	2 tablespoons lemon juice
dash pepper	1 pound fresh or frozen large
¼ cup oil	shrimp, shelled and deveined
2 tablespoons chopped parsley	

Preheat oven to 400 degrees. In a large heatproof skillet, melt butter. Add oil, 1 tablespoon parsley, garlic powder, salt, pepper, and lemon juice. Mix well. Add shrimp, tossing gently with butter mixture. Arrange in skillet in single layer. Bake 8 to 10 minutes or just until tender. Sprinkle with remaining parsley. Garnish with lemon wedges, if desired.

Bill Hecker

MARINATED SHRIMP

1 pound shrimp, shelled and deveined	2 tablespoons soy sauce
2 tablespoons dry sherry	2 tablespoons minced garlic
1 tablespoon fresh ginger	1 teaspoon sugar
2 tablespoons chopped scallions	2 tablespoons butter

Marinate shrimp in sherry, ginger, soy sauce, garlic and sugar for 15 minutes; then drain. Sauté shrimp in 2 tablespoons butter until pink. Serve on top of rice. Sprinkle with parsley and scallions.

Bridget DePasquale

SEAFOOD

SHRIMP SCAMPI

1 pound large shrimp, shelled,
   deveined, and butterflied
½ cup sweet butter or margarine
1 cup beef stock

1 clove garlic, minced
2 tablespoons chopped parsley
2 tablespoons bread crumbs

Sauté garlic in butter. Add parsley and beef stock; simmer for 2 minutes. Place shrimp in ovenproof casserole or pan. Sprinkle with breadcrumbs and pour sauce over the shrimp. Place under the broiler for a few minutes, until shrimp is done. Serve.

Marie Sluka

TUNABURGERS

2 7 ounce cans tuna, drained
1 cup breadcrumbs
1 cup chopped celery
4 tablespoons minced onion
⅓ cup mayonnaise

2 tablespoons chili sauce
1 teaspoon lemon juice
hamburger buns, optional
oil, as needed

Combine tuna, bread crumbs, celery and onion. Blend mayonnaise, chili sauce and lemon juice together. Add to tuna mixture. Form into 6 to 8 burgers. Fry in lightly oiled skillet for 5 minutes on each side, turning gently. Serve on buns, if desired. *Yield:* 6 to 8 servings.

The Committee

TUNA CAKES

2 6½ ounce sized cans tuna,
   drained
1 small onion, grated
unflavored bread crumbs, as
   needed

2 eggs
salt and pepper, to taste
oil for frying

In medium size bowl, blend all ingredients together until tuna mixture is like a dough. Heat oil in frying pan. Shape into cakes. Fry until golden brown, turning once. *Yield:* 6 to 8 servings.

Alison Nadolny

cakes

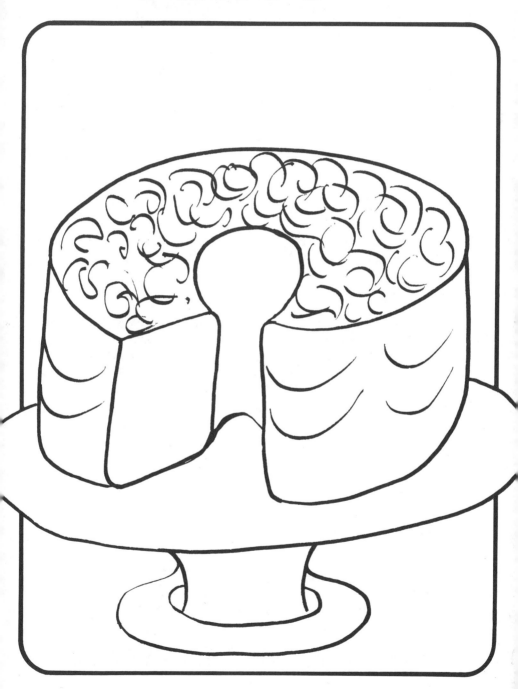

CAKES

APPLE CAKE

3 cups flour
2 cups sugar
3 teaspoons baking powder
4 cups sliced apples

1 cup oil
4 eggs
¼ cup apple juice
2 teaspoons vanilla

Mix liquid ingredients, then dry ingredients to make batter. Beat until smooth. Batter will be thick. Pour half of batter into ungreased tube pan. Place half of apples on top. Sprinkle with cinnamon and sugar. Add balance of batter, and apples, sprinkle with cinnamon and sugar. Bake at 350 degrees for 1 hour and 15 minutes.

Pauline Comando

APPLE WALNUT CAKE

4 cups coarsely chopped apples
½ cup oil
2 cups flour
1 teaspoon salt
1 cup chopped walnuts
2 cups sugar

2 eggs, slightly beaten
2 teaspoons vanilla
2 teaspoons baking soda
2 teaspoons cinnamon
1 cup raisins, optional

Preheat oven to 325 degrees. Beat eggs, oil and vanilla until smooth. Fold in apples. Mix together flour, baking soda, cinnamon, and salt, in a separate bowl. Stir into egg mixture alternately with apple mixture. Blend in raisins and walnuts. Pour into a greased and floured pan, 13x9x2 inch. Bake at 325 degrees for 1 hour. Let stand in pan until quite cool, turn out on rack when cool.

Pat Dowling

BANANA CAKE

3 or 4 ripe bananas
1 cup sugar
¼ cup margarine, melted
1 egg

1½ cups flour
1 teaspoon salt
1 teaspoon baking soda
1 cup chopped nuts

Combine mashed bananas with sugar then add egg and margarine. Add dry ingredients last and finally add nuts if desired. Mix with a fork. Bake in a lightly buttered and floured pan at 325 degree oven for 40 minutes or until cooked.

Mrs. Augustino

CARROT CAKE

2 cups sifted flour
2 cups sugar
2 teaspoons salt
2 teaspoons cinnamon
2 teaspoons baking soda

1½ cups oil
4 eggs
2 cups grated carrots
1 cup raisins, optional

Preheat oven to 350 degrees. Sift dry ingredients together. Add oil and mix well. Add eggs and mix well. Stir in carrots and raisins. Pour into a greased and floured 10 inch tube pan, or 9x13 inch pan. Bake 40 to 45 minutes in preheated oven. Cool. Frost with cream cheese frosting.

Cream Cheese Frosting:
2 3 ounce packages cream
   cheese
½ cup powdered sugar

¼ pound softened butter
2 teaspoons vanilla
1 cup chopped nuts, optional

Beat all ingredients, except nuts, until smooth. Frost cake. Sprinkle with nuts, if desired.

Linda Witanowski

CHEESECAKE

1 8 ounce package cream cheese,
   softened
8 ounces sour cream
1 pound ricotta
2 tablespoons flour

1 cup sugar
1 teaspoon vanilla
2 tablespoons lemon juice
5 eggs, separated

Crust:
1 cup plain bread crumbs
¼ cup butter

cinnamon, to taste

Beat egg yolks and whip egg whites. Mix together all above ingredients except egg whites until creamy. Fold in 5 egg whites. Mix crust ingredients together. Put in bottom of a greased springform pan. Pour cake mixture in pan. Bake at 325 degrees for 60 minutes. Close oven and let stay in oven for at least a ½ hour. Remove, cool completely and refrigerate overnight before serving. *Enjoy!*

Annette Laino

CAKES

CARROT PINEAPPLE CAKE

3 cups sifted flour
2 cups sugar
2 teaspoons cinnamon
1½ teaspoons baking soda
1½ teaspoons salt
1 teaspoon baking powder
1 8¾ ounce can crushed
  pineapple, drained, juice
  reserved

2 cups grated carrots
3 eggs, beaten
1½ cups oil
2 teaspoons vanilla or almond
  extract
1½ cups chopped nuts

Grease and lightly flour bundt pan. Mix together flour, sugar, cinnamon, baking soda, salt and baking powder. Add reserved juice to dry mixture. Add beaten eggs, oil and vanilla. Beat for 3 minutes. Stir in pineapple, carrots and nuts. Bake at 325 degree for 1½ hours. Cool for 10 minutes, before removing from pan.

Blanche McCabe

CHEESECAKE

Crust:
1½ cups graham cracker crumbs
1 cup sugar

4 to 5 tablespoons melted
  margarine

Filling:
24 ounces cream cheese
4 medium eggs
2 tablespoons vanilla
1 teaspoon lemon juice

1 cup sugar
1 pint sour cream
1 cup heavy cream
2 tablespoons flour

Grease bottom and sides of springform pan. Mix crust ingredients and pat firmly into pan. Place in freezer while making filling. Blend filling ingredients together with electric beater until smooth. Pour over crumbs. Bake in 325 degrees preheated oven for 20 minutes. Lower to 300 degrees for approximately 50 to 60 minutes until golden brown. Turn off oven. Leave cake in oven for 1 hour to cool. Refrigerate. Remove sides only when cake is cool enough. Can be made a day in advance.

Connie Nonnenmacher

CHEESECAKE

Crust:

1 box zwieback crackers, crushed fine
1 teaspoon cinnamon

1 cup sugar
½ cup melted butter or margarine

Filling:

4 eggs
1 cup sugar
4 8 ounce packages cream cheese, softened

1 teaspoon vanilla
1 teaspoon lemon juice

Topping:

2 cups sour cream
1 tablespoon lemon juice

1 tablespoon vanilla
4 tablespoons sugar

Preheat oven to 375 degrees. Crush crackers and mix with other crust ingredients. Set aside ¾ cup mixture for topping. Butter 9 inch springform pan and press mixture on bottom and sides. Place pan on cookie sheet, as it may drip. Bake 10 to 15 minutes.

Filling: beat eggs, sugar, lemon juice until light. Add softened cream cheese and beat until blended thoroughly. Pour filling into crust and bake for 20 minutes. Remove from oven and increase temperature to 475 degrees. Top the cake with mixture of sour cream, sugar and vanilla. Sprinkle with remaining cracker mixture, and bake 10 minutes. Cool and chill. Better if made 2 days before use.

Betty Wallin

RICOTTA CAKE

1 package yellow cake mix
4 eggs
1 teaspoon vanilla

2 pounds ricotta
¾ cup sugar
small chocolate chips, optional

Mix cake according to box directions, pour into greased 9x13 inch pan. Combine rest of ingredients and pour on top of batter in pan. Bake at 350 degrees for 1 hour and 15 minutes until golden.

Susan Wagner

CAKES

BANANA NUT CAKE

2¼ cups cake flour
1⅔ cups sugar
1¼ teaspoons baking powder
1¼ teaspoons baking soda
1 teaspoon salt
⅔ cups shortening

⅔ cup buttermilk
3 eggs
1¼ cups mashed very ripe
  bananas
⅔ cup finely chopped nuts

Measure all ingredients into large mixing bowl. Blend for ½ minute on low speed, scraping bowl constantly. Beat 3 minutes at high speed scraping bowl occasionally. Grease and flour baking pans. Pour into 13x9x2 inch pan or two 9 inch or 8 inch round layer pans. Heat oven to 350 dgrees, bake 35 to 45 minutes.

Cathy Vitelli

CHEESECAKE

1 pint sour cream
1½ cups sugar
5 eggs
4 tablespoons flour

4 8 ounce packages cream
  cheese
¾ cups milk
1 tablespoon vanilla

Soften cream cheese. Mix cream cheese well, mix in sugar and milk. Add eggs one at a time. Add sour cream, vanilla and flour. Mix for two minutes. Put into springform pan. Bake in oven at 375 degrees for 1 hour and 15 minutes. Open oven door and let cool in oven for ten minutes. Take out and let cool until room temperature, then refrigerate.

Gerry Daube

ROSALIE'S BLUEBERRY CHEESECAKE

2 8 ounce packages cream
  cheese
2 eggs, beaten
1 teaspoon vanilla
¾ cup sugar
½ teaspoon lemon juice

9 inch graham cracker crust
1 cup sour cream
3½ tablespoons sugar
1 teaspoon vanilla
1 21 ounce can blueberries

Mix first 5 ingredients well and put in graham cracker crust. Bake 25 minutes at 350 degrees. Let cool 5 minutes. Mix next 3 ingredients. Pour over pie. Bake again for 10 minutes. Cool pie and put blueberries on top.

Rosalie Toja

CALIFORNIA STYLE CHEESE CAKE

Crust:
1½ cups graham cracker crumbs   2 tablespoons sugar
⅓ cup melted butter

Cake:
1 pound cream cheese   2 tablespoons heavy cream
¾ cup sugar   2 teaspoons vanilla
2 eggs   3 tablespoons sour cream

Mix graham cracker crumbs, butter and sugar together. Press against bottom and sides of pie plate. Chill for 15 minutes. Begin to beat cream cheese with wooden spoon until smooth. Then switch to an electric mixer. Gradually add sugar (reserving 1 tablespoon), then add eggs one at a time. Beat for 5 minutes. Add heavy cream and 1 teaspoon vanilla. Beat 5 minutes longer. Pour ingredients into pie crust. Bake 20 minutes. Meanwhile, mix the sour cream with remaining sugar and vanilla. After 20 minutes baking time, increase temperature to 450 degrees. Remove cake from oven and spread sour cream mixture on top. Bake for 5 more minutes. Cool cake for one hour; then chill in refrigerator.

Deborah Zito

MARIE'S BRASS RAIL CHEESE CAKE

Crust:
3 cups graham cracker crumbs   8 tablespoons softened butter or
6 tablespoons sugar   margarine

Filling:
2 pounds cream cheese   1¼ cups sugar
1 pint sour cream   3½ tablespoons cornstarch
4 eggs   1 teaspoon vanilla

Beat cream cheese and sour cream together. Add eggs one at a time, add sugar, gradually; add cornstarch, vanilla and beat until smooth. Butter 10 inch springform pan. Carefully press graham cracker mixture around bottom and sides of pan. Slowly pour cheese mixture into crust lined pan. Preheat oven at 375 degrees. When cake is ready for oven, lower heat to 350 degrees. Bake 1 hour. Then turn off oven and leave cake in oven for 1 hour. Remove from oven. Let cake cool and then enjoy.

Marie Beyer

CAKES

DELUXE CHEESECAKE

1¼ cups flour
¾ cup butter or margarine, softened
2 cups sugar
3 egg yolks
grated peel of 2 fresh lemons, optional
grated peel of 1 fresh orange, optional

5 8 ounce packages cream cheese
5 eggs
¼ cup heavy cream
garnish, 1 cup sliced strawberries or 1 cup sour cream

Prepare cake, day before serving. In a small bowl, beat together on low speed, 1¼ cups flour, butter, ¼ cup sugar, 1 egg yolk, ½ of grated lemon peel, until well mixed. Refrigerate, covered for 1 hour. Preheat oven to 400 degrees. Press ⅓ of flour mixture onto bottom of 10 inch springform pan. Bake 8 minutes and cool. Increase oven temperature to 475 degrees. In large bowl, with mixer at medium speed beat cream cheese just until smooth. Slowly beat in 1¾ cups sugar, with mixer at low speed, beat in 3 tablespoons flour, 2 egg yolks, and remaining ingredients, except strawberries. At high speed, beat 5 minutes, occasionally scraping bowl with rubber spatula. Press rest of dough around side of pan to within 1 inch of top; do not bake. Pour cream cheese mixture into pan; bake 12 minutes. Lower oven to 300 degrees and bake 35 minutes longer. Turn oven off, let cheese cake remain in oven 30 minutes. Remove, cool in pan or on wire rack. Refrigerate.

To serve: Remove side of pan. With large spatula loosen cake from pan bottom; slide onto plate. Garnish with whole or sliced strawberries or spread top with sour cream. *Yield:* 16 servings.

Mrs. Lyons

CREAM CHEESE CAKES

3 ounces cream cheese
½ cup sweet butter
1 cup flour
1 cup chopped nuts

1 cup brown sugar
1 egg
1 teaspoon vanilla

Mix first three ingredients with fork. Roll into 24 balls. Press each ball into bottom and sides of miniature muffin tins. Two tins should be used. Combine remaining ingredients in small bowl. Fill each cup ½ way with mixture. Bake in preheated 425 degree oven for 20 minutes.

Eleanor McCann

PEACHES 'N CREAM CHEESE CAKE

Batter:

¾ cup flour
1 teaspoon baking powder
½ teaspoon salt
1 egg

1 package vanilla pudding mix - not instant
3 tablespoons butter, softened
½ cup milk

Filling:

1 15 to 20 ounce can sliced peaches or crushed pineapple, juice reserved
1 8 ounce package cream cheese

1 3 ounce package cream cheese
¾ cup sugar
5 tablespoons reserved fruit juice

Topping:

1 tablespoon sugar

½ teaspoon cinnamon

Combine batter ingredients in large bowl and beat 2 minutes at medium speed. Pour into greased and floured 9 inch pan. Place drained fruit over batter. Combine remaining filling ingredients in small bowl and beat 2 minutes at medium speed. Spoon to within 1/16 of edge. Sprinkle topping over cream cheese filling. Bake at 350 degrees for 30 to 35 minutes until crust is golden brown. Filling will appear soft. Refrigerate 2 hours before serving.

Eleanor Wittrup

NO BAKE BANANA SPLIT CAKE

2 cups crushed graham crackers
1 cup softened margarine
½ cup softened butter
2 cups powdered sugar
2 eggs
1 teaspoon vanilla

2 small cans drained crushed pineapple
3 bananas
whipped cream, as needed
chopped nuts, for garnish

Melt ½ cup margarine. Mix melted margarine with 2 cups graham cracker crumbs. Press mixture into bottom of 9x12 inch pan. In electric mixer, mix for 10 minutes: 2 eggs, 1 teaspoon vanilla, ½ cup butter, ½ cup margarine, 2 cups sugar. Spread this mixture over crust. Spread drained pineapple next, then spread sliced banana next. Top with whipped cream. Garnish with nuts. Chill.

Eleanor Wittrup

CAKES

CHOCOLATE SWIRL CHEESECAKE

1 cup chocolate cookie crumbs
¼ cup melted butter
3 tablespoons sugar
3 8 ounce packages cream
  cheese, room temperature
1 cup sour cream

2 tablespoons flour
3 eggs, separated
2 tablespoons cream de cocoa
1 6 ounce package semi-sweet
  chocolate chips, melted
1 cup sugar

Combine cookie crumbs, butter and sugar. Press evenly on bottom of a 9 inch springform pan. Chill. Preheat oven to 350 degrees. Beat cream cheese, sour cream, sugar and flour thoroughly. Add egg yolks one at a time blending well after each addition. Whip egg whites until almost stiff but not dry, and gently fold into cheese mixture. Fold in liqueur. Gently swirl slightly cooled chocolate through cheese mixture to give marbled effect. Transfer carefully to springform pan and bake 60 mintues. Turn off oven and let cool with door open. When cool, remove sides of springform. Refrigerate until serving time.

Margie Deegan

FLUFFY AND LIGHT CHEESECAKE

1½ cups graham cracker crumbs
1½ tablespoons sugar
2 tablespoons melted butter
15 ounces cream cheese
½ cup sugar
1½ tablespoons lemon juice

1 teaspoon vanilla
dash salt
5 egg yolks
2 cups sour cream
5 egg whites
½ cup sugar

Combine cracker crumbs, 1½ tablespoons sugar and margarine. Press on bottom of a 9 inch ungreased springform pan. In mixing bowl, beat cream cheese until softened. Beat in ½ cup sugar, lemon juice, vanilla and salt. Blend in egg yolks and sour cream. Do not beat. Beat egg whites until soft peaks form. Gradually add the remaining ½ cup sugar, beating until stiff peaks form. Fold the egg white mix into cream cheese. Mix. Carefully pour into springform pan. Bake in 325 degree oven for 1½ hours or until golden. Loosen cheesecake from edge of pan about ½ inch down, 10 minutes after taken out of oven. Let cool.

Dianna Ebe

BLUEBERRY TEA CAKE

½ cup softened butter
2 eggs, well beaten
pinch salt
1½ to 2 cups of blueberries
1 teaspoon vanilla

1 cup sugar
1½ cups flour
1 teaspoon baking powder
⅓ cup milk
powdered sugar

Cream butter and sugar, add eggs. Hand mixing is recommended. Mix and sift dry ingredients and add to creamed mixture, alternately with milk and vanilla. Fold in blueberries, pour into buttered 8 inch glass square pan and bake at 350 degrees for 35 minutes. Let cool for 15 minutes; remove from pan, when completely cool, sprinkle with powdered sugar.

Barbara Brennan

MELT-IN-YOUR-MOUTH CHEESECAKE

5 8 ounce packages cream
  cheese
5 eggs
1¾ cups sugar

1 teaspoon vanilla
3 tablespoons melted butter or
  margarine
1 pint sour cream

Preheat oven to 400 degrees. Grease and flour a 12 inch springform pan. In large bowl, mix together 1 egg and 1 package of cream cheese. Repeat until all eggs and cream cheese are mixed well. In a separate bowl, mix together sugar, butter and vanilla. Add to cream cheese mixture. Add sour cream and blend thoroughly. Pour into prepared pan. Place in oven for ½ hour. Turn off oven and leave pan in hot oven for one hour. Cool and serve. May be served with fruit topping of choice.

Carole Mahoney

BLENDER CUSTARD CAKE

½ cup sugar
5 eggs
½ cup buttermilk baking mix
1 teaspoon vanilla

¼ cup melted butter
2½ cups milk
1 cup coconut

Place ingredients in blender for 2 minutes on low speed. Pour batter in pie plate not pie shell. It makes its own shell. Bake in 350 degree oven for 50 minutes.

Kathy Turnbull

CAKES

DARK CHOCOLATE CAKE

1 package dark chocolate or
    devil's food cake mix
4 eggs
1 cup sour cream
¾ cup water

¼ cup oil
1 3 ounce package chocolate
    instant pudding
6 ounces chocolate chips

Mix all ingredients except chocolate chips in bowl at medium speed for 2 minutes. Grease and flour bundt pan. Fold in chocolate chips and pour mixture into pan. Bake for 50 to 60 minutes at 350 degrees, cool in pan for 25 minutes, then remove. Frost when fully cooled with dark chocolate frosting, of your choice.

Janice Byrne

BLACK MIDNIGHT CAKE

2¼ cups cake flour
1⅔ cups sugar
⅔ cup cocoa
1¼ teaspoons baking soda
1 teaspoon salt

¼ teaspoon baking powder
1¼ cups water
¾ cup shortening
2 eggs
1 teaspoon vanilla

Heat oven to 350 degrees. Grease and flour baking pan, 13x9x2 inch or two 9 inch layer pans. Measure all ingredients into large mixing bowl. Blend ½ minute on low speed, scraping bowl constantly. Beat 3 minutes at high speed. Pour into pan(s). Bake oblong pan about 45 minutes, layers 30 to 35 minutes or until wooden pick inserted in center comes out clean.

Erin and Kerri Darmody

DARK CHOCOLATE CAKE

2 cups flour
2 cups sugar
2 teaspoons baking soda
1 teaspoon baking powder
1 cup cocoa

2 cups hot water
2 teaspoons vanilla
½ cup oil
2 eggs

Put all ingredients into mixing bowl. Mix until well blended. It's not necessary to use electric beaters. Batter will be very thin. Preheat oven to 350 degrees. Lightly grease and flour either one 13x9x2 inch pan or two 9 inch layer pans. Pour into prepared pans and bake 30 minutes or until done.

Annette Saunders

FILLED COFFEE CAKE

1 20 ounce can pie filling
1½ cups sugar
1½ cups milk
1 teaspoon vanilla
1 teaspoon baking soda

3 cups flour
3 eggs
½ cup butter, softened
1 teaspoon salt
2 teaspoons baking powder

Topping:
⅔ cup flour
1 cup brown sugar
8 tablespoons margarine,
    softened

1 teaspoon cinnamon

Heat oven to 350 degrees; Grease a 13x9x2 inch pan. Mix flour, sugar and cinnamon. Cut in butter with pastry blender. Then beat flour, sugar, milk, butter, eggs, vanilla and baking powder, soda and salt together in large bowl on low speed. Scrape bowl constantly. Pour half of batter, about 2 cups, into greased pan. Repeat with remaining batter and pie filling mixture. Mix all topping ingredients until crumbly. Sprinkle topping on cake and bake 40 to 50 minutes at 350 degrees.

Mrs. Radman

CHOCOLATE CHIP CRUMB CAKE

2 cups self-rising flour
¾ cup sugar
½ cup softened shortening
1 cup milk

1 teaspoon vanilla
1 egg
6 ounces mini chocolate chips

Crumb Topping:
½ cup butter
1 cup flour

⅔ cup brown sugar
2 teaspoons cinnamon

Heat oven to 375 degrees. Sift together flour and sugar into bowl. Add shortening, milk, and vanilla. Beat until smooth. Add egg and beat 2 minutes. Grease and flour a 9x13 inch pan. Add chips to mixture. Pour mixture into greased pan. Sprinkle crumb mixture and bake for 20 to 25 minutes.

Vicky Reel

SOUR CREAM CHOCOLATE CAKE

2 cups flour
2 cups sugar
1 cup water
¾ cup sour cream
¼ cup shortening
1¼ teaspoons baking soda

1 teaspoon vanilla
½ teaspoon baking powder
2 eggs
4 ounces melted unsweetened
   chocolate, cooled
1 teaspoon salt

Heat oven to 350 degrees. Grease and flour oblong pan, 13x9x2 inch or two 9 inch or three 8 inch round layer pans. Measure all ingredients in large mixer bowl. Mix ½ minute on low speed, scraping bowl constantly. Beat 3 minutes on high speed, scraping bowl occasionally. Pour into pans. Bake oblong pan 40 to 45 minutes, layers 30 to 35 minutes or until top springs back when touched lightly with finger. Cool. *Note:* For cupcakes: fill tins ½ full and bake 20 to 25 minutes. *Yield:* 3 dozen.

Joanne Halloran

SOUR CREAM CHOCOLATE FROSTING

⅓ cup butter or margarine,
   softened
3 ounces melted unsweetened
   chocolate, cooled

3 cup powdered sugar
½ cup sour cream
2 teaspoons vanilla

Mix butter and cooled chocolate thoroughly. Blend in sugar. Stir in sour cream and vanilla; beat until frosting is smooth and of spreading consistency.

Joanne Halloran

MACE POUND CAKE

1 cup butter or margarine, room
   temperature
2 cups flour

1⅞ cups sugar
5 eggs
1 teaspoon mace

Cream butter, add sugar, beat until fluffy. Add eggs one at a time, beating after each egg. In another bowl, sift flour and mace. Add ingredients to first mixture. Pour into greased and floured loaf pan. Bake at 325 degrees for 1 hour and 10 minutes. *Variation:* Substitute vanilla extract for mace.

Carole Mahoney

JELLY ROLL

5 tablespoons shortening	1½ teaspoons baking powder
1 cup sugar	4 eggs
1 cup plus 2 tablespoons cake flour	1 teaspoon vanilla

Preheat oven to 375 degrees. Mix sugar, shortening, flour and baking powder. Do not use electric beater. Add 2 eggs and vanilla. Separate the 2 remaining eggs. Add yolks to mixture. Beat the whites until stiff and fold into the mixture. Pour on to a waxed paper lined 16x11 inch cookie sheet. Bake at 375 degrees for 15 minutes. Have a linen dish towel (not terry) well covered with powdered sugar. Flip cake on to towel when done. Cut the edges from all sides of cake. Spread with 1 jar of currant jelly and roll up.

Sharon Baudier

OLD FASHION GRANOLA CAKE

1½ cups boiling water	2 eggs
1 cup natural cereal	1 teaspoon allspice
1 cup sugar	1 teaspoon baking soda
1 cup brown sugar	1½ cups sifted flour
½ cup shortening	

Pour boiling water over natural cereal and let stand 10 minutes. Mix sugar, brown sugar, shortening, eggs, allspice and baking soda. Add natural cereal and flour. Pour into lightly greased and floured 9 inch tube pan. Bake at 375 degrees for 50 to 55 minutes. Dust with powdered sugar before serving.

Mrs. P. Gerkin

JEWISH POUND CAKE

1 cup margarine	2 teaspoons baking powder
2 cups sugar	1 teaspoon baking soda
4 eggs, beaten	1 teaspoon vanilla
1 pint sour cream	1 cup chopped nuts
3 cups flour	

Cream together margarine and sugar. Mix all other ingredients into creamed margarine and sugar and mix well. Place in greased 9 inch tube pan. Bake at 350 degrees for 1 hour. Cool in pan for ½ hour.

Barbara Romans

CAKES

LAZY CRAZY CAKE

3 cups cake flour
2 cups sugar
6 tablespoons cocoa
1 teaspoon salt
3 teaspoons baking soda

½ cup oil
2⅔ cups cold water
2 teaspoons vanilla
2 tablespoons vinegar

Sift dry ingredients into a large bowl. Make three wells in dry ingredients. Fill one with oil, one with vanilla and one with vinegar. Pour cold water over whole batter. Mix lightly until thoroughly mixed. Grease a 9 inch tube pan. Pour batter into pan and bake at 350 degrees for approximately 1 hour or until center is done. Remove from pan and cool on rack.

Edie Esposito

RED VELVET CAKE

1 cup butter
1½ cups sugar
2 eggs
2 teaspoons cocoa
2 ounces red food coloring
2 cups cake flour

1 teaspoon vanilla
1 teaspoon salt
1 cup buttermilk
1½ teaspoons baking soda
1 teaspoon white vinegar

Cream butter, sugar and eggs. Make paste of food coloring and cocoa and add to butter mixture. Add flour. Mix salt, vanilla and buttermilk together and put into mixture. Combine baking soda and vinegar together and quickly fold into the mixture. Lightly grease and flour two 9 inch pans or one 13x9x2 inch pan. Bake at 350 degrees for 25 to 30 minutes, or until done.

Annette Saunders

WHITE CAKE

1 cup shortening
1 cup sugar
3 eggs
1 teaspoon salt

1 teaspoon vanilla
4 teaspoons baking powder
2 cups flour
1 cup milk

Put first six items in bowl and beat well. Gradually add flour and milk. Beat well. Put into a greased oblong dish or two 8 inch cake pans. Bake at 325 degrees for 25 to 35 minutes.

Margaret Comerford

SOUR CREAM POUND CAKE

1 cup butter or margarine
6 eggs
2¾ cups sugar
3 cups flour
½ teaspoon salt
¼ teaspoon baking soda

1 cup sour cream
½ teaspoon lemon extract
½ teaspoon orange extract
½ teaspoon vanilla
powdered sugar

Bring butter and eggs to room temperature. Grease and flour a 10 inch tube pan. In small bowl, beat the butter until creamed. Gradually add sugar, beat until light and fluffy. Add eggs one at a time, beating 1 minute after each. Scrape the bowl frequently with spatula. Beat 2 minutes. Stir together flour, salt, and soda. Add to creamed mixture, alternating with sour cream, beginning and ending with flour. Beat in extracts until well blended. Bake at 350 degrees for 1½ hours or until a tooth pick inserted comes out clean and dry.

Nancy and Jennifer Vullo

PISTACHIO CAKE

1 package yellow cake mix
½ cup oil
4 eggs
1 cup club soda

1 cup chopped walnuts
1 box instant pistachio nut
  pudding

Frosting:
½ pint heavy cream
2 teaspoons sugar
1 cup milk

1 box instant pistachio nut
  pudding

Mix all cake ingredients together. Grease and flour tube pan. Bake at 350 degrees for 50 to 60 minutes.

For Frosting: Beat all ingredients until thick and cool before putting on cake.

Mrs. Augustino

GERMAN KUCHEN
(GERMAN OPEN FRUIT KUCHEN)

2 cups flour
1 egg
½ cup sugar
½ cup milk
½ cup butter or margarine,
   melted

3 apples, peaches or plums, cut
   in wedges (with skin)
cinnamon, to taste
sugar, to taste

Mix all ingredients together except fruit and cinnamon and sugar. Spread dough on a greased cookie sheet or pan about 10x14 inch. Then place cut up fruit in rows. Top with cinnamon, sugar, and bits of butter. Bake at 350 degrees for 45 minutes. Cut into rectangular pieces.

Ellen Kelly

CRUMB CAKE

2 cups flour
1 cup sugar
½ cup butter, softened
½ pint sour cream

2 eggs
1½ teaspoons vanilla
2 teaspoons baking powder
1¼ teaspoons baking soda

Crumb Topping:
½ cup butter, room temperature
1 cup flour

1 cup sugar

Cream butter and sugar until light and fluffy. Add sour cream and vanilla and mix until blended. Add all the dry ingredients and beat for 3 minutes. Grease a 13x9 inch pan and add cake mixture. In another bowl, combine crumb ingredients (add flour to butter and then add the sugar). Place topping on the cake. Bake at 350 degrees for 45 minutes. When completely cooled shake powdered sugar on top.

Alice Colloton

CHOCOLATE CHIP AND NUT CAKE

1 cup shortening	2 cups sugar
6 eggs	½ teaspoon almond extract
2 cups flour	1 cup chopped walnuts
1 cup chocolate chips	1 teaspoon salt

Mix together flour, salt, sugar, shortening and almond extract. Add eggs one at a time and beat well after each egg. Beat dough thoroughly. In a separate bowl, mix together the chocolate chips and walnuts. Add one cup of the chocolate chips and walnuts to cake mix. Stir thoroughly. Sprinkle the rest on top of cake. Grease and flour tube pan. Do not preheat oven. Set at 325 degrees for 15 minutes. Then put oven up to 375 degrees. Bake at 375 degrees for 50 to 60 minutes or until cake is done.

Maribeth Cozzi

AUNT JEAN'S TASTY CRUMB CAKE

2 cups flour, sifted	½ cup oil
½ teaspoon salt	1 egg
1 cup sugar	½ cup milk
2½ teaspoons baking powder	2 teaspoons cinnamon

Preheat oven to 350 degrees. Grease a square pan 8x8x2 inches. Mix flour, salt, sugar and baking powder in a large bowl. Add oil. Mix well with fork. Remove 1½ cups of mixture and put it into a medium size bowl. To the medium bowl add egg and milk. Mix well with spoon. Place into baking pan. Mix together 2 teaspoons sugar and 2 teaspoons cinnamon in small bowl. Mix with remaining dry ingredients in large bowl. (For moister crumbs add 2 teaspoons melted butter). Sprinkle evenly over top of batter in pan. Bake 30 minutes. *Yield:* 9 to 12 servings.

Silvia Waskewich

CAKES

RUM CAKE

1 cup chopped pecans or walnuts
1 package yellow cake mix
1 instant vanilla pudding mix
4 eggs

½ cup cold water
½ cup oil
½ cup dark rum

Preheat oven to 325 degrees. Grease and flour a 10 inch tube pan. Sprinkle nuts over bottom of pan. Mix all cake ingredients together. Pour batter over nuts. Bake 1 hour. Cool. Invert on serving plate. Prick top of cake with fork. Drizzle and smooth glaze evenly over top and sides. Allow cake to absorb glaze. Repeat until glaze is used up.

Glaze:
½ cup butter
½ cup water

1 cup sugar
½ cup dark rum

Melt butter in saucepan. Stir in water and sugar. Boil 5 minutes, stirring constantly. Remove from heat. Stir in rum. Glaze cake with warm mixture.

Judy Hein

STREUSEL COFFEE CAKE

1 egg
½ cup milk
¼ cup oil
1½ cups sifted flour

2 teaspoons baking powder
½ teaspoon salt
½ cup sugar

Streusel Topping:
½ cup sugar
⅓ cup sifted flour

½ teaspoon cinnamon
¼ cup butter, softened

Grease a 9 inch square pan. Preheat oven to 450 degrees. In a mixing bowl, beat egg slightly with a fork. Stir in milk and oil. Blend flour, baking powder, salt, and sugar in a large bowl. Add to liquid mixture. Stir just enough to moisten. Pour into pan. Blend all topping ingredients until crumbly, with pastry blender. Sprinkle topping over batter. Bake 20 to 23 minutes.

Mary Ellen Seus

WALNUT SOUR CREAM COFFEE CAKE

2 eggs
1 cup butter or margarine
1 cup sugar
1 teaspoon vanilla
2 cups flour

1 teaspoon baking soda
½ teaspoon salt
1 cup sour cream
1 teaspoon baking powder

Topping:
½ cup brown sugar
¼ cup sugar

1 teaspoon cinnamon
1 cup chopped walnuts

Cream butter and sugar until light and fluffy. Add eggs and vanilla; beat thoroughly. Add sifted dry ingredients and sour cream, alternately beating after each addition. Spread half batter in a greased and floured tube pan. Sprinkle half topping over dough. Add the rest of batter on top gently, and sprinkle with remaining topping. Bake at 350 degrees for 1 hour.

Alice Colloton

MINI CHEESE CAKES

1 box vanilla wafers
2 8 ounce packages cream
  cheese
½ cup sugar
2 eggs

2 teaspoons vanilla
1 21 ounce can cherry pie filling
  or your favorite filling
small foil cup cake holders

Beat cream cheese, sugar, eggs and vanilla for 5 minutes. Put one wafer into bottom of foil cup cake holder, and place on cookie sheet. Put approximately 1 heaping teaspoon of mixture on top of cookie and bake at 375 degrees for 15 minutes. Put desired amount of pie filling on top of each mini cheese cake as soon as removed from oven. Refrigerate until ready to use. May also be frozen for future use.

Vita Leggio

SOUR CREAM COFFEE CAKE

2½ cups flour
2 teaspoons baking powder
1 teaspoon baking soda
1 cup margarine
3 eggs, beaten

3 teaspoons cinnamon
1 cup sugar
4 ounces sour cream
½ cup brown sugar

Grease and flour 9 inch bundt cake pan. Cream margarine and sugar until smooth. Add beaten eggs and blend. Add dry ingredients alternately with sour cream blending well. Pour half of batter into cake pan and sprinkle with ½ of sugar and cinnamon mixture. Add remainder of batter and top with remaining sugar and cinnamon mixture. Bake at 350 degrees for 45 minutes to 1 hour. Cool 10 minutes and remove from cake pan.

JoEllen Schneider

CRUMB CAKE

1 yellow cake mix
4 eggs
⅔ cup oil

⅔ cup milk
3 teaspoons vanilla

Topping:
4 cups flour
3 teaspoons cinnamon
⅔ cup sugar

⅔ cup brown sugar
2 cups melted margarine

Mix batter according to directions. Spread on a greased 15x17 inch pan. Bake 15 minutes at 350 degrees. Spread on topping and return to oven 15 minutes. Cool. Sprinkle on powdered sugar.

Diane Darmody

ZUCCHINI CAKE

2 cups sugar
3 eggs
1 teaspoon vanilla
2 cups grated zucchini
1 cup oil
3 cups flour
1 teaspoon salt

¼ teaspoon baking powder
1 teaspoon baking soda
1 teaspoon cinnamon
½ cup white raisins
½ cup dark raisins
½ cup chopped nuts

Mix sugar, eggs, vanilla, zucchini and oil together. Sift flour, salt, cinnamon, soda and powder together. Add dry ingredients to zucchini mixture. Stir in raisins and nuts into mixture. Pour into well greased loaf pan or two coffee cans. Bake at 325 degrees for 60 minutes.

Dolores Gerkin

CAKES

cookies

ALMOND CRESCENTS

1 cup butter	⅓ cup sugar
2 teaspoons water	2 teaspoons vanilla
2 cups flour	1 cup chopped almonds
powdered sugar as needed	

Cream butter and sugar. Add water and vanilla and mix. Add almonds and flour. Mix all ingredients until a soft dough is formed. Cover dough and chill for 4 to 5 hours. Shape into crescents. Bake in 325 to 350 degree oven for 15 to 20 minutes on ungreased cookie sheet. When crescents are still warm, roll in powdered sugar.

Eleanor McCann

ALMOND ICEBOX COOKIES

2 cups butter	3 eggs, beaten
1 tablespoon cinnamon	5 cups flour
2 teaspoons baking soda	½ pound chopped almonds
1 cup sugar	1 cup brown sugar

Cream butter and sugars well. Add eggs, nuts and dry ingredients. Shape into a roll 2 inches thick. Chill. Cut into thin slices. Bake at 350 degrees for 10 minutes on a greased cookie sheet.

Carole DeCillia

LINZER COOKIES
GERMAN BUTTER COOKIES

1 cup sweet butter, softened	2 egg whites
½ cup sugar	½ teaspoon baking powder
2 egg yolks	2 teaspoons lemon juice

Mix all ingredients, except egg whites. Knead dough by hand; if too sticky add a little flour. Roll out on a board. Cut with cookie cutters. Dip or brush with egg whites. Add decorations of choice, if desired. Bake at 350 degrees for 10 minutes or until golden brown.

Linda J. Candia

VAN'S GREEN BROWNIES

½ cup sugar
½ cup butter, softened
4 eggs

1 cup flour
1 can chocolate syrup
1 teaspoon vanilla

Frosting:
½ cup butter, softened
2 cups powdered sugar

2 tablespoons green creme de
   menthe

Topping:
1 cup semi-sweet chocolate
   pieces

6 tablespoons butter

Cream ½ cup butter and sugar, beating until smooth. Beat in eggs, one at a time, until creamy. Add flour and mix well. Add syrup and vanilla and beat until mixed. Bake in greased 9x12 pan in preheated 350 degree oven for 25 minutes. Remove from oven and cool. Beat ½ cup butter, powdered sugar and creme de menthe together, until creamy. Spread frosting on cooled cake and refrigerate. Melt chocolate chips and butter together and pour green topping. Refrigerate until ready to serve. Cut into 1x2 inch brownies.

Nancy Besso

CANDY CANE COOKIES

½ cup butter or margarine,
   softened
1 cup powdered sugar
1½ teaspoons almond extract
2½ cups flour

½ teaspoon red food color
½ cup shortening
1 egg
1 teaspoon salt
1 teaspoon vanilla

Heat oven to 375 degrees. Thoroughly mix butter, shortening, powdered sugar, egg and flavorings. Blend in flour and salt. Divide dough in half; blend food coloring into one half. Shape one teaspoon dough from each half into 4 inch rope. For smooth, even ropes, roll them back and forth on a lightly floured board. Place ropes side by side; press together lightly and twist. Complete cookies one at a time. Place on ungreased baking sheet; curve top of cookie down to form handle of cane. Bake about 9 minutes or until set and very light brown. If desired, mix ½ cup crushed peppermint candy and ½ cup sugar. Immediately sprinkle cookies with candy mixture; remove from baking sheet. Cool. *Yield:* Approximately 4 dozen cookies.

Judy Flinn

COOKIES

CHOCOLATE CINNAMON BARS

2 cups flour
1 teaspoon baking powder
1⅓ cups sugar
4 teaspoons cinnamon
½ cup butter, softened

½ cup shortening
1 egg
1 egg, separated
6 ounce package chocolate chips

Mix and sift flour, baking powder, 1 cup sugar, 3 teaspoons cinnamon. Add butter, 1 egg and 1 egg yolk. Blend well. Press mixture into lightly greased 13x9 pan. Spread. Beat egg white and spread over mixture. Combine ⅓ cup sugar, 1 teaspoon cinnamon and chips and sprinkle over mixture. Bake at 350 degrees for 25 minutes. Cool. Cut into bars.

Patricia Brusca

CHOCOLATE CHIP COOKIES

2¼ cups flour
1 teaspoon baking soda
1 teaspoon salt
1 cup butter or margarine
¾ cup sugar
¾ cup brown sugar, packed

1 teaspoon vanilla
2 eggs
½ teaspoon water
1 12 ounce package chocolate
  morsels

Combine dry ingredients and set aside. Cream butter, sugars, vanilla and water. Add eggs and beat well. Add dry ingredients gradually. Fold in chocolate morsels. Grease cookie sheet and drop dough by teaspoonfuls onto cookie sheet. Bake at 375 degrees for 9 to 10 minutes.

Linda Pandalfi

JOANNE'S BROWNIES

1 cup sugar
2 eggs
2 squares unsweetened chocolate
½ cup butter

½ cup flour
1 teaspoon vanilla
½ cup chopped walnuts

Add sugar to eggs; beat. Melt chocolate and butter. Add to egg mixture. Blend in flour, add vanilla and nuts. Spread in greased 8x8x2 pan. Bake in moderate oven of 350 degrees for 30 to 35 minutes. Cool. This recipe may be doubled, but be sure to only use butter.

Joanne Halloran

CHOCOLATE KISS COOKIES

1 cup butter, softened
1 teaspoon vanilla
1 cup chopped pecans
powdered sugar, as needed

½ cup sugar
1¾ cups flour
1 9 ounce package chocolate
candy kisses

Cream butter and sugar together with vanilla. Add flour gradually, until well blended. Stir in pecans. Chill the dough. Mold about 1 teaspoon of cookie dough around each chocolate kiss, covering candy completely. Bake on cookie sheet at 375 degrees until they just turn golden around the edges, about 10 minutes. Let cool slightly before removing from cookie sheet. When completely cool, dust with powdered sugar. Store in airtight container. *Yield:* approximately 3 dozen.

Mary Wallin

GERMAN BUTTER COOKIE KISSES

2 cups sweet butter, room
   temperature
4½ cups flour

5 egg yolks
1 cup sugar
jam or prune butter, as needed

Preheat oven to 350 degrees. Mix first 4 ingredients well and form small balls. Make thumb impression in center of ball and fill with jam or prune butter. Place on ungreased pan and bake for 30 minutes.

Linda J. Candia

CHOCOLATE LASSIES

¾ cup butter
¾ cup sugar
1 egg, unbeaten
½ cup molasses
2½ cups flour
½ cup chopped walnuts

1½ teaspoons baking soda
½ teaspoon ginger
½ teaspoon cinnamon
1 6 ounce package semi-sweet
   chocolate pieces

Cream butter and sugar until fluffy. Beat in egg and molasses. Sift flour, baking soda and spices, together. Add to creamed mixture. Stir in semi-sweet chocolate pieces and walnuts. Drop by teaspoonfuls onto ungreased cookie sheets. Bake at 375 degrees 10 to 12 minutes.

Mary Deveau

COOKIES

JAM BUTTER COOKIES

1 cup butter
1 egg yolk
1 teaspoon vanilla
jam or jelly, optional

½ cup sugar
2 cups flour
1 teaspoon baking soda

Mix all ingredients together, except jam. When thoroughly mixed, roll into little balls and place on ungreased cookie sheet. Make thumbprint in cookie and fill with jelly or jam. Bake 15 minutes at 350 degrees. *Note:* This is a favorite with children and is great with raspberry jam.

Rosemarie DeRosa

CHOCOLATE PEANUT BUTTER PILE-UPS

1 cup peanut butter
½ cup sugar
1 egg

1 4 ounce package German
sweet chocolate, broken in
pieces

Mix peanut butter, sugar and egg until blended. Press or roll dough into a 10x7 inch pan or ungreased baking sheet. Bake at 325 degrees for 20 minutes. Remove from oven. Immediately arrange chocolate on top and cover lightly with aluminum foil. Let stand 3 minutes and remove foil. Spread melted chocolate over entire surface and immediately cut into 2x1 inch bars. Cool. *Yield:* approximately 30 bars.

Irene Francis

CHOCOLATETOWN CHIP COOKIES

¾ cup butter
1 cup packed brown sugar
2 eggs
1 teaspoonful baking soda
1 12 ounce package chocolate
   chips

½ cup sugar
1 teaspoonful vanilla
2 cups flour
1 teaspoon salt

Cream the butter, sugars and vanilla until light and fluffy. Add the eggs and beat well. Sift together, flour, baking soda and salt. Add to the creamed mixture. Add the chocolate chips and blend well. Drop by teaspoons onto lightly greased baking sheet. Bake at 375 degrees for 8 to 10 minutes. *Yield:* approximately 8 dozen.

Anne Stearns

156

MERRY CHEESE CAKES

Crust:

⅓ cup butter, softened
1 cup flour
½ cup brown sugar

½ cup chopped walnuts or
   pecans

Filling:

8 ounce cream cheese, softened
¼ cup sugar
1 egg

2 tablespoons milk
2 tablespoons lemon juice
½ teaspoon vanilla

Preheat oven to 350 degrees. Combine flour, butter and brown sugar. Blend at low speed, 2 to 3 minutes until particles are fine. Stir in nuts. Reserve 1 cup mixture for topping; pat remainder in ungreased 8 inch square pan. Bake in center of oven 8 to 10 minutes or until lightly browned. Prepare filling; blending until smooth. Spread over partially baked crust. Sprinkle with reserved crumb mixture. Return to oven for 25 to 30 minutes, or until golden brown. Cool. Cut into bars. Store in refrigerator.

Helen Kennedy

CREME DE MENTHE BARS

1 cup sugar
½ cup margarine
1 cup flour

1 16 ounce can chocolate syrup
1 teaspoon vanilla
4 eggs, well beaten

Frosting:

2 cups powdered sugar
½ cup margarine
2 tablespoons milk

½ teaspoon peppermint extract
green food coloring

Glaze:

1 cup chocolate chips

6 tablespoons margarine

Combine first 6 ingredients and put into ungreased 9x13 pan. Bake at 350 degrees for 30 minutes. Cool. Beat frosting ingredients until spreadable. Spread on cooled dough. Melt chips and margarine together to make glaze. When cool pour on top of green frosting. Refrigerate. Make sure each layer is cool before adding next layer. Cut into squares when glaze is set, but not hard.

Rachel Megna

CHRISTMAS COOKIES

1 cup butter, softened	2½ cups flour
1 cup sugar	¼ teaspoon salt
1 egg	¼ teaspoon baking soda
2 tablespoons heavy cream	1 teaspoon vanilla

Preheat oven to 400 degrees. Cream together gradually, butter, sugar, egg, heavy cream and vanilla. Sift together, flour, salt and baking soda in separate bowl. Gradually, add flour to creamed ingredients and beat until mixture is blended. Press onto cookie sheet with a cookie press. Bake for 10 to 12 minutes. *Note:* For chocolate cookies, add 3 squares of melted unsweetened chocolate to batter.

Gerry Daube

CREAM CHEESE COOKIES

1 cup shortening	1 3 ounce package cream cheese
1 cup sugar	1 egg yolk
½ teaspoon vanilla	2½ cups sifted flour

Cream shortening until fluffy, then gradually work in cream cheese and sugar, making sure mixture is creamy. Beat in yolk, vanilla and flour. If desired, cookies may be dropped by spoonfuls onto ungreased cookie sheets or chilled then rolled and cut with cookie cutters. Decorate with colored sugar, candies or sprinkles. Bake in a preheated 375 degree oven for 15 minutes. *Yield:* 4 dozen.

Judy Flinn

FRUITCAKE COOKIES

½ cup margarine	½ teaspoon baking powder
1 cup brown sugar	1 cup quick cooking oats
1 egg	1½ cups fruit cake, crumbled
1 cup flour	1 teaspoon salt

In large bowl mix butter and brown sugar until light and fluffy. Add egg and beat. Sift together flour, baking powder and salt. Add to creamed mixture. Stir in oats and fruit cake. Drop by teaspoonfuls, 2 inches apart, on well-greased baking sheet. Bake at 350 degrees for 8 to 10 minutes. *Yield:* 3 dozen cookies.

Christopher Mugno

MEXICAN BESITOS DE MERINGUE
(MERINGUE KISSES)

Review meringue making instructions from any cookbook before starting this recipe.

4 egg whites, room temperature
¼ teaspoon salt
¼ teaspoon cream of tartar
1 cup sugar

¾ teaspoon vanilla
1 packet pre-melted chocolate, (optional)
¼ teaspoon cinnamon

Preheat oven to 250 degrees. Line cookie sheets with foil. Beat egg whites on medium speed until foamy, add salt and cream of tartar; mix. Add sugar, 1 tablespoon at a time, beating well between each addition. Add vanilla and cinnamon. Beat at highest speed until glossy and very stiff peaks form. Gently fold in chocolate until nicely marbled. Drop by rounded teaspoons on foiled cookie sheets or pipe through pastry bag with medium tip; each kiss should be 1½ inches in diameter. Bake 40 to 45 minutes; turn oven off and cook 3 hours. Store airtight or they will get sticky.

Jean Buckridge

SHORTBREAD

1 cup butter, softened
½ teaspoon vanilla
32 unblanched almonds, optional

½ cup packed light brown sugar
2 cups flour, preferably cake flour
2 teaspoons sugar, optional

In a large bowl, cream butter with brown sugar and vanilla until light and fluffy. With rubber spatula gradually stir in flour, just until blended. Chill dough 30 minutes or until firm enough to handle. Cut in half. On center of ungreased cookie sheet, pat each half into a 7 inch, smooth, even circle. With fork, prick dough deep at ½ inch intervals. Make decorative border by pressing fork tines dipped in flour around edges. Press almonds 1 inch apart firmly into dough ½ inch from edges. Cover dough loosely with waxed paper and chill several hours or overnight. Bake in preheated 325 degree oven for 25 to 30 minutes or until firm to touch and edges are barely colored. Sprinkle each with 1 teaspoon granulated sugar. Cool on sheets on rack. Store in lightly covered container up to 2 weeks, or freeze up to 3 months.

Sister Jeannette Tenaglia

LEMON SQUARES

½ cup margarine or butter   1 cup flour
¼ cup powdered sugar

Topping:
2 eggs   1 cup sugar
2 tablespoons flour   2 tablespoons lemon juice

Garnish:
powdered sugar

Mix first 3 ingredients and press into 8 inch square greased pan. Bake at 350 degrees for 15 to 20 minutes, until tan in color. Beat together topping ingredients. Pour over hot crust and return to oven for 25 minutes. When cool, sprinkle powdered sugar on top.

Jackie Greene

CHRISTMAS PECAN BALLS

1 cup butter, melted   4 tablespoons sugar
2 teaspoons vanilla   2 cups flour
1 cup chopped pecans   powdered sugar, as needed

Mix butter, sugar and vanilla together. Mix flour and chopped pecans together. Combine both mixtures. Roll into small balls and bake at 350 degrees for 30 minutes on ungreased cookie sheet. Roll in powdered sugar when done.

Pam Falanga

CHRISTMAS COOKIES

1 cup shortening   2¼ cups flour
1 cup brown sugar   1 teaspoon baking soda
½ cup sugar   1 teaspoon salt
2 teaspoons vanilla   1½ cups candy coated chocolate
2 eggs   or mixed color chocolate

Blend shortening and sugar. Beat in vanilla and eggs. Add dry ingredients and blend. Stir in candies. Drop from spoon onto ungreased cookie sheet. Bake at 375 degrees for 10 minutes.

Amy Curcio

OATMEAL COOKIES

¾ cup shortening
½ cup sugar
¼ cup water
3 cups quick oats, uncooked
1 teaspoon salt
½ cup finely chopped nuts,
  optional
1 cup firmly packed brown
  sugar

1 egg
1 teaspoon vanilla
1 cup flour
½ teaspoon baking soda
nuts, raisins, chocolate chips or
  coconut, optional

Preheat oven to 350 degrees. Beat together shortening, sugar, brown sugar, eggs, water and vanilla until creamy. Mix remaining ingredients together well, then add to creamed ingredients. Mix well. Fold in any optional ingredients. Drop by rounded teaspoonfuls onto greased cookie sheet. Bake at 350 degrees for 12 to 15 minutes. *Note:* To make larger cookies use a tablespoon. *Yield:* 5 dozen small cookies; about 28 large.

Jennifer Vitelli

PALUSKI

½ cup butter, softened
1 cup flour

2½ tablespoons powdered sugar
½ cup chopped nuts

Mix all ingredients together. Shape into finger in the palm of your hand. Dip top into colored sprinkles. Place on cookie sheet at 350 degrees for 15 minutes or until done. Sprinkle with powdered sugar when ready to serve.

Joseph Karpowicz

PINOLI

½ cup sugar
½ teaspoon salt
1 8 ounce can pure almond paste
pinoli nuts, as needed

½ cup powdered sugar
¼ cup flour
2 egg whites

Preheat oven to 300 degrees. Crumble the paste, then add sugar, flour and salt. Mix well. Add egg whites one at a time and mix. Line cookie sheet with brown paper. Drop one tablespoon at a time and put pinoli nuts on top. Bake for 20 or 25 minutes. When cool, wet back of paper and remove cookies. Sprinkle with powdered sugar.

Rosanne De Lassio

COOKIES

SEVEN LAYER BARS

¼ cup sweet butter
1 cup graham cracker crumbs
1 cup shredded coconut
1 6 ounce package semi-sweet
   chocolate pieces

1 6 ounce package butterscotch
   pieces
1 14 ounce can sweetened
   condensed milk
1 cup chopped nuts

Preheat oven to 350 degrees. Melt butter in a 13x9x2 pan. Sprinkle crumbs evenly over the melted butter and press down. Sprinkle on the coconut, the chocolate, then the butterscotch pieces. Pour milk evenly over all. Sprinkle on the nuts and press lightly. Bake for 30 minutes. Cool in pan on wire rack. Cut into 1x2 inch bars. *Yield:* 48 bars.

Anne Stearns

TEA TESSIES

Shell:
3 ounces cream cheese
½ cup butter

1 cup flour

Filling:
¾ cup brown sugar
1 egg
1 tablespoon butter, softened

1 teaspoon vanilla
1 cup chopped nuts

Mix all of shell ingredients until ball forms. In small cup cake tins, press and flatten balls and build sides to form a shell. Fill with 1 teaspoon filling. Bake at 375 degrees for 30 to 35 minutes. Take out when cool and sprinkle with powdered sugar. *Yield:* 2 dozen.

Mrs. Nowicki

"NO-STIR" SQUARES

½ cup butter, melted
1½ cups graham cracker crumbs
1 cup coconut
12 ounces chocolate

14 ounces sweetened condensed
   milk
1 cup chopped walnuts

Arrange ingredients in layers in 11x8 pan in the order given. Bake in 350 degree oven for 35 to 40 minutes. Cut into squares when cooled.

Pam Falanga

ICE BOX COOKIES

2 cups butter or margarine, or 1 cup butter and 1 cup margarine
4 cups flour
1¾ cups powdered sugar

1 teaspoon vanilla
3 egg yolks
chocolate chips, as needed
chopped nuts, as needed

Cream together butter and sugar; add vanilla and egg yolks, one at a time. Beat after adding each egg yolk. Add flour gradually. Continue to add more flour until dough is easy to roll into a ball. Divide dough into 4 parts and roll into tubes about the diameter of a half dollar. Wrap in waxed paper. Refrigerate overnight or until ready to use. Slice to desired thickness. Place on cookie sheets. Bake at 350 degrees about 10 to 15 minutes. Melt chocolate chips and spread on cookies, then dip into chopped nuts.

Pauline Comando

SANDIES

1 cup butter or margarine, softened
2 teaspoons vanilla
2 cups sifted flour
⅓ cup sugar

2 teaspoons water
1 cup chopped pecans or walnuts
powdered sugar, optional
chocolate icing, optional

Mix first ingredients together in bowl. Stir in 1 cup chopped nuts. Bake on ungreased cookie sheet in slow oven of 325 degrees for 20 minutes. Remove to rack. Cool slightly. Roll in powdered sugar or, if desired, roll into fingers and dip one end in very thin chocolate icing.

Mrs. Blouin

THUMBPRINT COOKIES

2½ cups flour
½ teaspoon vanilla
1 cup butter

1 egg yolk
½ cup sugar

Filling:
jam, of choice

Cream sugar and butter. Add remaining ingredients. Form dough into small balls. Press with thumb on ungreased cookie sheet. Bake 15 to 20 minutes at 350 degrees. Fill with jam when cool.

Rosalie Toja

COOKIES

WALNUT CRESCENTS

1 cup butter or margarine,
  softened
½ cup powdered sugar
1¾ cups flour

1 cup chopped walnuts
¼ teaspoon salt
2 teaspoons vanilla extract
powdered sugar, as needed

Cream butter. Add ½ cup powdered sugar, vanilla and salt. Beat until light. Stir in nuts and flour until well blended. Wrap dough in waxed paper and chill well. Preheat oven to 300 degrees. Divide dough in 8 equal pieces. On lightly floured board, shape into thin rolls about ½ inch in diameter. Cut into 2 inch pieces. Taper off ends and shape into crescents. Put on ungreased baking sheets and bake 18 to 20 minutes. Remove to rack to cool. Sift powdered sugar over top. *Yield:* approximately 5 dozen.

Anne Stearns

MEXICAN WEDDING CAKES

½ cup butter
2 cups flour
1 cup chopped walnuts

½ cup shortening
1 teaspoon vanilla
6 teaspoons powdered sugar

Cream butter, shortening and vanilla. Stir in flour and walnuts. Mix well. Shape into small balls. Bake on ungreased cookie sheet in 400 degree oven for 10 minutes. Roll in powdered sugar while still warm, but not hot. Store overnight in waxed paper. *Yield:* 2 to 3 dozen.

Kathy Turnbull

SPRITZ COOKIES

4 hard boiled egg yolks
½ teaspoon salt
1 cup butter
½ cup sugar

½ teaspoon almond extract
2 cups sifted flour
maraschino cherries, for garnish

Thoroughly mash egg yolks. Mix well with remaining ingredients, except cherries. Shape cookies. Cut up cherries and place a piece in center of each cookie. Bake on cookie sheet at 375 degrees for 7 to 10 minutes.

Barbara Welsch

SPRITZ COOKIES

1 cup butter	½ cup sugar
1 egg	1 teaspoon vanilla extract
½ teaspoon almond extract	2½ cups flour

Chocolate Glaze:
1 cup chocolate chips   1 teaspoon shortening

Heat oven to 350 degrees. Cream butter and sugar until fluffy. Beat in egg and extracts. Gradually blend in flour. Using a press, place dough on cookie sheet. Bake 8 to 10 minutes. Make glaze by melting ingredients in saucepan. Be careful not to burn chocolate! When cookies are cool, dip in chocolate glaze. When cool, store in cookie tin.

Lucille Irving

VANILLA COOKIES

1 cup butter	½ teaspoon baking powder
⅔ cup sugar	⅛ teaspoon salt
1 egg	1 teaspoon almond or vanilla
2½ cups flour	extract

Cream butter and sugar. Add egg and mix thoroughly. Add dry ingredients, which have been sifted and mixed together. Add extract. Mix. Put dough through cookie press, and bake in 400 degree oven for 10 to 12 minutes.

Mary Deveau

STRUFOLI
ITALIAN HONEY BALLS

4 eggs
2 teaspoons salt
1¾ cups honey
1 teaspoon baking powder

oil, as needed
2½ cups flour
½ cup coarsely chopped walnuts

In large bowl, with fork or wire whisk, beat eggs, ½ cup oil and salt until well blended. Gradually stir in 2 cups flour and baking powder until well mixed. With hands, knead in remaining flour. Turn dough onto lightly floured surface. Cut dough into 20 equal portions. With palms of hands roll each into pencil shaped sticks. With floured knife, cut sticks into ¼ inch pieces. In a large skillet, heat about one inch oil to 370 degrees. Fry dough, a handful at a time. With slotted spoon, stir occasionally, for even browning. Remove and drain well on paper towels. Place in large bowl. In a sauce pan over medium heat, bring honey to boil. Stir in nuts and pour over fried dough. Toss well. Cover and refrigerate over night. *To serve:* Let fried dough stand at room temperature 1 hour to soften; toss well and shape in mound on plate.

Rosanne DeLassio

desserts

DESSERTS

FRUIT SALAD - AMBROSIA

2 cans pineapple chunks
2 11 ounce mandarin orange
  segments
½ pint sour cream

½ package flaked coconut
½ package miniature
  marshmallows

Drain fruit. Mix all ingredients and refrigerate.

Mary Ellen Giuliani

APRICOT SALAD MOLD

½ pint sour cream
1½ cups boiling water
1 cup apricot nectar juice
2 packages small apricot
  gelatin, or 1 large package

½ cup water
1 small can crushed pineapple
chopped walnuts, to taste

To gelatin, add hot and cold water, then add nectar and stir until dissolved. Chill this in your refrigerator for approximately 2 hours or until firm. Drain pineapple and add chopped walnuts to pineapple. Mix both ingredients into gelatin mixture. Place ½ mixture into a gelatin mold. Layer sour cream on top of gelatin mixture and fill the mold with remaining gelatin. Put top on mold and refrigerate overnight. To take the mold out, take off the small top and put on a serving tray. Shake out easily after you have removed the large top.

Gerry Daube

FRESH FRUIT MEDLEY

1 cup seedless green grapes
1 cup cantaloupe balls or
  pineapple cubes
1 cup strawberries

1 6 ounce can frozen fruit juice
  concentrate: pineapple,
  orange, lemonade, or
  cranberry juice cocktail,
  partially thawed

Divide fruit among 6 dessert dishes. Just before serving, spoon 1 to 2 tablespoons fruit concentrate into each serving. *Yield:* 6 servings.

Danielle Coffey

BLACK FOREST CREPES

Cherry Sauce:

2 16½ ounce cans sweet cherries in heavy syrup
½ cup granulated sugar

2 tablespoons cornstarch
¼ cup water
½ teaspoon almond kirsch

Crepes:

1 cup plus 2 tablespoons flour
¼ cup granulated sugar
3 tablespoons cocoa
dash salt
3 eggs, slightly beaten

1¼ cups milk
2 tablespoons melted butter
2 quarts vanilla ice cream
sweetened whipped cream and chocolate curls, for garnish

Soften ice cream slightly. To make sauce, drain cherries, reserving liquid. Chop cherries coarsely into chunks; set aside. Add sufficient water to reserved cherry liquid to measure 2 cups. Place in a 2 quart saucepan and add sugar. Heat and stir until sugar is dissolved. Mix cornstarch with water. Stir into boiling liquid and stir until thickened. Add almond flavoring. Remove from heat. Stir in cherries and kirsch.

To make crepes, combine flour, sugar, cocoa and salt. In the jar of a blender combine eggs, milk and butter and blend 10 seconds. Add dry ingredients and beat until smooth. Refrigerate at least 1 hour. Heat a small skillet, measuring 6 inches at the base, over medium heat. Brush lightly with melted butter. Pour in about 2 tablespoons of batter and immediately rotate skillet until bottom is completely covered. Cook 1 minute. Turn and cook other side for 30 seconds. Cool on a clean non terry cloth dish towel. Stack with small sheets of waxed paper in between.

To assemble, place a crepe on a serving dish. Spoon ½ cup softened ice cream down the center. Cover with ¼ cup cherry sauce. Fold crepe over ice cream and garnish with whipped cream and chocolate curls. *Yield:* 16 crepes.

Eleanor Wittrup

DESSERTS

BRANDIED PEACHES

8 pounds peaches
3 cups brandy
8 cups water
8 cups sugar

cloves, as needed
6 quart mason jars, or 12 pint
  jars
canner

Cut peaches in half. Remove pits. Leave skin on, but wipe off fuzz with a rough towel. Bring water and sugar to a boil, add peaches; boil again for 5 minutes. Put peaches in jars and add ½ cup brandy to each plus 2 whole cloves, cover with syrup. Put on seals and covers; process in boiling water bath for 25 minutes. Let stand in cool dark place for 3 months. *Yield:* 6 quarts or 12 pints.

Jean Sweeney

CRUSTLESS CREAMY CHEESECAKE

1 pound ricotta cheese
1 pound cream cheese
1 pound sour cream
1 teaspoon vanilla
½ cup butter, melted

3 tablespoons cornstarch
3 tablespoons flour
1½ cups sugar
4 eggs

Blend cheeses, sour cream, eggs, vanilla, and melted butter until smooth with electric mixer. Add cornstarch, flour and sugar. Grease inside of a 9 or 10 inch springform pan with butter before adding batter. Bake for 1 hour at 350 degrees, shut off oven and leave in for 2 hours. Top with cherry pie filling, if desired. Refrigerate until ready to serve.

Carole DeCillia

QUICK CHERRY CRISP

1 21 ounce can cherry pie filling
¾ cup flour
3 tablespoons brown sugar

¼ teaspoon cinnamon
6 tablespoons butter

Preheat oven 450 degrees. Spoon cherry pie filling into 9 inch pie plate. In bowl combine flour, brown sugar and cinnamon. With pastry blender cut butter into flour until mixture is crumbly. Sprinkle over filling. Bake 15 minutes. Reduce heat to 375 degrees; bake 10 minutes. Serve with whipped cream.

Linda Yarwood

170

CHERRY DELIGHT

1 cup flour
½ cup butter or margarine
1 cup coarsely chopped pecans
cream cheese filling

rice pudding filling
1 1 pound 5 ounce can cherry
  pie filling
non-dairy whipped topping

Cream Cheese Filling:
1 8 ounce package cream cheese
1 cup whipped topping

1 cup powdered sugar

Rice Pudding Filling:
½ cup rice
1⅓ cups water
½ teaspoon salt
½ teaspoon butter or margarine

4 cups milk
2 3⅝ ounce packages vanilla
  instant pudding mix

Beat together all ingredients for cream cheese filling and set aside. Cook rice according to package directions. Cool. Whip milk and instant pudding until thick. Fold in rice. Chill until firm. Preheat oven to 350 degrees. Lightly butter 13x9 inch pan. Cut butter into flour with pastry knife until resembles bread crumbs. Add pecans; mix well. Press into pan in an even layer. Bake until light brown about 20 minutes. Cool. When pastry is cooled spread cream cheese filling over crust. Cool. Spread rice pudding mixture over cream cheese layer. Chill until firm. Spoon cherry filling over pudding. Chill. Just before serving garnish each piece with whipped topping. *Yield:* 12 servings.

Janet Reynolds

CHOCOLATE YUMMY

2 cups milk
1 cup sugar
⅓ cup flour

⅛ teaspoon salt
⅓ cup cocoa
1 teaspoon vanilla

Heat 1½ cups milk in a double boiler. Mix dry ingredients together in bowl pressing the chocolate lumps against side of bowl. When thoroughly mixed, stir in remaining milk. Add to hot milk in double boiler. Stir until thickened. Remove from heat, stir in vanilla. Pour into individual containers. *Yield:* 4 servings.

Mary Nygaard

DESSERTS

COLD CHOCOLATE SOUFFLÉ

2 ounces unsweetened chocolate	½ cup powdered sugar
1 envelope unflavored gelatin, softened in 3 tablespoons cold water	¾ cup sugar
	1 teaspoon vanilla
	¼ teaspoon salt
1 cup milk	2 cups whipping cream

Start melting chocolate over low heat. Put gelatin in a small bowl with 3 tablespoons of cold water. Heat 1 cup milk. When chocolate is melted add powdered sugar and then gradually add hot milk, stirring gradually. It might lump, just keep stirring. Over low heat, stir until it reaches the boiling point, but do not boil. Remove from heat, stir in gelatin, sugar, vanilla and salt, mix well. Pour into large mixing bowl and refrigerate until slightly thickened, about 1 hour. Beat cream until whipped. Then beat chocolate mixture until light and fluffy. Fold cream into chocolate mixture and pour into serving dish or little dishes. Chill covered for 4 hours or overnight.

Vicky Reel

CHOCOLATE MOUSSE

4 eggs, separated	5 tablespoons coffee, brewed
6 ounces semi-sweet chocolate chips	3 teaspoons vanilla, or 2 tablespoons rum

Beat egg whites until foamy, to make meringue. Combine chocolate chips and coffee in blender. Blend until smooth. Add egg yolks and vanilla and blend. Fold above mixture into egg whites. Place in appropriate bowl. Refrigerate 2 to 3 hours. *Yield:* 6 servings.

Connie Nonnenmacher

FRUIT COCKTAIL AND CREAM DESSERT

½ pint heavy cream	2 tablespoons powdered sugar
1 large can fruit cocktail	sprinkles for garnish

Drain fruit cocktail, reserve juice for use in gelatin mix if desired. Whip cream and powdered sugar together until stiff. Add fruit cocktail and blend together. Spoon into individual dessert dishes and garnish with sprinkles.

The Committee

CREAM CHEESE TARTS

1 package foil midget muffin
  cups
2 packages chocolate snaps,
  crushed
2 8 ounce packages cream
  cheese, softened

2 eggs
½ teaspoon grated lemon peel
¾ cup sugar
1 teaspoon vanilla

Combine all ingredients (except 1 package of snaps) in bowl. Beat with electric mixer until smooth. In each muffin cup, put one whole snap upside down. Fill ¾ with cream cheese mixture. Place muffin tins on cookie sheet. Bake at 375 degrees for 10 minutes. Remove; cool completely.

Toppings:
Top with a variety of the following: Brush Apricot Glaze over the following: fresh strawberries, fresh grapes, fresh blueberries, canned pineapple tidbits.

Apricot Glaze:
Boil ½ cup of apricot preserves 225 to 228 degrees on candy thermometer. Thin with 1 to 2 tablespoons of hot water. Strain, then brush on tarts.

Helen McBride

JEWEL DESSERT

1 package orange gelatin
1 package cherry gelatin
1 package lime gelatin
lady fingers

1 cup pineapple juice
¼ cup sugar
1 pint heavy cream, whipped
1 package lemon gelatin

Prepare each flavor of first three gelatins by adding 1 cup hot water and ½ cup of cold water to each. Pour each flavor into an 8 inch pan, chill until firm. Mix 1 cup pineapple juice and ¼ cup sugar, heat until sugar dissolves. Remove from the heat and dissolve lemon gelatin in hot juice, add ½ cup of cold water. Chill until slightly thickened. Meanwhile line serving pan with lady fingers, cut gelatin into ½ inch cubes. Prepare 1 pint heavy cream, whipped, blend lemon and pineapple juice into whipped cream, fold in gelatin cubes and pour into pan. Chill and refrigerate for 5 hours.

Sister Jeannette Tenaglia

DESSERTS

BANANA DONUTS

2 cups flour
2 teaspoons baking powder
2 tablespoons sugar
2 eggs
1 teaspoon vanilla

1 cup milk
2 teaspoons lemon juice
½ cup raisins
1 or 2 bananas

Mix flour with baking powder. Add the eggs, sugar, vanilla, milk and lemon juice. When you have a paste, add cut up pieces of banana and the raisins. Take a little portion of the dough on a spoon and dip in hot shortening until brown.

Ann Marcic

CREAM PUFFS

1 cup water
½ cup margarine or butter
1 cup flour

¼ teaspoon salt
4 eggs

In a saucepan, bring water to boiling. Stir in butter until melted. Add flour and salt at once. Stir vigorously. Cook and stir until mixture forms a ball that doesn't separate. Remove from heat; cool slightly. Add eggs one at a time. Beat vigorously after each addition until smooth. Drop by heaping teaspoon 3 inches apart on a greased baking sheet. Bake in 400 degree oven until golden brown, about 30 minutes. Remove from oven and split.

Carmela Cerullo

4 LAYER DESSERT

1 cup flour
½ cup finely ground pecans
½ cup butter, softened
1 cup powdered sugar
2 cups whipped topping

8 ounces cream cheese, softened
6 ounce package chocolate
  pudding
grated chocolate, as needed

Mix together flour, pecans and butter and press into bottom of 9x13 inch glass dish. Bake at 375 degrees for 15 minutes. Chill. Blend sugar, 1 cup whipped topping and cream cheese and spread on crust. Chill. Prepare chocolate pudding. Cool and pour over mixture. Chill. Cover with 1 cup whipped topping and top with grated chocolate. *Yield:* 12 servings.

The Committee

FRUIT GELATIN

1 tablespoon unflavored gelatin
¼ cup cold water
¾ cup boiling water

1 cup fruit juice
sugar

Soak gelatin in cold water to soften. Dissolve in boiling water, stirring. Add one cup of any of the following juice: orange, grapefruit, apricot, cranberry, grape, peach, raspberry, or *canned* pineapple. Taste, if not sweet enough add sugar to taste. Pour into bowl or individual cups. Chill until soft. *Note:* Do not use fresh pineapple juice as gelatin will not set. *Yield:* 4 servings.

Madeline Mara Evancie

GLAZED PEACH CREME

2 packages, 3 ounces each,
   gelatin, peach flavor
2 cups boiling water

¾ cup cold water
1 pint vanilla ice cream
1 8¾ ounce can sliced peaches

Dissolve one package gelatin in 1 cup boiling water. Add cold water. Chill until slightly thickened. Gelatin will have the consistency of unbeaten egg whites. Dissolve second package gelatin in remaining boiling water. Add ice cream and stir until melted and smooth. Pour into serving bowl. Chill about 1 hour, or until set but not firm. Arrange canned or fresh peach slices on gelatin ice cream mixture. Top with clear gelatin. Garnish with whipped topping, if desired. *Yield:* 10 servings.

Stephanie Rabuse

STRIPED GELATIN MOLD

4 gelatins: red, yellow, green,
   orange
1¼ cups sugar
1 pint sour cream

1 pint heavy cream
2 envelopes plain gelatin,
   softened in ½ cup cold water

Bring sugar and heavy cream to a boil. Add gelatin and cool; then add sour cream. Dissolve gelatins in 1½ cups water each, ¾ cup hot and ¾ cup cold. Rub a mold with oil, 12 cup size loaf shape. Keep cream mixture soft over warm water in double boiler pan. Put ¾ cup cream mixture in mold, covering bottom evenly. Harden in freezer 15 minutes and alternate colors with cream using ¾ cup each layer. 15 layers. Refrigerate overnight.

Kathy Smith

ICE BOX CAKE

1 3 ounce box chocolate
pudding, cooking type
1 3 ounce box vanilla pudding,
cooking type
1 box graham crackers

milk, as needed
9x9 square baking dish,
preferably glass as leftovers
remain in refrigerator
sliced bananas, optional

Place graham crackers in bottom of pan to form crust being sure to fill in all areas. Cook vanilla pudding according to package directions. When done, pour into baking dish and let cool. When cooled, place another row of graham crackers on top. At this time, if desired, sliced bananas can be added. Cook chocolate pudding according to package directions and pour into baking dish on top of next row of graham crackers. Let cool and sprinkle graham cracker crumbs on top. Refrigerate. This makes a nice dessert for company or just the family after dinner. When serving, slice as a cake.

Rosemarie DeRosa

DONUT HOLES

1 pound of ricotta cheese
6 eggs
4 cups of warm milk
8 teaspoons baking powder

10 tablespoons sugar
1 teaspoon cinnamon
flour as needed

Beat all together until smooth, then add as much flour as necessary for the right consistency. Consistency should be thick so that it can easily be dropped into hot oil. Drop by teaspoon into hot oil. Top with honey, cinnamon or powdered sugar.

Pauline Comando

HAWAIIAN DELIGHT

1 6 ounce package lemon gelatin
1 cup canned crushed pineapple,
juice reserved
1 cup boiling water

4 ounces cottage cheese
1 cup heavy cream
½ cup maraschino cherries
½ cup shredded coconut

Dissolve gelatin in boiling water and reserved pineapple juice. Chill until partially set. Fold in remaining ingredients and chill.

Angel Byrnes

EASY FRESH PEACH COBBLER

8 medium peaches, sliced

Topping:

1 cup flour	1 pinch salt
1 cup sugar	melted butter, as necessary

Place sliced peaches in a 9x13 ovenproof pan. Combine topping ingredients. Crumble topping over peaches and drizzle with melted butter. Bake at 350 degrees for 30 to 40 minutes. Serve warm with vanilla ice cream sprinkled with cinnammon on top.

Kathryn Slaska

CHEESE CAKE PIE

1 pie shell, brushed inside with melted butter	1 can crushed pineapple, well drained

Filling:

½ cup sugar	1 teaspoon vanilla
1 tablespoon flour	3 eggs
⅛ teaspoon salt	½ cup heavy cream
½ pound cream cheese	¼ teaspoon cream of tartar

Spread crushed pineapple in pie shell. Set aside. Mix sugar, flour, salt and cream cheese thoroughly. Add vanilla and yolks of eggs and beat. Add cream and mix again. Beat egg whites with a pinch of salt and ¼ teaspoon cream of tartar until they form peaks. Fold into mixture. Pour into a prepared pan. Bake at 350 degrees until center is set, about 45 minutes to 1 hour. Serve cold.

Beverly Maccari

MELTAWAYS

½ cup butter, softened	5 tablespoons powdered sugar
1 cup flour	1 cup chopped walnuts

Combine ingredients; form into ball. Place in refrigerator for 15 minutes. Take small pieces off ball. Place on ungreased cookie sheet. Bake at 350 degrees for 20 minutes. Let cool and roll in powdered sugar.

Eileen Kalkhof

DESERTS

APPLE CRUMB PIE

5 to 7 tart apples
1 9 inch unbaked pie shell
½ cup sugar
1 teaspoon cinnamon

½ cup sugar
¾ cup flour
⅓ cup butter, softened

Pare apples, cut into eights. Arrange in unbaked pie shell. Mix ½ cup sugar with cinnamon, sprinkle over apples. Mix other ½ cup sugar with flour, cut in butter until crumbly, sprinkle over apples. Bake in 400 degree oven for 40 minutes. Cool. Spoon whipped cream on top if desired.

Cathy Theodorakis

MERINGUES

4 egg whites
1½ cups sugar
⅓ cup walnuts

1 cup bittersweet chocolate chips

In a large bowl, let egg whites warm to room temperature. Preheat oven to 300 degrees. With mixer at high speed, beat egg whites until soft peaks form. Add sugar, 2 tablespoons at a time, beating well. Continue beating until stiff peaks form. Fold in chocolate chips and walnuts. Drop mixture by teaspoonful onto a lightly greased cookie sheet; bake 25 minutes until golden. Cool. Store in a container. Bon appetite!!

Arleen G. Eberhardt

CHERRY CREAM CHEESE PIE

1 6 ounce graham cracker pie crust
1 8 ounce package of cream cheese

1 8 ounce container heavy cream
1 cup powdered sugar
1 teaspoon vanilla extract

Topping:
1 21 ounce can cherry pie filling

Let cream cheese stand at room temperature until softened. In a medium size mixing bowl, beat cream cheese, heavy cream, powdered sugar and vanilla extract. Beat all these ingredients until light and fluffy. Pour filling into pie crust. Chill several hours and then top with cherry pie filling.

Denise Gonzalez

DESSERTS

CHERRY PIE SUPREME

9 inch unbaked pie shell
1 1 pound 5 ounce cherry pie
  filling
4 3 ounce packages cream
  cheese, softened

½ cup sugar
2 eggs
½ teaspoon vanilla
1 cup sour cream

Preheat oven to 425 degrees. Prepare pie shell. Spread half of cherry pie filling in bottom. Set rest of filling aside. Bake shell 15 minutes or until crust is golden. Remove from oven. Reduce oven temperature to 350 degrees. Meanwhile, in small bowl, beat cheese with sugar, eggs, and vanilla until smooth. Pour over hot cherry pie filling; bake 25 minutes. Filling will be slightly soft in center. Cool completely on wire rack.

To serve: Spoon sour cream around edge of pie. Fill center with remaining cherry pie filling. *Variation:* Substitute 1 1 pound 5 ounce can blueberry pie filling.

Antonia DeLisi

CREAM CHEESE PIE

Crust:
¼ cup butter or margarine
3 tablespoons sugar
1 egg

1 cup flour
1 teaspoon baking powder

Filling:
8 ounces cream cheese
⅓ cup plus 1 tablespoon flour
1½ cups milk
2 eggs

juice of 1 lemon
1 teaspoon vanilla
cinnamon, to taste

Start recipe by assembling crust first. Mix sugar and butter. Add egg, flour and baking powder. Mix well. Mixture will be crumbly. Place in a 9 inch pie plate and pat on bottom and sides. Mix cream cheese with sugar. Add flour then eggs, one at a time, mixing well after each addition. Stir while adding milk gradually. Add vanilla then lemon juice. Pour into unbaked pie shell. Sprinkle with cinnamon. Bake at 325 degrees for 1 hour.

Jean Ciano

DESSERTS

LIME CHIFFON PIE

1 envelope, unflavored gelatin
½ cup sugar
¼ teaspoon salt
4 egg yolks
½ cup fresh lime juice
¼ cup water
1 teaspoon grated lemon peel
few drops green food coloring

4 egg whites
½ cup sugar
1 cup heavy cream, whipped
additional whipped cream, for
  garnish
grated lime peel, for garnish
1 baked 10 inch pie shell

Mix together gelatin, ½ cup sugar and salt in a sauce pan. Beat together egg yolks, lime juice and water; stir into gelatin mixture. Cook over medium heat stirring constantly until boiling. Remove from heat; stir in grated lemon peel and food coloring. Chill, stirring occasionally until mixture mounds slightly when dropped from spoon. Beat egg whites until soft peaks, gradually add ½ cup sugar beating to stiff peaks. Fold gelatin mixture into egg whites. Fold in whipped cream. Pour into baked pie shell and chill until firm. Spread with additional cream and edge with grated lime peel. *Note:* This pie requires a lot of different bowls in the preparation, but it is so delicious that you'll find it is well worth it.

Barbara Brennan

IMPOSSIBLE FRENCH APPLE PIE

6 cups sliced apples
1¼ teaspooons cinnamon
1 cup sugar
¾ cup milk

½ cup buttermilk baking mix
2 eggs
2 tablespoons butter or
  margarine, softened

Preheat oven to 325 degrees. Grease a 10 inch pie plate. Mix apples, cinnamon and sugar. Place in pie plate. Beat remaining ingredients until smooth. Pour over apples. Sprinkle with streusel topping. Bake 55 to 60 minutes in preheated oven until knife inserted in center comes out clean.

Streusel Topping:
1 cup buttermilk baking mix
½ cup chopped nuts
1 cup brown sugar, firmly
  packed

3 tablespoons butter or
  margarine

Mix all ingredients until crumbly. Sprinkle on pie.

Patricia Stepanik

PUMPKIN ICE CREAM PIE

½ teaspoon vanilla
1 baked 9 inch pie shell
1 quart vanilla ice cream
1 cup cooked pumpkin
¾ cup sugar

½ teaspoon salt
¾ teaspoon pumpkin pie spice
1 cup heavy cream
½ cup brown sugar
½ cup dark corn syrup

Spread ice cream in cooked pie shell. Use deep pie shell or less ice cream. Place in freezer until hard. Blend pumpkin, sugar, salt and spice. Whip cream until stiff and fold into pumpkin mixture. Spoon into frozen pie shell over ice cream. Replace in freezer until ready to use. *Note:* When serving, cover with additional whipped cream and drizzle the following syrup over top: Boil ½ cup brown sugar, ¼ cup dark corn syrup and ¼ cup hot water until it starts to thicken. Don't let it get too thick. When cool, add ½ teaspoon vanilla.

Colleen Maguire

FRENCH APPLE PIE

2 frozen pie crusts
1 box of pie crust mix
⅔ cup brown sugar

1 12 ounce package butterscotch
  morsels
2 20 ounce cans apple pie filling

Mix pie crust mix and the sugar until finely crumbled. Reserve 1½ cups crumby mixture. Stir in butterscotch pieces. Mix remaining crumbly mixture with apples. Pour into pie shells. Sprinkle reserved crumbly mixture on top. Cover edge of pie shell with 2 inch strip of aluminum foil to prevent excessive browning; remove foil last 15 minutes of baking. Bake 40 to 45 minutes in a 425 degree oven. *Yield:* 2 pies.

Helen Kennedy

LOW CALORIE FRUIT PIE

20 ounce can crushed pineapple
½ cup boiling water
2 packages unflavored gelatin
2 teaspoons vanilla

2 teaspoons lemon juice
4 packages low calorie
  sweetener
1½ cups powdered milk

Place pineapple, water and gelatin in blender for 2 minutes. Add the remaining ingredients and blend for 3 more minutes. Pour into 9 inch pie plate and refrigerate until firm.

Regina Whitaker

DESSERTS

SNOW PUDDING WITH CUSTARD SAUCE

1 package gelatin, any flavor   2 tablespoons sugar
3 eggs, separated

Prepare gelatin according to package directions. Refrigerate until consistency of heavy cream. Separate 3 eggs, reserving yolks for custard
sauce. Beat egg whites, gradually adding sugar until stiff peaks form. Beat
gelatin by tablespoons into whites until all gelatin is mixed into egg whites.
Refrigerate.

Custard Sauce:
1½ cups scalded milk   ⅛ teaspoon salt
¼ cup sugar   ½ teaspoon vanilla
3 reserved egg yolks

Beat yolks slightly with a fork. Add sugar and salt. Gradually add hot milk,
while stirring constantly. Cook in a double boiler until mixture thickens
and coats a wooden spoon. Strain, mix in vanilla and chill. Serve sauce over
gelatin pudding.

Angel Byrnes

RASPBERRY RIBBON PIE

1 9 inch baked pie crust   1 tablespoon lemon juice
1 3 ounce package raspberry   1 3 ounce package cream cheese
   flavored gelatin   ⅓ cup powdered sugar
¼ cup sugar   1 teaspoon vanilla extract
1¼ cups boiling water   1 cup heavy cream
1 10 ounce package frozen   fresh raspberries, or whipped
   raspberries   cream, for garnish

Prepare pie crust. In bowl, stir gelatin and sugar with boiling water until
dissolved; add frozen raspberries and lemon juice. Stir mixture until
berries thaw. Cover and refrigerate, stirring frequently, until mixture
mounds when dropped from a spoon. In a bowl, mix cream cheese with
powdered sugar, vanilla extract until smooth. In a bowl with mixer at
medium speed, beat heavy cream into soft peaks, gradually fold cream
cheese mixture into cream. Spread half of the whipped cream mixture in
the pie crust, then spoon half of raspberry mixture over it. Repeat with
rest of cream mixture and berries. Refrigerate until set, then garnish with
berries or whipped cream.

Mira Harbulak

STRAWBERRY ICE CREAM PIE

1 10 ounce package frozen
  strawberry halves, defrosted
1 package, 3½ ounces,
  strawberry gelatin
¾ cup liquid, juice from berries
  plus water

1 pint vanilla ice cream
1 9 inch graham cracker pie
  crust

Defrost berries, then drain their juice into a measuring cup. Add water to the juice to make ¾ cup liquid. Set aside berries for later. In a small saucepan, bring the liquid to a boil. Turn off heat and add the gelatin powder to the hot liquid. Stir well until the gelatin is dissolved. Add the ice cream and mix thoroughly with a large spoon. Chill the mixture until it is almost set, about 20 minutes, then fold in the strawberries. Spoon into graham cracker pie shell and chill for at least 2 hours.

Cathy Sterling

STRAWBERRY FROZEN PIE

1 8 ounce package cream cheese,
  softened
1 cup sour cream

2 10 ounce packages frozen
  sliced strawberries, thawed
1 graham cracker crust

Blend cream cheese and sour cream. Reserve ½ cup berries and syrup; add remaining berries to cheese mixture. Pour into graham cracker crust. Freeze firm. Remove from freezer 5 minutes before serving. Cut in wedges, spoon reserved berries and syrup over top.

Kvet Kleven

RASPBERRY DESSERT

2 boxes frozen raspberries,
  thawed

1 pint heavy cream
½ teaspoon vanilla

Whip cream until stiff. Add vanilla. Drain raspberries. Fold into whipped cream. Pour into 8 sherbert glasses. Chill and serve cold. *Yield:* 8 servings.

Helen Evancie

DESSERTS

OLD FASHIONED RICE PUDDING

6 cups milk	3 egg yolks, beaten
¾ cup long grain rice	2 teaspoons vanilla extract
1 cup heavy or whipping cream	¼ teaspoon salt
¾ cup sugar	1 teaspoon cinnamon

Pour milk in medium saucepan and bring to boil over medium heat. Stir in rice and return to boil. Reduce heat and simmer uncovered until rice is tender, about 55 minutes, stirring occasionally. In a small bowl, combine cream, sugar, egg yolks, vanilla and salt; set aside. When rice is tender, stir in cream mixture until completely combined; heat to a boil. Remove from heat and pour into 2 quart serving dish. Sprinkle top generously with cinnamon. Chill at least 4 hours. *Yield:* 6 cups.

Pat Di Palo

CREAMY RICE PUDDING

½ cup rice	½ cup sugar
1 quart milk	2 teaspoons vanilla
3 eggs, separated	cinnamon, to taste
salt, pinch	

Cook rice in milk in a covered pot until rice is tender. Mix egg yolks with sugar and vanilla. Add to rice and cook on low heat, until well mixed. Cool rice mixture. Beat egg whites until stiff. Fold egg whites into rice mixture. Top with cinnamon. Serve.

Gerry Accardo

FROZEN LEMON PIE

1 box vanilla wafers	½ pint heavy cream
3 eggs	½ cup sugar
3 tablespoons lemon juice and lemon rind	

Line pan, 11x15 with waxed paper. I use an old ice cube tray. Crush wafers and pat firmly in pan. Leave enough to sprinkle on top. Separate egg yolks and add half of the sugar, ¼ cup. Cook yolks in double boiler for 2 minutes, yolks will be thick. Beat egg whites, lemon juice and rind. Pour into tray, sprinkle wafers on top. Freeze.

Joan Higgins

STRAWBERRIES ROMANOFF

2 pints fresh strawberries
⅓ cup plus 2 tablespoons sugar
⅓ cup Grand Marnier or
   Cointreau

1 orange
¾ cup heavy cream

Remove the stems from the strawberries. Rinse well and drain. Pat dry with paper towels. Place the strawberries in a bowl and add ⅓ cup sugar and Grand Marnier. Using a swivel-bladed potato peeler, cut around the orange to produce a very thin spiral of peel. Do not cut into the white pulp. Cut the peel into wafer-thin shreds. Add to the strawberries and fold together, gently. Use the remaining orange in another dish. Cover the bowl and refrigerate until ready to serve.

To serve, whip cream and flavor with the remaining 2 tablespoons of sugar. Serve with cream on top of strawberries. *Yield:* 8 servings.

Sister Jeannette Tenaglia

IMPOSSIBLE PIE

4 eggs
¼ cup melted butter
2 cups milk
½ cup sugar

½ cup coconut
½ cup buttermilk baking mix
1 teaspoon vanilla

Place all ingredients in blender. Blend 2 minutes. Pour into buttered and floured 9 inch pie dish. Sprinkle with nutmeg and a little extra coconut. Bake at 350 degrees for 45 minutes, or until knife inserted comes out clean. Chill 3 hours.

Pat Sullivan

RICE PUDDING

½ cup uncooked rice
½ cup sugar
1 quart milk

1 egg, separated
1 teaspoon vanilla
pinch salt

Place rice, milk, salt and sugar in a large pot. Bring to boil, cover and reduce heat. Cook 45 minutes, stirring frequently. Beat egg yolk with 1 teaspoon water. Add to rice. Beat egg white and vanilla. Place rice pudding in serving bowl. Add egg white and mix. Serve warm or cool.

Dolores Chuco

DESSERTS

SOUR CREAM TWISTS

1 package active dry yeast	2 eggs, slightly beaten
¼ cup very warm water	1 teaspoon salt
4 cups sifted flour	1 teaspoon vanilla
1 cup margarine, melted	1 cup sugar
1 cup sour cream	1 teaspoon cinnamon

Sprinkle yeast into very warm water; stir until dissolved. Combine flour, margarine, sour cream, eggs, salt and vanilla in a large bowl. Stir in dissolved yeast; beat until smooth. Cover with a damp cloth. Refrigerate at least 2 hours or up to two days. Best if left overnight. Combine sugar and cinnamon. Sprinkle on a board. Roll dough into rectangle about 15x18. Turn so both sides are coated to prevent sticking. Fold over in half and then three times as you would a letter. Roll into rectangle ¼ inch thick using up all sugar. Cut into strips 1x4. Twist and place on greased baking sheet. Bake in a moderate oven, 375 degrees for 15 minutes.

Diane Szarek

WALNUT CREAM ROLL

4 eggs, separated	¼ cup sifted flour
1 teaspoon vanilla	½ cup walnuts, finely chopped
½ teaspoon salt	1 cup heavy cream, whipped
½ teaspoon sugar	powdered sugar

Beat 4 egg yolks, until thick and lemon colored. Set aside. Combine 4 egg whites, vanilla, and salt. Beat until soft peaks form. Gradually add sugar, beating until stiff peaks form. Fold egg yolks into whites. Carefully fold in sifted flour and walnuts. Spread batter evenly in a greased and floured 15½x10½x1 inch jelly roll pan. Bake in 375 degree oven for 12 minutes or until done. Immediately loosen sides and turn out on a clean towel sprinkled with powdered sugar. Starting at narrow end, roll cake and towel together. Cool on a rack. Unroll and spread with sweetened whipped cream. Roll cake and chill.

Donna Appleby

TRIFLE

sponge cake, or 1 layer of
  yellow cake mix
1 28 ounce can of pears,
  drained, juice reserved
1 6 ounce package of raspberry
  gelatin

1 6 ounce package of vanilla
  pudding
whipped cream, as needed
rum or sweet sherry, as needed
maraschino cherries, as garnish

Whipped cream, sweetened: for each cup of heavy cream, use ½ pint, add 1 to 2 tablespoons sugar and 1 teaspoon vanilla extract. Beat until stiff peaks form. In a 2½ quart dish, with more or less vertical sides, spread a layer of sponge cake about 1 inch thick. Add rum or sweet sherry to the cake, to taste. Form a layer of fruit on top of the cake reserving juice for gelatin. Make the gelatin, substituting fruit juice for the cold water. Pour over fruit and cake and chill until set. This is best done a couple days beforehand. When set, cook vanilla pudding and form a layer about 1 inch thick on top of the gelatin. Chill until set. The night before is best. Before serving, whip cream and add sugar and vanilla extract. Form a layer of whipped cream and garnish with cherries.

Eugenia W. Savarese

ethnic cooking

SPICY TRIPLE DELIGHT
Chinese

½ pound chicken cutlets, cubed
½ pound small shrimp, cleaned
and deveined
½ pound pork, cubed
5 scallions, cut into 1 inch
sections

3 ounces sliced bamboo shoots
5 tablespoons oil
cornstarch and water mixture

Marinade:
2 eggs, beaten
3 tablespoons cornstarch
1 teaspoon sugar
¼ cup sherry

¼ teaspoon salt
¼ cup light soy sauce
2 teaspoons sesame oil
⅛ teaspoon white pepper

Sauce:
3 tablespoons brown bean sauce
2 tablespoons hoisin sauce
½ teaspoon red pepper flakes
1 fresh red hot pepper, cut into
rings

1 teaspoon sugar
¼ teaspoon salt
¼ cup black or dark soy sauce
¼ cup light soy sauce
¼ teaspoon grated ginger

Marinate chicken, pork and shrimp about 2 hours, in marinade ingredients. Place 5 tablespoons oil in wok over high heat and stir-fry the pork first, then chicken and then shrimp, bamboo shoots and scallions. Stir-fry about 2 minutes. Blend in the sauce mixture and continue to stir-fry until all ingredients are well coated. Glaze, if necessary with a little cornstarch mixture to thicken sauce.

Sister Jeannette Tenaglia

ORIENTAL STRING BEANS
Chinese

1 pound fresh string beans,
sliced
1 tablespoon oil
2 cloves garlic, minced

1 medium onion, sliced
2 tablespoons soy sauce
1 cup chicken broth

Sauté garlic and onion in oil in a frying pan. Add green beans, soy sauce and chicken broth. Simmer for 8 to 10 minutes or until tender.

Huy Dinh

SHRIMP WITH LOBSTER SAUCE
Chinese

24 shrimp, shelled and deveined
salt, dash
pepper, dash
1 teaspoon cornstarch
½ pound ground pork or beef
2 eggs
5 tablespoons oil
2 cloves garlic, minced

4 green oinions, or regular
   onions, cut in 1 inch slices
2 tablespoons soy sauce
1 teaspoon sugar
1 tablespoon cornstarch mixed
   with 1 tablespoon water
1 cup chicken broth, or water

Mix soy sauce and sugar together. Place shrimp in bowl, mix with a dash of salt, pepper and 1 teaspoon cornstarch. Heat 3 tablespoons oil, fry garlic and onion 1 minute, remove. Cook shrimp 1 minute or until pink.

Heat 2 tablespoons oil and stir fry pork until white, or beef until brown. Add soy sauce and sugar mixture. Cook 1 more minute. Add shrimp mixture and heat all. Add broth or water, and bring to a boil. Add cornstarch and stir until thick. Pour eggs over all. Turn off heat and allow eggs to set. Serve.

Joanne Nimsger

SWEET AND SOUR PORK
Chinese

½ teaspoon salt
¼ teaspoon pepper
¼ cup powdered sugar
2 tablespoons cornstarch
1 pound lean pork, cut in cubes
2 tablespoons peanut oil
2 tablespoons water
1 tablespoon butter

1 cup finely chopped onion
1 8 ounce can bamboo shoots,
   drained
1 1 pound can of peas, drained
juice of one lemon or 3
   tablespoons lemon juice
¼ cup soy sauce

In small bowl combine salt, pepper, powdered sugar and cornstarch. Coat pork. Heat oil in wok. Add pork and stir fry for 10 minutes. Reduce heat to simmer; add water, cover and simmer for 30 minutes until pork is tender. Remove cover and turn up heat. Push pork up side, add butter. When melted, add onion and bamboo shoots. Stir fry 2 minutes. Add peas, lemon juice and soy sauce. Cook 2 minutes. Serve with rice or noodles.

Susan Jencen

CHINESE SWEET AND SOUR PORK
Chinese

1 package sweet and sour sauce
  mix
1 10½ can chicken broth
2 cloves garlic, finely minced
1½ to 2 pounds lean pork, cut
  into one inch cubes
1 tablespoon soy sauce
¼ cup vinegar

2 to 3 carrots, sliced
2 onions, cut in 1 inch squares
1 cup pineapple cubes, drained
2 scallions, sliced
⅛ pound snow pea pods
2 tablespoons peanut oil
2 tablespoons cornstarch

Mix cornstarch and soy sauce in mixing bowl. Add pork cubes and stir until well coated. Preheat wok. Add peanut oil. When hot, add pork cubes along with minced garlic and ginger root. Stir fry over medium heat until brown. Add ¼ to ⅓ cup chicken broth, ¼ cup vinegar and packaged sauce mix. Add to wok along with carrots, green pepper and onion. Bring to boil; reduce heat and simmer covered 10 minutes, stirring frequently. Add pineapple cubes, sliced scallions and snow peas and cook till heated through. Serve with rice.

Madeline A. Thorpe

CHOW MEIN
Chinese

2 tablespoons oil
1 cup thinly sliced onions
2 cups diced celery
½ cup chicken gravy or bouillon
1 10½ ounce can cream of
  mushroom soup
¼ cup soy sauce

1½ cups slivered chicken, pork,
  turkey or shrimp, cooked
1 16 ounce can bean sprouts,
  drained
1 tablespoon cornstarch in ½
  cup water

In hot oil in a large skillet, sauté onion and celery stirring occasionally until onion is golden, about 10 minutes. Add gravy, soup and soy sauce. Bring to a boil. Add meat and bean sprouts. Return to a simmer. Cover and simmer 5 minutes. Add cornstarch in water. Mix well in skillet. Bring to a boil. Simmer 5 minutes until mixture thickens. Serve over rice along with Chinese noodles. *Yield:* 6 servings.

Beverly Maccari

PORK WITH BLACK BEAN AND GARLIC SAUCE
Chinese

½ pound pork, cut into bite-size cubes
½ fresh tomato, cut into 5 segments
10 snow pea pods, blanched

1 scallion, cut into ½ inch sections on a bias
cornstarch mixture
oil for deep-frying

Batter:
1 cup flour
½ teaspoon salt
½ teaspoon baking soda

½ teaspoon vinegar
enough water or stock to form a light batter

Sauce:
1 cup chicken stock
1 teaspoon thick molasses soy sauce
1 teaspoon oyster sauce

¼ teaspoon sesame oil
¼ teaspoon sugar
¼ teaspoon salt

Seasonings:
1 tablespoon black bean sauce
1 teaspoon minced garlic

1 tablespoon dry sherry

Mix batter ingredients. Coat pork cubes in batter and deep-fry in 350 degree oil until golden brown. Drain oil. Set pork aside. Add 1 tablespoon oil to wok over high heat and add garlic and black bean sauce. Stir-fry 15 seconds. Add snow peas, scallions and tomato. Sizzle in sherry and stir-fry to combine. Blend in sauce and add cornstarch mixture to glaze sauce. Mix in pork cubes and serve hot.

Sister Jeannette Tenaglia

EGG ROLLS WITH CHICKEN
Chinese

Egg Roll Skins:

2 cups flour
1½ cups water
2 eggs

salt, pinch
oil, for frying

Mix first 4 ingredients to a smooth batter. Place small amount of oil in a 6 to 7 inch frying pan. Fry small amounts, approximately ⅓ cup of batter in pan, turning to cook both sides of crepe. Drain and reserve as each skin is cooked.

Filling:

1 boned chicken breast, cooked
1 teaspoon salt
1 teaspoon sugar
1 teaspoon cornstarch
2 teaspoons oil
2 tablespoons soy sauce
1 4 ounce can mushrooms,
    chopped

1 cup bean sprouts
2 scallions, chopped
½ cup sliced onion
¼ cup chopped bamboo shoots
1 egg beaten

Dice chicken breast and mix with salt, sugar, cornstarch and soy sauce. Reserve. Sauté mushrooms, bean sprouts, scallions, onion and bamboo shoots in the 2 tablespoons oil for several minutes. Add chicken and cook for 5 minutes. Fill each egg roll skin with a generous tablespoon of chicken filling. Roll filled skin lengthwise, tucking ends in and brush with beaten egg to help seal edges. Deep fry egg rolls several at a time until golden brown. Drain well and serve with soy sauce, hot mustard, duck sauce. *Yield:* 8 to 10 servings.

My Hoa Dinh

CHICKEN WITH NUTS IN HOISIN SAUCE
Chinese

2 tablespoons dry sherry
2½ tablespoons hoisin sauce
3 whole chicken breasts,
  uncooked
½ pound fresh mushrooms
2 medium sized dried Chinese
  mushrooms

2 tablespoons cornstarch
2 tablespoons peanut or corn oil
juice of ¼ lemon
¼ cup fried peanuts or cashew
  nuts, not dry roasted

Soak Chinese mushrooms in hot tap water about ½ hour. Discard hard stems and squeeze out excess water from caps and slice into thin strips.

Cut raw chicken breasts into 1 inch square slices. Marinate in 2 tablespoons sherry and 2 tablespoons cornstarch for 30 minutes. Mix and coat chicken thoroughly. Heat 2 tablespoons oil in frying pan over high flame, for 30 seconds. Add chicken and stir-fry about 2 minutes or until chicken turns white. Be sure to stir continuously so chicken will not stick to the pan. You may need to add more oil as you progress. Cook only a small amount of chicken at a time and remove. Set cooked chicken aside.

Add all mushrooms to pan and stir-fry for about 3 minutes. Return chicken to pan with mushrooms and peanuts. Add sherry, lemon juice and 2½ tablespoons hoisin sauce. Mix thoroughly. Sprinkle with scallions and serve.

Sister Jeannette Tenaglia

195

TUNG TING LAKE SHRIMP
Chinese

½ pound large shrimp, peeled,
   halved lengthwise, cleaned
   and dried

1 pint oil
2 egg whites, lightly beaten
1 ounce sliced, smoked ham

Marinade mixture:
½ tablespoon cornstarch
½ teaspoon salt

½ egg white

Vegetables:
8 canned straw mushrooms
5 broccoli flowerettes

5 canned baby corn
4 water chestnuts, sliced

Sauce mixture:
½ teaspoon sugar
1 teaspoon dry sherry wine
¼ teaspoon salt

½ cup chicken stock
½ teaspoon cornstarch

In a bowl, combine shrimp with marinade ingredients for at least 20 minutes and then arrange shrimp and vegetables neatly on a large platter and keep nearby.

Combine sauce ingredients in a bowl. Add 1 pint of oil to wok and heat to 325 degrees. Gently place egg whites into oil in wok and stir-fry until egg whites bubble and are firm. Remove egg whites to serving platter with strainer to remove excess oil. Collect shrimp from platter and add to 350 degree oil in wok and stir gently for about 5 seconds to separate the shrimp. Immediately add vegetable ingredients to the shrimp in the oil. Gently stir and fry for 30 seconds. Remove all ingredients from the oil with a strainer to remove excess oil. Remove all the oil from the wok. Return all shrimp and vegetables to the hot wok, and add sauce ingredients; stir fry for about 5 seconds. Transfer all ingredients from the wok and place over the egg whites on serving platter. Rearrange the broccoli flowerettes on the edge of the platter for a decoration. Serve immediately.

Sister Jeannette Tenaglia

HOUSKA
Czechoslovakian

5 to 6 cups unsifted flour
½ cup sugar
1 teaspoon salt
1 teaspoon grated lemon peel
¼ heaping teaspoon ground
    mace
2 packages dry yeast
1 cup milk
⅔ cup water

juice of ½ lemon at room
    temperature
¼ cup sweet butter
⅔ cup blanched almonds,
    slivered
1 cup golden seedless raisins
12 glaced cherries
corn oil
2 eggs, room temperature

Frosting:
1 cup sifted powdered sugar
1 tablespoon milk

1 tablespoon lemon juice

In a large bowl thoroughly mix 1½ cups flour, sugar, salt, lemon peel, mace and undissolved dry yeast.

Combine milk, water and butter in a saucepan. Heat over low heat until liquids are very warm (120 to 130 degrees). Butter does not need to melt. Gradually add to dry ingredients and beat two minutes at medium speed of electric mixer, scraping bowl occasionally. Add lemon juice. Add eggs and ½ cup flour. Beat at high speed two minutes, scraping bowl occasionally. Stir in almonds, raisins and enough additional flour to make a stiff dough. Turn out onto lightly floured board and knead until smooth and elastic, about 8 to 10 minutes, adding glaced cherries evenly throughout dough as you knead. Cover with plastic wrap, then a towel. Let rest 20 minutes.

To make large braid: Divide dough into four equal pieces. Roll 3 pieces into ropes 14 inches long. Braid together on greased baking sheet. Tuck ends under to seal. Divide remaining piece into two equal pieces. Roll into ropes 11 inches long. Twist together. Place small twisted rope on large braid. Tuck ends under to seal.

To make medium braids: Divide dough in half. Shape each half as above.

Cover loosely with wax paper brushed with corn oil, then top with plastic wrap. Refrigerate 2 to 24 hours. When ready to bake, remove from refrigerator. Uncover dough carefully. Let stand at room temperature 10 minutes. If not using frosting, brush the braid with an egg white beaten lightly with 1 tablespoon cold water before baking. Bake at 375 degrees for 35 minutes for large braid; 25 minutes for small braids. Remove from baking sheet and cool on wire rack. While warm, frost.

Marie Sluka

CHICKEN, SHRIMP AND SCALLOP PROVENCALE
French

½ cup olive oil
½ pound shelled shrimp
¼ pound scallops
6 whole chicken breasts, 5 to 6
  pounds
2 pounds onions, sliced
2 green peppers, sliced
2 red peppers, sliced
1 cup chicken broth

1 cup canned tomatoes, drained
  and seeded
3 tablespoons tomato paste
6 garlic cloves, finely chopped
1½ teaspoons salt
½ teaspoon pepper
¼ teaspoon basil
¼ teaspoon oregano

In a large skillet, heat oil over medium heat. Sauté shrimp just until pink; and scallops just until firm. Remove and set aside. Add chicken to skillet and cook until done. Remove and set aside.

To drippings in pan, add onions and peppers. Sauté until soft, but not brown. Add remaining ingredients and all juices from shellfish and chicken. Bring mixture to a boil and then simmer. Cut up chicken breasts into strips. Add to simmering sauce. Add shrimp and scallops just before serving. Serve with rice or pasta.

Carol Lohmann

FINNISH PANCAKES
Finland

8 large eggs
4 to 5 tablespoons sugar
1 cup flour

1 quart milk
1 teaspoon salt
½ cup butter

Melt ½ cup butter and put into a 12x16 inch pan. Beat eggs and milk lightly. Add sugar, salt and flour. Pour mixed batter over melted butter. Bake in 450 degree oven for 20 to 23 minutes. Serve with maple syrup, jelly or butter.

Marlene Pepe

EPIPHANY CAKE
Region of Brittany and France

1½ cups flour
1 cup sugar
5 egg yolks and 1 for glazing
½ cup sweet butter, room
  temperature

½ cup salted butter, room
  temperature
1 teaspoon baking powder
1 teaspoon vanilla extract

Mix butter and sugar first; add yolks and vanilla. Mix in flour and baking powder. Grease a large pie pan or large quiche dish. Place dough in pan. Glaze the top of the dough with egg yolks. Poke holes on top with fork into a design. Put in a hot oven for 7 minutes at 400 degrees. Then lower to 300 to 350 degrees for 45 to 50 minutes. *Note:* Cake will not rise much and should not brown.

Tradition: On the 6th of January, a small button wrapped in foil is baked into the dough. Equal portions are divided among guests and the person who gets the button is King and is given a paper or cardboard crown. He represents one of the Wise Men who visited the Christ Child. If a woman gets the button, she chooses a King.

Edie Lyons

CHICKEN CORN SOUP
German - Amish

3 quarts chicken broth
1 onion, diced
1 cup diced cooked chicken
8 ears cooked corn or 2 cans
  corn

½ pound wide noodles
parsley, chopped, for garnish
pepper, to taste

Bring broth to boil. Remove corn kernels from cobs and place into bowl. When soup boils, add onion and noodles. Boil gently until noodles are done, about 20 minutes. Lower to simmer and add chicken and corn. Simmer 1 to 2 minutes until hot throughout. Sprinkle with parsley and pepper. Serve hot. *Note:* If fresh corn is used, add to broth when the noodles are added. *Yield:* 8 servings.

Helen Evancie

SAUERBRATEN
German

5 to 6 pound bottom or rump roast of beef	2 bay leaves
4 large onions, sliced	8 whole cloves
6 ribs celery, sliced	1½ cups white vinegar
2 large carrots, peeled and sliced	1 cup white vinegar
3 tablespoons salt	½ cup sugar
2 tablespoons pickling spice	3 quarts cold water
	24 ginger snaps

Prepare 3 to 5 days before serving. Place water, onions, celery, carrots, vinegars, salt, sugar and herb seasonings in a large pot. Bring to boil for 5 minutes. Place meat in a stone crock or pot, (not aluminum) large enough to accommodate meat and cooked stock. Pour hot stock over meat. Let cool, cover and refrigerate or keep in a cool place for 3 to 5 days, turning meat in stock once or twice a day. On serving day, remove meat from stock and dry with toweling.

Brown meat in 2 to 3 tablespoons oil or shortening, in a large Dutch oven. Do not skimp on browning. Turn meat frequently, and brown on all sides. Place vegetables and stock over meat. Bring to a boil, then reduce heat. Cover and cook slowly for 2 to 2½ hours. Remove meat and strain stock, reserving vegetables. Return stock to pot to prepare gravy. Purée vegetables carefully, in blender and add to stock. Bring to a boil and add crumbled ginger snaps to thicken. Cook until ginger snaps are melted. Slice meat and serve with gravy, potato dumplings and cooked red cabbage.

Judy Hein

KARTOFFELKLOSSE
POTATO DUMPLINGS
German

6 medium potatoes, peeled and
   cooked
2 eggs, beaten
1 teaspoon salt

¼ teaspoon pepper
¼ teaspoon nutmeg
⅔ cup flour
boiling water

Mash or rice cooked potatoes. Cool. Add eggs, salt, pepper and nutmeg to cooled potatoes. Mix in flour. Shape into balls, approximately 2 inches in diameter. Use floured hands to help shape balls and retain shape. Place on waxed paper. Chill 1 hour.

Bring water to boil in a large pot. Carefully, drop dumplings into boiling water and let cook 15 minutes and until they rise in pot. Remove with slotted spoon and keep warm until serving time. *Yield:* approximately 1 dozen dumplings.

Judy Hein

KARTOFFEL PFANNKUCHEN
POTATO PANCAKES
German

6 medium or large sized
   potatoes
1 small onion, grated
2 tablespoons flour
2 eggs, beaten

¼ teaspoon pepper
½ teaspoon grated nutmeg
3 or 4 tablespoons butter
2 tablespoons chopped parsley

Wash and peel potatoes. Keep in bowl of cold water and cover. Drain. Grate and drain water that collects in potatoes. Add onion and mix. Add flour, beaten eggs, pepper, nutmeg and parsley. Mix well. Heat butter on a griddle. Place large spoonfuls of potato mixture on the hot griddle. Cook until brown and crisp on each side, turning with pancake turner. Keep warm on a platter. Serve with applesauce.

Helen Evancie

SPATZLE
EGG NOODLES
German

1 egg, beaten	½ cup milk
1 teaspoon salt	1½ cups flour

Combine egg and salt in a medium size bowl. Alternately add flour and milk, mixing well after each addition, until all ingredients are combined. Dough batter should be a soft, sticky consistency.

Bring water to a boil in a large pot. Drop dough into boiling water by teaspoonfuls. After using all dough, allow noodles to cook until they rise to top of water, approximately 10 minutes. Drain.

Serve in soup or with a roast and its gravy. Noodles may also be sautéed in butter and served as a side dish.

Judy Hein

HOPPELPOPPEL
Germany

6 medium potatoes unpeeled	1 cup minced onions
(leftover firm, boiled potatoes	8 eggs
may be used)	2 tablespoons milk
3 cups cubed ham or smoked	chopped parsley, to taste
tenderloin, cooked	pepper, to taste

Boil potatoes until done but firm. Sauté onions in bacon fat or butter, until golden, stirring frequently. Drain potatoes, peel, and cut into cubes. Add to onions and cook turning occasionally until light brown. Turn into rectangular, greased pan. Stir in ham. Beat eggs, milk, parsley, and pepper in small bowl. Pour over potatoes and ham. Combine slightly. Bake in 350 degree oven until eggs are set, 45 to 60 minutes. Serve hot. *Yield:* 4 servings.

Helen Evancie

WIENER SCHNITZEL
German

6 veal cutlets	½ cup butter
½ cup flour	6 lemon slices
2 eggs, beaten	¼ cup chopped parsley
1½ cups plain breadcrumbs	

Flatten cutlets with mallet or rolling pin to ¼ inch thickness. Dip cutlets into flour, then eggs and finally into breadcrumbs, coating well and pressing crumbs onto cutlets. Refrigerate cutlets on waxed paper for 20 to 30 minutes.

To cook cutlets, melt butter in a large skillet and cook veal until golden brown on both sides. Keep warm in oven. Serve with parsley garnish and lemon slices. *Yield:* 6 servings.

Judy Hein

SPANA KOPETA - SPINACH PIE
Greek

Filling:

1 large onion, chopped	½ pound crumbled feta cheese
3 tablespoons oil	3 eggs, beaten
¼ cup chopped, fresh dill	salt and pepper, to taste
5 packages frozen chopped spinach, thawed and drained	

Pastry:

1 cup melted butter	1 package fillo dough

Sauté onion in oil until soft. Add dill and drained spinach, stir and simmer 3 minutes. Drain off any liquid. Add feta cheese and beaten eggs. Mix well. Add salt and pepper to taste. In large baking pan, 11½x17½ inches, layer ½ the box of fillo, brushing each sheet with melted butter. Spread spinach mixture evenly over fillo and continue to layer the rest of the dough over the mixture, buttering each sheet. Fold over fillo that is overlapped and brush with butter. Score top diagonally. Do not go through to bottom. Bake in a pre-heated 400 degree oven for 25 to 30 minutes or until golden brown.

Cathy Theodorakis

GRILLOT
Haitian

1 fresh ham, boned
hot water
¼ cup vinegar
juice of 1½ lemons
¼ cup orange juice
thyme, to taste

chopped parsley, to taste
minced garlic, to taste
salt, to taste
chopped scallions, to taste
black pepper, to taste
oil, for frying

Cut pork into several pieces. Rinse pieces with combination of hot water, lemon juice and vinegar. Drain. Mix herbs and rub into pork. Add orange juice and mix well. Place pork in large pot with enough water to cover. Bring to a boil and cook until tender. Remove pork and reserve stock for sauce. Fry pork in oil until golden. Garnish with parsley, lemon juice and sliced onions. Serve with Sauce Ti Malice.

Marie Gilles

SAUCE TI MALICE
Haitian

Reserved stock from pork
⅓ cup oil
2 tablespoons tomato paste

hot peppers, chopped, to taste
2 tablespoons butter
1 medium onion, sliced

In a saucepan heat oil and stir in tomato paste. Add pork stock, bring to a boil and add hot peppers. Lower heat, add butter and simmer to desired consistency. Remove from heat and add onion. Cover pan. The heat of the sauce will cook the onion. Serve over Grillot.

Marie Gilles

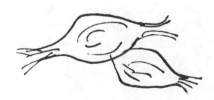

RIZ ET POIS NATIONAL
RICE AND BEANS
Haitian

1 cup kidney beans	thyme, to taste
2 cups white rice	salt and pepper, to taste
2 slices bacon, diced	parsley, to taste
4 cups water	garlic, to taste
¼ cup oil	3 cloves

Cook kidney beans until fork tender, in a large pot with generous amount of water. Do not overcook. Drain and reserve 3 cups cooking stock.

Using a large pot, sauté thyme, parsley, black pepper, garlic and bacon in oil. Add kidney beans, 3 cups of bean stock and 4 cups water, salt to taste and cloves. Cook on medium heat for 10 to 15 minutes. Add butter, stir and cover. Lower heat and simmer for 20 to 30 minutes. Serve with Grillot. *Yield:* 3 to 4 servings.

Marie Gilles

CABBAGE AND HALUSKA
Hungary

1 egg	1 small head cabbage
3 potatoes, peeled	salt
salt and pepper, to taste	butter, to taste
flour, as needed	diced onion, to taste

Grate raw potatoes. Mix egg, grated potatoes, salt, pepper and enough flour to make a thick consistency. Drop by teaspoonfuls in boiling salted water. Cook 5 to 10 minutes until dumplings plump, rise and are soft. Drain and run under cold water. Set aside.

Grate cabbage. Salt the cabbage and let stand. Squeeze excess water out of cabbage. Melt 3 tablespoons butter in large pan. Add cabbage and diced onion and cook. When browned, add cabbage to haluska (dumplings), and serve.

Diane Mulhern

PALACZYNTA
Hungarian Crepes

1 egg
¼ teaspoon salt
2 tablespoons sugar
1 cup flour

1½ cups milk
½ teaspoon vanilla
oil or butter, for frying

Mix egg, salt, sugar, flour, milk and vanilla to make a thin batter. Pour small amount of batter into oiled 7 inch frying pan. Fry on one side, then the other. Continue with remaining batter. Thin batter with small amount of milk to sustain consistency, if necessary. When all crepes are cooked, roll with jam or farmer's cheese mixed with egg, vanilla and sugar to taste. *Yield:* 20 crepes.

Diane Mulhern

ITALIAN FIG COOKIES

Fig Filling:
2 packages Italian figs
1 teaspoon vanilla
1 teaspoon ground cloves
1 teaspoon cinnamon
honey, ½ of a small bottle
¼ glass water

grated orange peel, to taste
sliced almonds, approximately
   ½ cup
1 egg white
colored nonpareils

Dough:
5 cups flour
¾ teaspoon baking soda
2 cups powdered sugar

1 pound margarine, softened
2 eggs
2 teaspoons vanilla

Make filling: grind up figs into a minced texture. In a bowl, mix together minced figs, vanilla, ground cloves, cinnamon, honey, water, grated orange peel and sliced almonds. The mixture will become very sticky.

Prepare dough: Mix all dry ingredients first, then add wet ingredients. Mix until dough is smooth. *Note:* This dough is very flaky so you cannot handle it. Place a small amount of dough in the palm of hand, and spread to cover palm. Place about a teaspoon of fig filling on dough and cover with remaining dough. Shape into small crescents; slit sides of crescents with about two slits on each side. Place on cookie sheet. Brush cookies with egg white and sprinkle with colored nonpareils. Bake at 375 degrees for 10 to 12 minutes. Cool on wire rack.

Vita Leggio

ITALIAN COOKIES

3 cups flour	2 eggs
3 teaspoons baking powder	¾ cup sugar
½ teaspoon salt	1 teaspoon lemon extract or any
½ cup oil	flavor
¼ cup milk	

Preheat oven to 400 degrees. Mix flour, baking powder and salt. In separate bowl, mix oil, milk, eggs and sugar. Gradually, add flour mixture into egg mixture. Mix well. Roll dough into small balls the size of walnuts. Bake on cookie sheet 10 to 12 minutes. Remove. Glaze.

Glaze:
powdered sugar	food coloring, optional
hot water	

Combine enough powdered sugar and small amounts of hot water together to make a thin glaze. Add food coloring if desired. Drizzle on warm cookies.

Anthony Cerullo

CHICK PEAS AND MACARONI
Italian

1 small onion, chopped	Italian seasoning, to taste
1 15 ounce can tomato sauce	1 pound macaroni (small shells,
1 19 ounce can chick peas	elbows, or ditali)
oil, as needed	grated cheese, to taste
salt and pepper, to taste	

Brown onion in a little oil. Add tomato sauce and a small amount of water and let cook for about ½ hour, with cover half off to thicken. Add chick peas, undrained, and let cook for another ½ hour; leave cover half off again to thicken. Cook macaroni to taste, drain and mix with chick peas, salt and pepper. Sprinkle grated cheese on top and serve with Italian bread and butter.

Rosemarie DeRosa

FETTUCCINE ALFREDO
Italian

1 pound fettuccine pasta
4 tablespoons butter
¾ cup heavy cream

½ cup grated Parmesan cheese
pepper, to taste

Cook fettuccine in 6 quarts salted boiling water until al dente. Drain. In a large skillet, melt butter. Add fettuccine and toss until well coated. Combine the cream and Parmesan cheese and pour over pasta. Heat until cream is hot, stirring constantly. Serve with pepper and extra cheese. *Yield:* 4 to 6 servings.

Eleanor McCann

ITALIAN MEAT SAUCE

1½ pounds chopped meat
1 pound Italian sausage
2 32 ounce cans crushed
   tomatoes
1 29 ounce can tomato sauce
1 can tomato paste

2 cloves garlic, minced
1 small onion, chopped
basil, parsley, oregano, salt,
   pepper, sugar, to taste

Brown meat, sausage, onion and garlic. Place in large pot. Add tomato paste. Bring to boil. Add tomatoes and sauce. Stir and return to boil. Add herbs and seasonings to taste. Simmer 2½ hours.*Yield:* enough for 2 pounds pasta.

Virginia Castellano

SPAGHETTI CARBONARO
Italian

¼ pound prosuitto ham, diced
2 tablespoons olive oil
3 medium onions, diced
½ cup sweet butter
1 pinch each salt and pepper

1 teaspoon parsley
2 egg yolks
½ cup grated cheese
1 pound spaghetti, cooked

Brown prosuitto in oil, add onion. Simmer on slow flame for 20 minutes. Add butter, salt, pepper, parsley and 1 cup water. Simmer 20 minutes. Add eggs and cheese. Pour over one pound cooked spaghetti.

Mary Lou Giampietro

ZITI AL FORNO - BAKED ZITI
Italian

2½ cups tomato sauce,
  homemade or canned
3 sweet Italian sausages,
  optional
1 pound ricotta cheese
½ teaspoon salt
½ teaspoon pepper

½ teaspoon ground nutmeg
1 tablespoon chopped parsley
¼ cup grated Parmesan cheese
1 egg
6 ounces mozzarella cheese,
  diced
1 pound ziti

Prepare tomato sauce, or use canned sauce. Remove casings from sausages, break up meat and brown in small skillet. Place in strainer for fat to drain off. Set aside. Combine ricotta with nutmeg, salt, pepper, parsley, Parmesan cheese, egg and mozzarella cheese. Set aside. Cook and drain ziti according to directions on box. Spoon 1 cup tomato sauce into a 13x9x2 inch baking dish. Layer on half the ziti. Cover with all the sausage meat. Spoon on an even layer of the ricotta mixture. Cover with remaining ziti, then the remaining sauce. Sprinkle with Parmesan cheese. Bake covered in 350 degree oven about ½ hour.

Marie Sluka

MACARONI AND BROCCOLI
Italian

1 pound ziti
1 medium head broccoli
salt

¼ cup vegetable oil
½ cup Parmesan cheese

Cook ziti as per package directions. Wash broccoli and remove any very thick stems. Bring 2½ cups water to boil. Add 1 teaspoon salt and broccoli. Cover. Cook 8 to 10 minutes until tender. Drain macaroni. Add oil and Parmesan cheese. Mix. Do not drain broccoli. Add broccoli with cooking water to macaroni and mix gently. Pass extra Parmesan cheese and enjoy!

Ellen Brusca

BAKED SPAGHETTI AND CHEESE
Italian

1½ pounds spaghetti   ½ pound shredded Swiss cheese

Prepare spaghetti according to directions, drain and rinse. Layer spaghetti and cheese in a baking pan starting with a layer of spaghetti and ending with cheese. Bake in 300 degree oven until cheese melts. Place in broiler until cheese browns. Serve with your favorite spaghetti sauce. *Yield:* 6 to 8 servings.

Eileen Czarniecki

POTATO KUGEL
Lithuanian

5 pounds baking potatoes   4 eggs
½ pound pork cutlets   1 large onion, grated
2 tablespoons flour   1 teaspoon salt
1 teaspoon baking powder   2 tablespoons butter

Cut pork cutlets into small pieces. Melt butter in frying pan adding pork and onion; sauté until brown. Set aside. In large bowl grate potatoes and add the rest of the ingredients, including cooked pork, mixing well. Grease a 13x9 inch pan. Place mixture in pan. Bake in 350 degree oven for about 1½ hours until golden brown. Serve with sour cream or apple sauce.

Eileen Rathgaber

PICADILLO
Mexican

2 pounds ground beef   ¼ teaspoon oregano
2 onions, chopped   ⅛ teaspoon cinnamon
2 garlic cloves, chopped   ⅛ teaspoon ground cloves
1 large can whole tomatoes in   ⅛ teaspoon cumin
   purée   ¾ teaspoon salt
⅓ cup raisins   ⅛ teaspoon pepper
⅓ cup sliced stuffed olives

Brown beef, onions and garlic. Drain fat, break up any meat clumps. Add remaining ingredients. Cook at least 5 minutes on medium-low, stirring occasionally. Serve over rice or as filling for tacos.

Jean Buckridge

FLAN
Mexican

Caramel:

3 tablespoons sugar ½ tablespoon water

Custard:

1 14 ounce can sweetened
  condensed milk
1 5 ounce can evaporated milk
5 ounces whole milk

3 eggs
1 teaspoon vanilla
3 tablespoons sugar
dash grated lemon rind

Put sugar and water in top of double boiler. Over medium heat melt sugar carefully until mixture turns to caramel color. Turn pan to coat bottom and sides with caramel sauce. Put all custard ingredients into a blender. Pulse 3 to 4 times to mix custard. Pour into top of double boiler. Place double boiler top over water that is simmering, cover pan and cook about 1 hour. Custard is done when knife inserted midway in center comes out clean. Cool custard, then invert custard onto dish.

Jean Buckridge

FLAN WITH CHEESE
Spanish

1 cup sugar
3 eggs
1 13 ounce can evaporated milk
1 14 ounce can sweetened
  condensed milk

8 ounces cream cheese
1 tablespoon vanilla

Brown sugar in saucepan or double boiler pan. Place eggs, evaporated milk, condensed milk, cream cheese and vanilla in blender and blend well. Pour blended mixture over brown sugar in double boiler pan or a flan pan. Heat oven to 350 degrees. Place pan in ovenproof double boiler with water in bottom. If using flan pan, set in another shallow pan of water. Bake 1 hour or until knife inserted in center comes out clean. Cool. Loosen edges with knife and invert onto serving plate.

Brandon Nazario

PAELLA
Spanish

1 chicken, cut up
1¼ pounds Italian hot sausage
¾ pound pork, cubed
1½ pounds large shrimp, shelled
   and deveined
6 mussels, steamed open
6 clams, steamed open
1 28 ounce can plum tomatoes,
   drained and chopped

3 large onions, minced
5 ounces defrosted peas
6 cups chicken broth
3 cups uncooked rice
3 garlic cloves, minced
2 tablespoons sherry
green and red pepper strips, for
   garnish
oil, for frying

Paste:
1 teaspoon vinegar
1 garlic clove
2 tablespoons oil

2 peppercorns
1 teaspoon oregano

Early in day, crush paste ingredients and rub into chicken pieces. *Note:* A mortar and pestle is helpful to make paste. Let chicken stand to absorb flavors. Brown chicken in ¼ cup oil for 10 to 15 minutes. Remove. Slice sausage and brown in same pan. Remove. Wipe pan. Brown pork in ¼ cup oil. Add tomatoes, onions and garlic. Sauté, stirring constantly and briskly, until liquid evaporates. Set aside. About ½ hour before serving, preheat oven to 400 degrees. Mix 3 cups rice with the pork mixture. Bring 6 cups chicken broth to boil and add 2 tablespoons sherry. Place pork and rice mixture into a large ovenproof casserole. Pour broth over and bring to boil on top of stove, stirring constantly. Remove from heat. Add shrimp, chicken, sausage on top of rice. Place on lowest rack in oven. Bake uncovered 25 to 30 minutes in preheated oven. Remove from oven and cover with clean towel for 5 to 8 minutes. Place warm, steamed clams, mussels, peas and fresh pepper strips on top of casserole at serving time. *Yield:* 6 to 8 servings.

Jennifer Hoyes

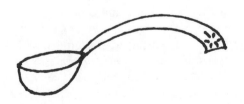

BEEF AND RICE FIESTA
Spanish

1 pound ground beef
1 medium onion, sliced
1 cup beef bouillon
1 15 ounce can whole kernel
   corn

1 teaspoon chili powder (more,
   if you like it spicy)
1 28 ounce can crushed tomatoes
1 green pepper, cut in strips,
   chunks, or rings

Brown beef in skillet, leaving meat in chunks. Remove meat from skillet. Add onion and green pepper to skillet and sauté until tender. Add bouillion, corn, chili powder and crushed tomatoes. Bring to a boil. Simmer for 5 minutes, stirring occasionally. Serve over rice. *Yield:* 4 to 5 servings.

Adrienne V. Wheatley

SWEDISH MEATBALLS
Swedish

Meat Mixture:
1 pound ground beef
¼ pound ground pork
½ cup fine breadcrumbs
1 cup milk
½ teaspoon salt

¼ teaspoon white pepper
1 egg
2 tablespoons finely chopped
   onion

Gravy:
2 tablespoons margarine or
   butter
1 cup Half and Half, or beef
   stock

1 tablespoon cornstarch
2 tablespoons cold water

Combine meat mixture ingredients; beat with fork. Shape mixture into 40 to 50 small meatballs. Heat margarine in large skillet over moderate heat. Brown meatballs on one side about 2 minutes; turn and brown other side. Reduce heat to low and cover pan, simmer for 8 minutes. Remove meatballs, pour off fat. Add Half and Half, or beef stock. Blend cornstarch and water; add to pan. Stir over moderate heat until mixture comes to a boil, taste and if necessary, add salt and pepper. Serve gravy with meatballs.

Marlene Pepe

kids Korner

APPLE CRISP

4 to 5 apples, sliced
1 cup sugar
1 cup flour
dash salt
1 teaspoon baking powder

1 egg
½ cup butter or margarine,
  melted
cinnamon

Place apples in buttered 9 inch pie plate. Mix all dry ingredients with egg until moistened by egg. Sprinkle over fruit (close to edge of pie plate). Sprinkle melted butter or margarine over top. Sprinkle with cinnamon. Bake at 350 degrees for ½ hour until brown and crisp.

Kathy Tarantino

FRENCH CHEESE BREAD

1 loaf of French or Italian bread
butter, softened, as needed
pepper, to taste

Romano cheese, sliced or
  grated, to taste

Preheat oven to 400 degrees. Make diagonal cuts, 1 inch apart in loaf of bread, but do not cut all the way through the bread. Spread butter into each cut. Cut cheese slices into fourths and tuck ¼ of a slice of cheese into each cut. If using grated cheese, sprinkle desired amount into each cut. Sprinkle top of loaf with pepper and place on a baking sheet. Heat in oven until cheese melts, about 5 minutes.

Genine Swanzey

CHEWIES

2 cups brown sugar
½ cup butter or margarine
3 eggs
¼ teaspoon salt
12 ounces chopped nuts

12 ounces chocolate chips
2 cups sifted flour
1 teaspoon baking powder
1 teaspoon vanilla

Cream brown sugar, butter and vanilla, then mix in eggs. Sift flour, baking powder and salt. Combine all ingredients and mix well. Pour into 13x9x2 inch pan. Bake at 350 degrees for 25 minutes. When cooled cut into squares.

Karen McManus

BETTY OR BARNEY BREAD

1 slice bread
peanut butter or cream cheese
jelly

cheerios
raisins
apple slice

Cover one side of bread with either peanut butter or cream cheese. Put jelly around 3 edges (Betty) or just top edge (Barney). Place 2 cheerios for eyes; raisin for nose; and apple slice for mouth.

Kimberly and Courtney Dougherty

KID'S BROCCOLI CASSEROLE

½ cup sour cream
1 10 ounce can cream of chicken
  soup
1 tablespoon minced onion
  flakes

1 tablespoon flour
¼ teaspoon salt
⅛ teaspoon pepper

Combine all ingredients and put in a 1½ quart casserole. Make topping, cover and bake at 350 degrees for 30 minutes.

Topping:
2 cups herb seasoned stuffing
½ cup melted butter or
  margarine

Combine thoroughly and spread on broccoli before baking.

Ann Marie Kane

CATHY'S CLAM DIP

1 6½ ounce can minced clams
20 crushed snack crackers
¼ cup melted butter or
  margarine

oregano, to taste
garlic powder, to taste

Melt butter and add spices. Add snack crackers. Drain clams slightly and add to mixture. Stir and put in baking dish. Cover and bake at 375 degrees for 15 minutes, until bubbly.

Catherine Tagle

KATHY'S KARROTS

2 or 3 large fat carrots
3 ounces cream cheese or cream
cheese with chives

Pare carrots and cut into 2 inch chunks. Core center of each chunk with a vegetable peeler. Stuff with cream cheese. Chill. *Yield:* 1 to 2 servings.

Kathleen Hein

BROWNIES

1 box chocolate cake mix or
brownie mix
1 8 ounce package light
caramels
⅔ cup evaporated milk

1 12 ounce package semi-sweet
chocolate chips
¾ cup walnuts or pecans
¾ cup butter, melted

Melt caramels in ⅓ cup evaporated milk in double boiler or heavy sauce pan over low heat. Put aside after it is melted. In mixing bowl, mix the dry cake with the butter. Place ½ of cake mixture in a greased 9x13 inch pan and bake at 350 degrees for 6 to 8 minutes. Remove from oven and pour caramel mixture over brownies. Sprinkle chocolate chips over caramels. Sprinkle nuts over chocolate chips. Top with remaining ½ of brownie mixture. Bake at 350 degrees for 16 to 18 minutes. Cool and cut into bars. *Yield:* 16 bars.

Denise Cadet

BUTTER CRUNCH

1 cup chopped walnuts or pecans
1 cup butter or margarine
1 cup firmly packed brown
sugar

1 cup semi-sweet chocolate
morsels

Line a 9x13 inch baking pan with aluminum foil. Butter foil. In a heavy medium saucepan melt butter. Add sugar and cook, stirring constantly, to 290 degrees on a candy thermometer (hard crack stage). Pour toffee on buttered aluminum foil and sprinkle with chocolate morsels. When chocolate begins to melt, spread evenly with spatula and immediately sprinkle with chopped nuts. With the back of a spoon, gently press nuts into chocolate. Cool and refrigerate to set. Crack into pieces.

Christine Sluka

CHOC-OAT BARS

2 cups oats
½ cup brown sugar
½ cup melted butter
¼ cup dark corn syrup
½ teaspoon salt

1 teaspoon vanilla
1 6 ounce package semi-sweet
   chocolate pieces, melted
¼ cup chopped nuts

Heat oven to 400 degrees. Grease baking pan, 9x9x2 inches. In medium bowl, mix oats and brown sugar. Stir together butter, syrup, salt and vanilla. Mix thoroughly into oat mixture. Press dough evenly into bottom of pan. Bake 8 to 10 minutes or until top bubbles. Cool. Spread melted chocolate on top. Sprinkle nuts on top of chocolate. Chill. Cut into bars, about 2x1 inch.

Anne Carey

CHOCOLATE COOKIES

½ cup butter
1½ cups sugar
1 egg, well beaten
¼ teaspoon salt
2 squares unsweetened
   chocolate, melted

2½ cups flour
2 teaspoons baking powder
¼ cup milk

Cream butter and sugar. Add well beaten egg, salt and chocolate. Beat well. Sift flour with baking powder and add alternately with milk. Beat again. Chill several hours. Roll very thin. Shape with a small cutter. Bake on a greased cookie sheet in a moderate oven, 350 degrees for 10 minutes.

Vanessa Rog

CHOCOLATE CREAM PIE

1 ready made pie crust
2 packages chocolate pudding

whipped cream, as needed
chocolate decorations, optional

Make chocolate pudding according to directions and pour into pie crust. Cool in refrigerator for 10 minutes. Take out and top with whipped cream. Optional decoration: Take one chocolate bar and using grater, make chocolate shavings. Sprinkle over pie topping. Refrigerate.

Susan Keane

KID'S KORNER

CARROT CAKE

2 cups sugar
1½ cups vegetable oil
4 eggs
1 cup chopped nuts
3 cups grated carrots

2 cups flour
1 teaspoon salt
2 teaspoons baking soda
2 teaspoons cinnamon

Cream Cheese Topping:
1 pound box powdered sugar
⅓ cup butter or margarine
2 teaspoons vanilla

1 8 ounce package cream cheese
1 cup chopped nuts

Preheat oven to 350 degrees. Mix sugar, oil and eggs. Beat at high speed. Sift dry ingredients and mix with egg mixture. Add carrots and nuts. Bake in three 9 inch pans or oblong pan, until cake is done and tester comes out dry. If still moist, leave in oven 5 more minutes. Time 9 inch pans - 30 minutes, oblong pan - 45 minutes.

For topping: soften butter and cheese to room temperature and cream together. Mix sugar and vanilla with butter and cheese until smooth. Add nuts. Spread on cooled cake. *Note:* Cake tastes best if prepared 2 days before serving.

Kathleen and Michelle Aurigemma

HOMESTYLE FRANK AND CHEESE DINNER

8 ounce package of egg noodles
¼ cup butter or margarine
⅓ cup finely chopped onion
¼ cup flour
1 teaspoon salt
½ teaspoon dry mustard

2½ cups milk
¾ teaspoon Worcestershire
  sauce
2 cups shredded Cheddar cheese
1 pound frankfurters, cut into 1
  inch pieces

Preheat oven to 350 degrees. Cook noodles according to package directions. Meanwhile, in medium skillet, melt butter and cook onion until tender. Stir in flour, salt and mustard blended with milk and Worcestershire sauce. Bring to the boiling point, then simmer, stirring constantly, until sauce is thickened, about 5 minutes. Stir in 1¼ cups cheese until melted. In a greased 3 quart casserole, combine noodles, frankfurters, and sauce. Top with remaining cheese. Bake 25 minutes or until heated through. *Yield:* 6 servings.

Lynn Gach

FOOLPROOF CHOCOLATE FUDGE

3 6 ounce packages semi-sweet
  chocolate chips
1 14 ounce can of sweetened
  condensed milk

1½ teaspoons vanilla extract
½ cup chopped nuts, optional
dash salt

In heavy saucepan, over low heat, melt chips with condensed milk. Remove from heat; stir in remaining ingredients. Spread evenly into waxed paper lined 8 inch square pan.

Chill 2 to 3 hours or until firm. Turn fudge onto cutting board; peel off paper and cut into squares. Store, loosely covered at room temperature. *Yield:* approximately 1¾ pounds.

Sandra Gach

CHOCOLATE COOKIE TREATS

½ cup margarine
2 cup graham cracker crumbs
chopped walnuts, to taste
1 6 ounce package semi-sweet
  chocolate morsels

4 ounces coconut
1 14 ounce can sweetened
  condensed milk

Melt margarine and spread in 13x9x2 inch pan to coat bottom. Cover with graham cracker crumbs. Sprinkle with chopped walnuts, chocolate morsels and coconut. Pour condensed milk over top. Bake at 325 degrees for 25 minutes. Cut into about 30 squares.

Margie Weir

PEANUT FUDGE

12 ounces peanut butter chips
14 ounce can sweetened
  condensed milk

¼ cup butter
½ cup chopped peanuts
6 ounces chocolate chips

Melt peanut butter chips, 1 cup sweetened condensed milk and 2 tablespoons butter in heavy saucepan. Stir in peanuts. Spread in an 8 inch square pan lined with waxed paper.

Melt chocolate chips and remaining condensed milk and butter. Spread over peanut butter mix. Chill. Cut into squares.

Francesco Lupis

KID'S KORNER

COUNTRY STYLE GRANOLA SNACK

5 cups rolled oats
1½ cups wheat germ
1 cup shredded coconut
1 cup unsalted chopped peanuts
½ cup whole wheat bran

½ cup packed brown sugar
½ cup oil
⅓ cup water
2 teaspoons vanilla

Stir together oats, wheat germ, coconut, peanuts, wheat bran and brown sugar. Combine oil, water and vanilla. Pour over dry mixture and stir thoroughly. Turn into a 15x10x1 jelly roll or cookie sheet pan. Bake at 350 degrees for one hour, stirring every 15 minutes. Cool and store in covered container. *Yield:* 10 cups.

Christine Hein

ORANGE OATMEAL COOKIES

½ cup margarine
1 egg
½ cup sugar
½ cup brown sugar
1 tablespoon fresh orange peel
2 tablespoons orange juice

1 cup flour
1 cup oatmeal
½ teaspoon salt
½ teaspoon baking soda
½ cup raisins or grated carrot

Mix all ingredients together. Drop from spoon onto ungreased cookie sheet. Bake 12 to 15 minutes in preheated oven at 350 degrees. *Yield:* approximately 3 dozen.

Danielle Radman

FUDGE CAKE

4 eggs
1 cup sour cream
¼ cup oil
1 box chocolate cake mix
1 package instant vanilla
   pudding

½ cup warmed milk
1½ cups semi-sweet chocolate
   chips

Grease and flour tube pan. Beat all ingredients except chocolate chips; stir in last. Bake in a preheated 350 degree oven for 1 hour.

Tommy Blouin

DORMIR SOÑADO

1 cup orange juice
1 teaspoon sugar
2 ice cubes

1 teaspoon vanilla extract
¾ cup milk

Combine all ingredients in blender, mix well. If you'd like the orange taste stronger, decrease the amount of milk to ½ cup.

Alexandro Nazario

HOMEMADE CRACKER JACKS

1 pound popcorn
1 cup margarine or butter
½ cup honey

1 cup lightly packed light brown
   sugar
1 teaspoon vanilla

Preheat oven to 250 degrees. In a small sauce pan melt butter, add honey and brown sugar. Bring to a boil without stirring for about 5 minutes. Take off stove and add vanilla. Place popcorn in a baking dish and pour mixture over it. Place in oven for 1 hour stirring once every 15 minutes.

Cecilia Lupis

GELATIN BLOX

4 envelopes unflavored gelatin
3 3 ounce packages flavored
   gelatin, of choice

4 cups boiling water

In large bowl, mix unflavored gelatin with flavored gelatin. Add boiling water and stir until gelatin is completely dissolved. Pour into 13x9 inch baking pan. Chill until firm. To serve, cut into 1 inch squares.

Matthew Cerullo

HOMEMADE PEANUT BUTTER

1 cup shelled unsalted peanuts
3 tablespoons vegetable oil

½ teaspoon salt

Put all ingredients into the container of an electric blender. Blend for 1 minute. Eat.

Eugene Swanzey

KID'S KORNER

PRETZELS

2 packages yeast
1½ cups warm water
2 tablespoons sugar
1 teaspoon salt

4 cups flour
1 egg, beaten
coarse salt, as needed

Add sugar to ½ cup water. Stir in yeast with wooden spoon. Let stand 5 to 10 minutes. Let bubble, then add rest of water, salt and then flour, gradually. Put plastic wrap over bowl. Place in a cool, dark place to rise. Beat down and let it rise again. Form into any shape. The children like to make initials or animal forms. After formed, brush with beaten egg and then sprinkle coarse salt over. Bake at 325 degrees until golden brown.

Pat Rayfield

8 MINUTE LIGHT 'N FRUITY PIE

1 3 ounce package gelatin, any
flavor
⅔ cup boiling water
2 cups ice cubes
1 8 ounce container non-dairy
whipped topping, thawed

1 cup diced fruit, optional
9 inch graham cracker crumb
crust

Completely dissolve gelatin in boiling water, stirring about 3 minutes. Add ice cubes and stir constantly until gelatin is thickened, about 2 to 3 minutes. Remove any unmelted ice. Using wire whisk, blend in whipped topping, then whip until smooth. Fold in fruit. Chill if necessary, until mixture will mound. Spoon into pie crust. Chill 2 hours.

Kathleen Keane

GINGER SNAPS

¼ cup butter
¼ cup sugar
1 egg
¼ cup molasses

¼ tablespoon ginger
¼ teaspoon baking soda
1¼ cups flour

Cream the butter and sugar. Add egg and molasses. Then add the ginger, soda and flour. Mix well. Roll very thin on a floured board. Cut into desired shapes. Bake on a greased cookie sheet in a 350 degree oven for 10 to 12 minutes.

Vanessa Rog

A CHILD'S SUMMER SALAD LUNCH

1 carrot
1 stalk celery
1 small bell pepper
1 medium tomato
any favorite salad dressing
1 slice ham, turkey, or chicken

2 to 4 black olives, (optional)
lettuce, of choice
2 dill pickle slices
2 slices American, Swiss or any
  favorite cheese

All ingredients should be cold. Clean vegetables. Slice carrot and celery into small chunks. Slice pepper into long thin strips. Cut tomato into small wedges. Slice meat and cheese into small pieces. Arrange lettuce after tearing into bite size pieces into a serving dish. Put carrot, celery, pepper, tomato, meat and cheese on top. Add pickle and olives. Pour on dressing to taste. *Yield:* 1 serving for older child. 2 servings for small children.

Angela McGivney

RICE CEREAL TREATS

¼ cup margarine
1 10 ounce package
  marshmallows

6 cups rice cereal

Melt margarine in a large pan over low heat. Add marshmallows and stir until completely melted. Remove from heat. Add rice cereal. Stir until well coated. Using buttered spatula or wax paper, press mixture evenly into buttered 13x9x2 inch pan. Cut into squares when cool.

Peter Cerullo

REUBEN SANDWICHES

party rye bread
corned beef, cut into small, thin
  slices

sauerkraut, canned or package
Russian dressing
Swiss cheese

Place small amount of corned beef on cocktail rye bread. Place small amount of sauerkraut on top of meat. Add some Russian dressing and cover with a slice of Swiss cheese. Place on cookie sheet and heat until cheese is melted. If desired, toast bread first.

Matthew Tagle

STRAWBERRY-ORANGE ICE

1¾ cups orange juice
½ cup lemon juice
3 pints hulled strawberries

1¾ cups sugar
⅛ teaspoon salt

In covered blender at high speed, mix all ingredients until smooth, blending about half at a time. Pour strawberry mixture into a 13x9 inch baking pan and mix well. Cover pan with foil or plastic wrap and freeze until partially frozen, about 4 hours, stirring occasionally. Spoon strawberry mixture into chilled large bowl, and with mixer at medium speed, beat until smooth but still frozen. Return strawberry mixture to baking pan. Cover with foil or plastic wrap and freeze mixture until firm, about 3 hours. To serve, remove mixture from freezer and let stand at room temperature 10 mintues for easier scooping. *Yield:* 20 servings.

Diane Szarek

POPEYE SALAD

1 pound fresh spinach
1 teaspoon grated onion
½ teaspoon salt
2 hard boiled eggs, chopped

4 slices bacon, diced
4 tablespoons malt vinegar
2 teaspoons sugar

Wash and trim spinach. Dry and chop. Add onion, salt and chopped eggs. Fry bacon until crisp. Drain and add to salad. Combine vinegar and sugar and pour over salad. Toss well.

Daniel Heffernan

PEANUT BUTTER ROLLS

1 cup peanut butter
½ cup powdered milk

¼ cup honey
rice cereal, as needed

Mix peanut butter, powdered milk and honey in a bowl. Roll marble sized balls and then roll into rice cereal.

Robert Bardunias

GIANT SNICKERDOODLES

½ pound butter or margarine
1½ cups, plus 2 tablespoons
sugar
2 eggs
2¾ cups flour

2 teaspoons cream of tartar
1 teaspoon baking soda
¼ teaspoon salt
2 teaspoons cinnamon

In large mixing bowl with electric mixer at medium speed, cream butter or margarine, 1½ cups sugar and eggs until light and fluffy, scraping sides of bowl occasionally. In a separate bowl, combine flour, cream of tartar, baking soda and salt. Add to creamed mixture until well blended. Refrigerate dough for 30 minutes. Dough refrigerated overnight is easier to work with. Preheat oven to 375 degrees. Combine remaining 2 tablespoons sugar and cinnamon in a shallow bowl. Shape dough into 2 inch balls and roll in cinnamon-sugar. Place 3 inches apart on ungreased cookie sheets. Bake 12 to 15 minutes until golden brown. Snickerdoodles will puff up at first, then flatten out during baking. Remove from cookie sheet and cool on wire rack. May be frozen up to 3 months. *Yield:* 2 dozen.

Eileen M. Rielly

SAFETY RULES FOR YOUNGSTERS

The following are 10 safety rules for cooking in the kitchen.

1. Use pot holders when placing food in the oven or taking it out.
2. Always use a dry pot holder, never a wet or damp one.
3. Turn all handles of pans or pots inward over the stove.
4. Use a chopping board for cutting or chopping foods.
5. If you have to reach for something on a high shelf, use a step-stool or a sturdy chair.
6. Wipe up all spills right away to avoid any slips or falls.
7. If a glass should break, call your parent.
8. Never use the electric mixer or blender without a parent standing next to you.
9. For cutting or paring foods, use a small paring knife that has a saw-toothed edge.
10. When stirring hot liquids, always use a long-handled spoon.

HOUSE FRAGRANCE

1 quart pineapple juice
1 quart water
1 quart apple cider
4 cinnamon sticks

16 whole cloves
½ teaspoon allspice
4 teaspoons ginger

Mix together and bring to a boil. *Note:* Wonderful to use at Christmas time, makes house smell delightful. Just keep heating it each day. Leave on a back burner. Lasts about 10 days.

Barbara Valeri

beverages, microwave, and misc.

BEVERAGES

GARDNER'S APPLE CIDER COOLER

½ gallon apple cider
1 bottle of dry champagne
10 cloves

5 cinnamon sticks, or 1 teaspoon
  ground cinnamon
1 sliced lemon

Marinate spices in cider overnight; or place in a pot and slowly bring to a boil. Let cool at room temperature; then chill. When ready to serve, add sliced lemons; then champagne and serve. Great and refreshing!

Mary Gardner

BLACKBERRY BRANDY

4 cups fresh blackberries
2 cups brandy
¾ cup sugar

¾ teaspoon whole allspice
12 whole cloves

Wash fruit; drain. In gallon screw-top jar, mix fruit and remaining ingredients. Cover tightly. Invert jar; let stand 24 hours. Turn jar upright; let stand 24 hours. Repeat turning process until sugar is dissolved. Store in cool, dark place at least 2 months. Strain through cheesecloth into a decanter. Cover. *Yield:* 3½ cups.

Judy Hein

HOMEMADE IRISH CREAM

1 13 ounce can evaporated milk
1 14 ounce can sweetened
  condensed milk
6 eggs

1 tablespoon coffee
1 teaspoon vanilla
1 cup rye

Blend and refrigerate at least 12 hours.

Pat Rayfield

CHAMPAGNE PUNCH

1 large bottle champagne
1 bottle ginger ale
2 cans punch

pineapple chunks or frozen
  strawberries
½ gallon raspberry sherbert

Mix all ingredients together except the sherbert. Chill. Pour into punch bowl. Add sherbert just before serving.

Linda J. Candia

COFFEE LIQUOR

6 cups sugar
6 cups water
½ cup vanilla extract

½ cup instant coffee granules
½ gallon vodka

Mix sugar, water and coffee together in a large pot. Bring mixture to boil, then simmer for 2 hours. Stir in vanilla and set aside, covered, for at least 12 hours. Stir in vodka. May be used at once. *Yield:* 1¼ gallon.

Judy Hein

EGG NOG

6 eggs
¾ cup sugar
2 pints half and half

¾ cup rum
nutmeg, to taste

Separate eggs. Beat egg whites; set aside. Mix sugar and egg yolks together, then add half and half and rum. Mix well. Fold in egg whites. Sprinkle nutmeg on top. *Yield:* 4 to 6 servings.

Pat Rayfield

JOANNE'S EGGNOG

8 eggs, separated
1 cup sugar
3 ounces rum

2 cups brandy
1 pint heavy cream
1 quart milk

Beat yolks and whites of 8 eggs separately. Add 1 cup sugar to whites, beat until stiff. Combine beaten yolks and whites and mix thoroughly. Add rum and brandy. Beat mixture. Add 1 pint heavy cream and 1 quart milk. Mix. Chill well. Serve with a light sprinkling of nutmeg on top.

Joanne Halloran

PAT'S ORANGE COOLER

1 6 ounce can frozen orange
   juice
1 cup milk
1 cup water

½ cup sugar
1 teaspoon vanilla
12 ice cubes, cracked fine

Place all ingredients in a blender and mix until smooth, about 1 minute.

Patricia Stefanik

ORANGE LIQUOR

4 medium oranges
2 cups sugar

2 cups vodka or rum

Squeeze juice from oranges; reserve peel from one orange. Scrape white membrane from reserved peel. Cut peel into strips. Add water to juice to make 2 cups. Bring orange juice mixture, peel and sugar to boiling. Reduce heat; simmer over low heat 5 minutes. Cool. Pour into large screw-top jar. Stir in vodka. Cover. Let stand at room temperature 3 to 4 weeks. Strain into decanters. Cover. *Yield:* 5 cups

Eileen Rathgaber

SUMMER PUNCH

3 cups orange juice
1½ cups lemon juice
3 quarts pineapple juice
⅓ cup lime juice
2½ cups sugar
1 cup mint leaves

4 quarts chilled ginger ale
2 quarts chilled club soda
1 pint fresh strawberries
lemons and limes, sliced, for
  garnish

Combine juices, sugar and mint leaves. Chill several hours and strain. Pour over ice in punch bowl. Slowly pour ginger ale and club soda down side of bowl. Add strawberries and float lemon and lime slices. *Enjoy! Enjoy! Yield:* 60 servings.

Ginette Leveque

PLUM CORDIAL

3 pounds of fresh purple plums,
  halved and pitted

4 cups sugar
4 cups gin

In a gallon screw-top jar, mix all ingredients. Cover tightly. Invert jar; let stand 24 hours. Turn jar upright and let stand 24 hours. Repeat turning until sugar dissolves. Store in cool, dark place 2 months. Strain through cheese cloth into decanters. Cover.

The Committee

SPICED FRUIT PUNCH

6 cups sugar	2 dozen lemons, juiced
1 quart water	2 dozen oranges, juiced
3 dozen whole cloves	cherries
2 sticks cinnamon	2 bottles of ginger ale

Bring to boil first 4 ingredients for 10 to 15 minutes. Strain and add the juice of lemons and oranges. Add 2 bottles of ginger ale. Garnish with fruit slices and cherries.

The Committee

STRAWBERRY DAIQUIRI

1 10 ounce package frozen strawberries, thawed	4 ounces lemon juice
6 ounces light rum	3 tablespoons sugar
	2 cups crushed ice

Mix all ingredients in blender. *Yield:* Four 6 ounce servings.

Eileen Rathgaber

1 MINUTE GARLIC BREAD

½ cup of butter or margarine	1 one pound loaf Italian bread,
3 cloves garlic	sliced ¾ inch thick
½ teaspoon oregano	grated Parmesan cheese, to
½ teaspoon basil	taste

Place butter in a small glass mixing bowl and microwave on Medium-Low, 30%, or defrost 1 minute. Using a garlic press, squeeze garlic into butter and add residue from pulp. Blend in oregano and basil. Spread on bread and assemble slices to form a loaf. Line a microwave-safe wicker basket with six paper napkins or paper towels. Place bread in utensil and cover with paper napkins. Microwave on High for 1 minute just before serving. *Yield:* 20 slices.

Anne Stearns

MICROWAVE

APPLE BETTY

2 cans of canned apples
2 cups graham cracker crumbs
¼ cup sugar
1 cup brown sugar

1½ teaspoons cinnamon
½ teaspoon nutmeg
½ cup melted margarine, or
  butter

Mix dry ingredients, then fold in apples. Place in an oven proof glass pan. Pour melted margarine over top of mixture. Microwave on High for 12 minutes.

Ellen Kelly

MINI PIZZA

1 English muffin
¼ cup shredded mozzarella
  cheese

spaghetti sauce or pizza sauce,
  as needed

Split English muffin and put halves on a paper plate. Spread sauce on each half. Sprinkle cheese over sauce. Microwave on High 1 minute or until cheese melts.

Annabelle Pilkington

CHILI

1 pound ground beef
1 medium onion, chopped
½ cup chopped green pepper
1 6 ounce can tomato paste
1 15½ ounce can kidney beans,
  undrained

½ cup water
1 teaspoon salt
¼ teaspoon garlic powder
2 to 3 teaspoons chili powder

Crumble ground beef in 2 quart glass casserole. Stir in onion and green pepper. Cover with a glass lid. Microwave for about 5 minutes on High, or until meat is browned. Drain and stir in remaining ingredients; cover. Microwave for 14 to 16 minutes, on Roast or until hot, about 150 degrees Farenheit. Let stand, covered 5 minutes before serving. *Note:* Sprinkle shredded Cheddar cheese over bowls of chili, if desired. *Yield:* 4 to 6 servings.

Ann Bardunias

CHICKEN CUTLETS MOZZARELLA

1 pound boneless chicken breast
½ cup Italian seasoned bread
  crumbs

1 cup prepared meatless
  spaghetti sauce
4 slices mozzarella cheese

Separate chicken breasts into four portions and pound to flatten slightly. Coat well in bread crumbs. Arrange breasts around sides of an 8 inch baking dish. Cover with waxed paper. Microwave on High for 5 to 6 minutes. Pour ¼ of the sauce over each portion. Place a slice of cheese on top of each breast and garnish with crumbs, if desired. Cover with waxed paper and microwave on Medium-High, 70%, for 3 to 4 minutes, or until sauce is hot and cheese is melted. *Yield:* 4 servings.

Anne Stearns

CHOCOLATE PUDDING

½ cup milk
½ of 1 ounce square, semisweet
  baking chocolate

2 teaspoons cornstarch
1 teaspoon sugar

Pour milk into a 2 cup glass measuring cup. Add chocolate. Microwave milk and chocolate on High 1 minute. Remove from oven and stir to mix chocolate and milk. Combine cornstarch and sugar in a cup. Pour into milk mixture and stir. Microwave on High 30 seconds. Check to see if mixture has thickened and begun to boil. Remove from oven. Stir pudding and spoon into a bowl.

Annabelle Pilkington

NACHOS

16 large tortilla chips
¾ cup shredded Monterey Jack
  cheese

¼ cup shredded Cheddar cheese

Spread tortilla chips on a 10 inch plastic or wax coated paper plate. Sprinkle with cheese. Microwave at Medium, 50% 1½ to 2½ minutes. Microwave just until cheese softens. It will finish melting by internal heat. Rotate twice during heating. *Yield:* 16.

Anne Stearns

MICROWAVE

LASAGNE

1 pound ground beef	10 uncooked lasagne noodles,
36 ounces spaghetti sauce	narrow, straight edges, not
15 ounces ricotta cheese	curly
1 egg	Parmesan cheese, to taste
8 ounces mozzarella cheese, shredded	

Crumble beef into microwave colander. Place colander in a bowl to catch drippings. Cook on High power 3 minutes. Let stand 2 to 3 minutes. Drain. Add meat to sauce in a bowl. Mix ricotta cheese with egg in another bowl. Place ⅓ meat sauce in bottom of 12x8 dish. Place 5 noodles on top of sauce. Spoon ⅓ ricotta cheese on dry noodles. Add ½ mozzarella cheese, sprinkle with Parmesan. Repeat with next ⅓ of sauce, 5 noodles, cheese. Finish off with remaining sauce. Sprinkle Parmesan cheese on top. Cover TIGHTLY with plastic wrap. Cook on High power 10 minutes. Cook 50% power 2 to 3 minutes. Release wrap in one corner when done. Let stand covered 10 minutes.

Mary Smith

HAMBURGER MEDLEY

1 pound ground beef	1 cup uncooked elbow macaroni
½ cup chopped green pepper	dash hot pepper sauce
½ cup chopped onion	1 cup water
16 ounces tomato sauce	
1 12 ounce can whole kernel corn, drained	

In a three quart casserole dish, crumble ground beef. Add chopped pepper and onion. Heat on High for 6 minutes or until beef is browned. Stir once and drain. Stir in tomato sauce, corn, macaroni, hot pepper sauce and water. Mix well. Cover with glass lid. Heat on High 8 minutes and then Medium-Low 12 minutes, until macaroni is tender. Stir twice during cooking. Let stand 10 minutes before serving. *Yield:* 4 servings.

Marie Hecker

HOME STYLE POT ROAST

3½ to 4 pounds beef chuck roast
¼ cup water
1 large onion, sliced
1 cup chopped celery
3 medium carrots, cut into
 chunks

1 bay leaf
3 medium potatoes, quartered
1 4 ounce can mushroom stems
 and pieces
2 teaspoons salt
¼ teaspoon pepper

Place roast and water in 4 quart ceramic dutch oven; cover with glass lid. Microwave for 20 minutes on High. Turn meat over; add remaining ingredients and recover. Microwave for 55 to 60 minutes, on simmer, or until meat is fork tender. Let stand covered, 10 minutes before serving.

Ann Bardunias

APPLESAUCE

4 medium cooking apples, pared,
 quartered and cored
1 cup water

½ cup packed brown sugar
¼ teaspoon cinnamon
⅛ teaspoon nutmeg

Heat apples and water over medium heat to boiling. Reduce heat; simmer, stirring occasionally, 5 to 10 minutes or until tender. Stir in brown sugar, cinnamon and nutmeg. Heat to boiling. *Yield:* 4 cups.

Mary DiPaola

BARBECUE SAUCE

½ cup catsup
1 teaspoon mustard
1 teaspoon Worcestershire sauce
⅓ cup white vinegar

¼ cup molasses
dash garlic powder
salt and pepper, to taste

Combine all the ingredients above and blend well. Barbecue sauce is great for chicken, pork, beef and lamb.

Eileen Rathgaber

MISCELLANEOUS

ED'S BARBECUE SAUCE

1 40 ounce jar duck sauce
1 32 ounce bottle catsup
1 16 ounce bottle dark corn
  syrup
1 cup French dressing
3 tablespoons lemon juice

2 teaspoons hot sauce
2 teaspoons Worcestershire
  sauce
1 tablespoon garlic powder
2 teaspoons liquid smoke

Combine all ingredients in a large bowl. May be used as a marinade and basting sauce for chicken, ribs or steak. May be frozen in containers or preserved in canning jars and put through a 10 minute water bath. *Yield:* approximately 2 quarts.

Dr. Edward Hiross

HOT FUDGE SAUCE

8 squares unsweetened chocolate
2 cups sugar
1 12 ounce can evaporated milk

2 tablespoons strong coffee
1 teaspoon vanilla
dash salt

Melt chocolate in top of double boiler. Add sugar and mix well. Cover and cook over boiling water for 30 minutes. Add evaporated milk, coffee, salt and vanilla. Beat until smooth. Refrigerates for weeks when tightly closed.

Jennifer Hoyes

BEER MARINADE FOR BEEF

1½ cups beer
½ cup minced scallions
⅓ cup olive oil
3 tablespoons soy sauce
2 tablespoons sugar

1 clove minced garlic
cayenne pepper, to taste
3 pounds beef, cut up for shish
  kabobs, or steaks for barbecue

In a ceramic or glass dish, combine the first 7 ingredients, mixing well. Add the beef and marinate overnight in the refrigerator, stirring several times. Barbecue meat on grill and use the marinade to baste meat as it cooks.

Nancy Besso

THREE DAY MARMALADE

1 grapefruit
1 orange

1 lemon
sugar

First day: Cut fruit in half and remove seeds. Cut away and discard ends. Slice fruit as thinly as possible. Cover, barely, with cold water in a bowl. Leave overnight covered, at room temperature. *Second day:* Put mixture in enamel or stainless steel pan and boil for 30 minutes. Cover and leave at room temperature. *Third day:* Measure fruit mixture. Add an equal amount of sugar. Cook over a slow flame, stirring frequently, to prevent sticking and burning, for about 1 hour. Test on a cold saucer for thickness. If too thin, cook a little longer. Pour into sterilized jar and seal, or keep in refrigerator. *Yield:* 1 pint.

Helen Mara Evancie

PERSONAL PIZZAS

1 tablespoon flour
2 teaspoons shortening
1 package ready made
   refrigerated biscuits

1 8 ounce can pizza sauce
1 cup shredded mozzarella
   cheese

Grease 2 baking sheets with shortening. Pull the biscuits apart to make 4 inch circles. Coat with flour. Place these biscuits on the greased baking sheet. Spoon 1½ tablespoons of pizza sauce into the center of each biscuit. Sprinkle each with 1½ tablespoons of cheese. *Optional toppings:* Use pepperoni slices, sliced olives, or chopped green peppers. Bake at 450 degrees for 10 to 15 minutes, until brown and bubbly.

The Committee

WELSH RABBIT

8 tablespoons butter
2 quarts milk
white pepper, to taste
paprika, to taste

8 tablespoons flour
1 pound shredded American, or
   Cheddar cheese

Melt butter in top of double boiler. Stir in flour, to make a smooth paste. Stir or whisk continously while over heat until smooth and thickened. Add cheese, stirring until melted. Sprinkle with pepper and paprika. Place over bottom of double boiler and hot water. Cover and keep hot over low heat. Serve over toast.

Helen Evancie

MISCELLANEOUS

PEANUT BRITTLE

2 cups sugar
1 cup light corn syrup
⅓ cup water

1 pound salted peanuts
1 tablespoon butter
1 tablespoon baking soda

Grease two cookie sheets and keep in low heat oven. Place sugar, corn syrup and water in large pot and cook to rolling boil, stirring down until soft ball stage forms. Stir in peanuts. Reduce heat to medium; continue to stir. Stir in butter and baking soda. Mix well, stirring constantly. Pour half of mixture onto each pan. Spread to ¼ inch thickness. Cool and break into pieces. *Yield:* approximately 2 pounds.

The Committee

MIRACLE FROSTING

1 cup sugar
1 egg white, unbeaten
¼ teaspoon cream of tartar

½ cup boiling water
½ teaspoon vanilla

Mix sugar, egg white, cream of tartar. Add boiling water and beat on high speed, add vanilla. *Note:* This is a quick and inexpensive marshmallow type frosting.

Carol Lourich

CREAMY TOMATO SAUCE TOPPING

3 tablespoons butter
1 to 2 tablespoons flour
salt, to taste

1 8 ounce can tomato sauce
sugar, to taste

Melt butter in pan with flour. Add approximately 4 ounces water and stir until smooth. Add tomato sauce, sugar and salt to taste. This sauce is delicious over mashed potatoes, pork chops, hamburgers, or when you are serving a "dry meat dish", such as meatloaf.

Diane Mulhern

for your information

FOR YOUR INFORMATION

"THE COOK'S A B C 'S"

Al dente - Italian term used to describe food, especially pasta, cooked firm to the bite. Frequently used in reference to vegetables.

Bard - Wrap meat with a fat (salt pork or bacon) so it won't dry out and done to improve the flavor.

Baste - Moisten food as it cooks, with sauce, pan drippings, or fat.

Bind - Hold a mixture of foods together with egg, cream, mayonnaise or a sauce.

Blanch - Cook in, or cover with, boiling water for a few minutes.

Blaze (Flambe) - Pour warm spirits over a given dish and ignite with a match.

Braise - Cook covered in a small amount of liquid, in the oven or on top of the range.

Bread - Coat a food (meat, fish, croquettes) in bread crumbs.

Caramelize - Cook sugar over moderate heat, stirring constantly until it turns into a golden syrup.

Coat - Cover food completely with flour, grated cheese, or crumbs. Food is also "coated" with aspic or a sauce.

Cream - Work shortening and sugar together until light and fluffy using spoon, electric beater or hands.

Cube - Cut food into precise cubes.

Cut in - Work the shortening into the flour with two knives or a pastry blender.

Dice - Cut into very small cubes.

Dredge - Cover food completely with a dry ingredient such as flour, cornmeal, or crumbs.

Fillet - In it's simplest sense, a cut of meat or fish without bones. Fillet as a verb is to bone a piece of meat or fish.

Fold - Blend beaten egg whites or whipped cream into a thicker, heavier mixture, using a gentle under-and-over motion that does not break down the air bubbles.

Fricassee - French word for "medley" generally understood as stew with a thickened sauce.

Grate - Pulverize food by rubbing it on, or putting it through a grater.

Herb bouquet (Bouquet garni) - "Bunch" of herbs tied together with string or secured in a cheesecloth bag. Used to flavor soups and stews during cooking and then discarded before the dish is served.

Julienne - Cut foods into long thin strips.

Knead - Means of mixing and blending, by hand, a dough that is too stiff to mix with the average implement.

Marinate - Soak in a liquid containing an acid such as lemon juice, vinegar or wine, plus seasonings and sometimes oil.

Mask - Coat or cover food completely with a sauce or aspic.

Parboil - Precook until partially done.

Pare (Peel) - Remove the outer skin by means of a small sharp knife or vegetable peeler. (You pare fruit but you peel both fruit and vegetables).

Poach - Cook eggs, fish, chicken, fruit and other delicate foods in hot liquid at a temperature below the boiling point.

Puree - Reduce food to smooth, uniform consistency by pressing it through a sieve or food mill or by whirling in a blender.

Reduce - Decrease amount of liquid by boiling uncovered over high heat. Done to intensify flavor.

Refresh - Stop the cooking process by plunging cooked foods into cold water. Helps retain flavor and sets the color.

Roast - Cook by dry heat in an oven; or on a spit in an oven, or over charcoal or in a electric rotisserie.

Sauté - Fry quickly in a small amount of fat.

Scald - Heat liquid, usually milk to temperature just below the boiling point.

Score - Partially gash the surface of foods, e.g., hams and steaks, to make decorative lines.

Sear - Brown quickly at high temperature.

Shred - Cut or pull apart a meat or vegetable into thin strips, especially for Chinese dishes.

Simmer - Cook foods in a liquid heated to just below the boiling point.

Sliver - Chop a food, especially nuts, into thin strips.

Steam - Cook a meat, fish, vegetable or pudding in a steamer or pan placed over boiling water.

Steep - Extract the essence from a food by soaking in a hot liquid.

Stew - Simmer or cook slowly. Word also means the food itself e.g., beef stew or lamb stew.

Stir-fry - Constantly stir or toss foods while cooking in a little oil over fairly high heat. An essential technique in Chinese cooking, stir-frying is most easily done in a wok.

Veronique - Garnish with white seedless grapes.

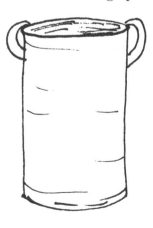

FOR YOUR INFORMATION

HERBS AND SPICES

Herbs - are the leaves of various plants grown in the temperate regions of the world. The following is a description of the more commonly used herbs which the French label "les fines herbes".

The Accent Herbs:

Chervil - more delicate and ferny than parsley, it is an aromatic, sweet herb which is prevalent in French cuisine. Use it with chicken and veal, in omelets, in Bearnaise sauce or as a garnish with green salads.

Chives - have a delicate onion flavor and are used as garnish for eggs, vegetables, salads and in hot or cold sauces.

Mint - a fragrant plant whose leaves are used to flavor salads and cold soups. A touch of mint is good with cooked green beans or peas, and it makes an excellent addition to a marinade for lamb.

Summer Savory - is similar in taste and fragrance to thyme. Finely minced, it is very good in a vinaigrette. It is usually found in prepared poultry seasonings.

Sweet Basil - a plant of the mint family with a pleasantly sweet flavor. Its use is associated with tomatoes. France has a basil paste called Pistou that is used in vegetable soups. Italians have a specialty called Pesto Genovese which is a garlickly basil sauce used as a topping for spaghetti. Use in marinades, sauces, sausages and stews.

Sweet Marjoram - tiny, slightly gray leaf of a member of the mint family, it is used in Middle European cooking for flavoring roasts, and in the famous Hungarian Goulash.

Parsley - all-around herb used in cooking as well as for garnish. It goes well with every other herb. The flat Italian type has the most flavor.

Dill - a member of the parsley family whose seed is a must for Scandinavian cooking. It has a natural affinity for radishes, cucumbers, shrimp and salmon.

Thyme - a slightly pungent herb used for stews, soups and pates. "Bouquet garni" contains a sprig of thyme.

Pungent Herbs:

Rosemary - in legend, the symbol of fidelity, its dried leaves look like pine needles. It's used with lamb and pork in Italian, Southern, French and Spanish cooking. It is also used in marinades, but remember to use sparingly.

Sage - a perennial mint which has a warm, and somewhat bitter flavor, it is very popular in British recipes, especially in stuffings. It goes well with fatty meat like pork, sausage, duck and goose.

Tarragon - an herb used predominately in French cooking. It serves as a base for Sauce Bernaise and is used in cooking, chicken and veal. In combination with other minced fresh herbs, it is excellent in crepe batter or omelettes. Tarragon butter is great on grilled fish or steak, and of course, it is used in making tarragon vinegar.

Two other very popular herbs that must be considered are the bay leaf and oregano.

Bay leaf - comes from the laurel tree and is used in stocks, sauces, marinades and in Bouquet Garni.

Oregano - is wild marjoram. Its crushed olive green leaves have a pungent flavor which is commonly used in Southern Italian Cooking.

Spices - are parts of certain plants-the bark, the root, the flower buds, that grow in the tropical regions of the world. The following are the most commonly used spices.

Cloves - the dark brown, unopened bud of a tree flower found in Zanzibar and Madagascar that has a spicy, sweet, penetrating flavor. It is sold whole or ground.

Cinnamon - is the inner bark of Cinnamon zeylancium which is found in Ceylon. It has a mild flavor and is sold in sticks or ground.

Nutmeg - is the kernel of fruit of the Myristica tree, grown in Indonesia. It is sold whole or ground.

Mace - is the network around the nutmeg kernel; it is light orange in color when dried and ground. It is of course similar to nutmeg in aroma but has a different flavor.

Ginger - the root of an herbaceous plant which comes in two forms: black ginger and white ginger.

Allspice - is the dried berry of the pimento tree whose flavor resembles a combination of cloves, cinnamon and nutmeg.

FOR YOUR INFORMATION

KITCHEN TIPS

To store unused garlic cloves: Peel and store in salad oil in covered jar. Garlic remains fresh; oil may be used in salad dressing.

Immerse garlic cloves in very hot water for 5 minutes. They'll peel easily. This also works for onions, as well as peaches and tomatoes.

To pulverize a garlic bud without a press, put the bud, skin included, between 2 thicknesses of waxed paper and hit it several times with a hammer.

To locate garlic clove in salad dressing or other dishes stick a toothpick through the clove. In this way, you can easily locate it when it is to be removed.

Use grapefruit juice in place of vinegar in oil-vinegar salad dressing for an unusual flavor.

Add ½ to 1 teaspoon baking powder to frying batter *or* substitute buttermilk baking mix for flour. Fish, chicken, etc., will have a delicious crust. Also, a tablespoon of sherry or brandy is particularly delicious in frying fish and seafood.

Or add a little sherry to the egg if you use it as a coating for fried fish.

Chicken or meat pieces, chilled for an hour or more before being breaded or floured, will retain the coating much better during cooking.

Want a crisp, brown crust on your roast or broiled chicken? Rub mayonnaise over the skin first or coat with Italian Salad dressing and sprinkle with paprika.

Prick cooking bacon thoroughly with a fork. It will lie flat.

Mix ½ can of beer with small can of tomato paste or purée and add to beef stew and pot roast for a delicious gravy.

Substitute coffee for water in making gravy; adds color and a richer taste; *or* add a bit of instant coffee powder.

To reheat rolls or biscuits without having them harden, dip fingers in cold water and sprinkle into a brown paper bag. Do this several times (do not get bag more than damp). Put in rolls, twist bag tightly closed, and put in 300 degree oven about 15 minutes. Same applies to bread.

A leftover baked potato can be reheated if dipped in water and allowed to re-bake in a 350 degree oven for 20 minutes.

Bacon dices easily when frozen. Stack frozen slices and cut with scissors.

When broiling meats such as bacon or hamburgers on a rack, place a slice or two of dry bread in the broiler pan to soak up the dripped fat. This not only helps to eliminate smoking fat but reduces the chance of the fat catching fire.

For a more tender pie crust, use less water than is called for.

Always peel off paper liners from cupcakes or muffins while they are still hot.

Freeze an angel food cake; then thaw it. You will be amazed how easily it slices.

Nut, pumpkin, cranberry breads slice better if put in freezer for about an hour before; or use knife whose blade has been held over gas flame. This method is a sure bet for fruit cake.

Cake pans need only be greased on the bottoms, not on the sides. Most cakes rise more evenly when they can cling to ungreased sides while baking. The sides can be loosened with a thin knife before removal from the pans.

For a beautiful, unfrosted cake, place lacy paper doily on the top of the cake. Sift powdered sugar on top of the doily. Carefully remove doily for a lacy sugar pattern.

Bake brownies 5 minutes less than box requires and leave overnight, covered. They cut more easily and are more fudgie.

Forget to take eggs out of refrigerator? Either put them in warm water for a few minutes, or if you wish to boil them, stick a pin into the pointed end of each egg. They will not crack.

Easy way to peel hard boiled egg: Roll it under your hand on a hard surface while it is still hot. Peel under cold water. The finer the cracks the easier the shells will come off.

To slice hard cooked eggs without crumbling the yoke, first dip knife in water.

For tender hamburgers: add one grated raw potato for each pound of ground meat for luscious, juicy hamburgers; or add salt to taste to four tablespoons of ice water to one pound of chopped meat, or add same amount of club soda; or put an ice cube in center of uncooked hamburger.

Freeze fresh cranberries before you grind them. Ground frozen, you will have no mess. The same is true of oranges, if you plan to combine them with the cranberries for relish.

FOR YOUR INFORMATION

Dates, figs, etc. cut or chop more easily if you freeze them for 1 to 2 hours before cutting. Knife or scissors dipped in hot water frequently, while cutting helps, too.

A bit of sugar added to paprika accentuates its flavor.

Spray gelatin mold with vegetable oil before filling for easier unmolding.

Cheese grates more easily if placed in freezer for an hour. Cheese grater sprayed inside and out with vegetable oil washes more easily.

Use warm water in making ice cubes. They freeze quicker and are crystal clear.

For perfect lettuce leaves: core head of lettuce; place in colander and place under running cold water. Force of water separates leaves. Allow to drain and then pull apart.

Allow meat to "rest" 15 minutes after it comes from the oven. This gives juices time to settle and makes carving easier.

Leftover whipped cream will retain its lightness, height and texture a day or more (refrigerated) if when whipping you add 1 teaspoon light corn syrup to each ½ pint of cream or one envelope of unflavored gelatin for each pint.

To have membrane - free orange sections: let orange stand, covered with boiling water for 5 to 10 minutes before being peeled.

You can reuse cooking fat. Add a few slices of raw potato, bring to boil and strain through a few thicknesses of cheesecloth.

Leftover soups put into blender make delicious and different sauces for vegetables or meats and fish. Try combining several kinds.

Fresh lima beans have a delicious taste if they are cooked together with a whole onion.

Ever try, baking whole, fresh beets? Delicious!

To coat a casserole evenly with butter or shortening, first chill the casserole well, then apply melted butter or shortening with a brush.

Always wash unhulled strawberries. If hulled first, they will soak up water.

Also wash mushrooms in cold water to which 2 to 3 teaspoons of flour has been added. They will stay white and not absorb the water.

For a high meringue: add ½ teaspoon of baking powder to room temperature egg whites before beating.

SIMPLE SUBSTITUTES

For These	*Use These*
1 whole egg, for thickening or baking	2 egg yolks; *or* 2 tablespoons dried whole egg plus 2½ tablespoons water.
1 cup butter or margarine for shortening	⅞ cup lard, or rendered fat, with ½ teaspoon salt; *or* 1 cup hydrogenated fat (cooking fat sold under brand name) with ½ tablespoon salt.
1 square (oz) chocolate	3 or 4 tablespoons cocoa plus ½ tablespoon fat.
1 teaspoon double acting baking powder	1½ teaspoons phosphate baking powder; *or* 2 teaspoons tartrate baking powder.
Sweet milk and baking powder for baking	Equal amount of sour milk plus ½ teaspoon soda per cup. (Takes the place of 2 teaspoons baking powder and 1 cup sweet milk).
1 cup sour milk for baking	1 cup sweet milk mixed with one of the following: 1 teaspoon vinegar; *or* 1 tablespoon lemon juice; *or* 1¾ teaspoons cream of tartar.
1 cup whole milk	½ cup evaporated milk plus ½ cup water; *or* 4 tablespoons dry whole milk plus 1 cup water; *or* 4 tablespoons nonfat milk plus 2 teaspoons tablespoons fat and 1 cup water.
1 cup skim milk	4 tablespoons nonfat dry milk plus 1 cup water.
1 tablespoon flour for thickening	½ teaspoon cornstarch, potato starch, rice starch, or arrowroot starch; *or* 1 tablespoon granulated tapioca.

FOR YOUR INFORMATION

1 cup cake flour for baking	Up to ½ cup bran, whole-wheat flour, or corn meal plus enough all purpose flour to fill a cup.
For 1 cup white sugar	1 cup powdered sugar *or*, 1¾ cups powdered sugar *or*, 1 cup packed brown sugar *or*, 2 cups corn syrup *or*, ¾ cup honey *or*, ¾ cup maple syrup *or*, 1 cup molasses

TIMETABLE FOR BRAISING

Cut	Average Weight or Thickness	Cooking Time
Beef		
Pot Roast	3-5 pounds	3-5 hours
Swiss Steak	1½-2½ inches	2-3 hours
Short Ribs	Pieces 2 x 2 x 4 inches	1½ hours
Round Steak	¾ inch	45-60 minutes
Pork		
Chops	¾-1½ inches	45-60 minutes
Spareribs	2-3 pounds	1½ hours
Tenderloin (Whole)	¾-1 pound	45-60 hours
Tenderloin (fillets)	½ inch	30 minutes
Lamb		
Breast - Stuffed	2-3 pounds	1½-2 hours
Breast - Rolled	1½-2 pounds	1½-2 hours
Shanks	½ pound each	1½ hours
Veal		
Breast - Stuffed	3-4 pounds	1½-2 hours
Breast - Rolled	2-3 pounds	1½-2 hours
Birds	½ x 2 x 4 inches	45-60 minutes
Chops	½ x ¾ inch	45-60 minutes
Chops - Breaded	½ x ¾ inch	45-60 minutes
Steaks or cutlets	½ x ¾ inch	45-60 minutes
Shoulder chops	½ x ¾ inch	45-60 minutes

TIMETABLE FOR BROILING

		Minutes	
	Weight	Rare	Medium
Beef			
Filet mignon - 1 inch	⅓	5	7
Filet mignon - 1½ inches	½	9-10	12
Filet mignon - 2 inches	¾	15	18
Club steak - 1 inch	1	9-10	12-14
Club steak - 1½ inches	1¼	14-16	18-20
Club steak - 2 inches	1½	18-22	24-30
Sirloin steak - 1 inch	3	10-12	14-16
Sirloin steak - 1½ inches	4¼	15-20	20-25
Sirloin steak - 2 inches	5¾	20-25	25-30
Porterhouse steak - 1 inch	2	9-10	12-15
Porterhouse steak - 1½ inches	2½	14-16	18-20
Porterhouse steak - 2 inches	3	18-22	25-30
Ground patties (1 x 3 inches)	4 ounces	15	25
Lamb			
Shoulder chops - 1 inch	3 ounces	10	12
Shoulder chops - 1½ inches	6 ounces	15	18
Rib chops - 1 inch	2 ounces	10	12
Rib chops - 2 inches	3 ounces	18	22
Loin chops - 1 inch	3 ounces	10	12
Loin chops - 2 inches	6 ounces	18	22
Pork			
Ham Slice - ½ inch	¾-1 pound	*	20
Ham Slice - 1 inch	1½-2 pounds	*	25-30
Ham Slice - tenderized		*	
Ham Slice - ½ inch	¾-1 pound	*	16-20
Ham Slice - 1 inch	1½-2 pounds	*	10-12

*Ham is always cooked well done.

FOR YOUR INFORMATION

TIMETABLES FOR ROASTING

Meat	Weight (Pounds)	Oven Temp.	Meat Reading	Time per Pound in Minutes
Beef				
Standing Ribs (3 ribs)	7-8	300	140*	18-20
			160**	22-15
			170***	27-30
Rolled ribs	6-8	300	140*	32
			160**	38
			170***	48
Rump	5-7	300	150-170	25-30
Whole Tenderloin	4-6	300	140*	25
			160**	30-35
Pork, Fresh				
Loin - Center	3-4	350	185	35-40
Loin - Whole	8-15	350	185	15-20
Loin - End	3-4	350	185	50-55
Shoulder - Whole	12-14	350	185	30-35
Shoulder - Boned and Rolled	4-6	350	185	40-45
Spareribs	1½-1¾	350	185	40-45
Pork Butt	4-6	350	185	45-50
Ham	10-18	350	185	30-35
Pork, Smoked				
Ham - Whole	10-12	300	170	25
Ham - Half	6	300	170	30
Ham - Picnic	3-10	300	170	35
Lamb				
Leg	6½-7½	300	175-180	30-35
Shoulder - Rolled	3-4	300	175-180	40-45
Shoulder	4½-5½	300	175-180	30-35
Rack of Ribs (6-7 ribs)	2	300	175-180	45-50
Crown (12-15 ribs)	4	300	175-180	30-35
Veal				
Leg roast	7-8	300	170	25
Loin	4½-5	300	170	30-35
Rack (4-6 ribs)	2½-3	300	170	30-35
Shoulder	7	300	170	25
Shoulder - Rolled	5	300	170	40-45

*Rare
**Medium
***Well done

FOR YOUR INFORMATION

FOLLOW THIS *LOW* CALORIE DIET MENU AND *EAT ALL* THE *ICE CREAM* YOU WANT!

Monday
Breakfast: weak tea
Lunch: (1) bouillon cube in half cup diluted water
Dinner: one pigeon thigh; 3 ounce prune juice (gargle only)

Tuesday
Breakfast: scraped crumbs from burnt toast
Lunch: one doughnut hole (without sugar), one glass of dehydrated water
Dinner: three grains cornmeal (broiled)

Wednesday
Breakfast: shredded egg shell skin
Lunch: one half dozen poppy seeds
Dinner: bee's knees and mosquito knuckles sautéed in vinegar

Thursday
Breakfast: boiled out stains of old table cloths
Lunch: belly button of a navel orange
Dinner: three eyes from Irish potatoes (diced)

Friday
Breakfast: two lobster antennas
Lunch: one tail of a sea horse
Dinner: rotisserie broiled guppy filet

Saturday
Breakfast: four chopped banana seeds
Lunch: broiled butterfly liver
Dinner: jelly vertebrae a la centipede

Sunday
Breakfast: pickled humming bird tongue
Lunch: prime rib of tadpole; aroma of empty custard pie plate
Dinner: tossed paprika and clover leaf salad

Note: a 7 ounce glass of steam may be consumed on alternate days to help in having something to blow off.

INDEX

INDEX

APPETIZERS
Almond Prune Appetizers 8
Artichoke Pie 8
Wrapped Bread Sticks 8
Easy Buffalo Wings 9
Cheese Ball 9
Cream Cheese Balls 9
Chopped Chicken Liver and Eggs 16
Delicious Chopped Chicken Liver 10
Baked Clams 10
Baked Clams 13
Clam Dip 11
Hot Clam Dip 11
Clam Pie 12
Clam Spread 13
Crabmeat Appetizer 13
Crabmeat Mold 14
#1 Crabmeat Spread 14
Hot Crab Spread 14
Escargots 15
Sweet and Pungent Cocktail Franks 15
Grape Appetizers 16
Guacamole Dip 16
Guamanian Cheese Canapes 15
Herb Dip 17
Quiche Lorraine 17
Party Meatballs 24
Misto Fritto 25
Italian Garlic Mozzarella Bread 24
Meat Filled Mushroom Caps 25
Pickled Mushrooms 19
Stuffed Mushrooms 17
Olive Cheese Ball 18
Toasted Onion Canapes 18
Sweet Red Pepper Relish 18
Pizza Roll 19
Russian Pashka 21
Hot Sausage and Cheese Puffs 20
Sausage and Spinach Pie 20
Shrimp Spread 21
Shrimp Dip For Vegetables 22
Hot Spinach Balls 21
Spinach Dip 22
Spinach Pie 22
Taco Dip 23
Walking Taco 23
Zucchini Appetizers 23
SOUPS AND SALADS
SOUPS
Barley Soup 28
Yankee Bean Soup 28
Broccoli Soup 29
Cream of Celery Soup 29
Chicken Soup 30

Easy Clam Bisque 31
Chick Corn Soup 30
Fish Chowder 30
Blender Gazpacho 31
Lentil Soup 31
Minestrone Soup 32
Mushroom Barley Soup 32
Onion Soup 35
French Onion Soup 33
Pea Soup 33
Split Pea Soup 34
Creamed Potato Soup 34
SALADS
Three Bean Salad 35
Broccoli Salad 36
Carrot Salad 36
California Chicken Salad 37
Cold Chicken and Pasta 37
Cole Slaw 36
Cole Slaw 38
Cranberry Gelatin Salad 38
Creamy Cranberry Mold 39
Cucumber Aspic 38
Marinated Cucumber Salad 39
Five Cup Salad 39
Macaroni Salad 40
Orzo Salad 40
Cold Pasta Salad 40
Mexican Pineapple Cabbage Salad 42
Pistachio Coconut Surprise 42
Basic Potato Salad 43
Rotelli Salad 41
Spinach Salad 41
Spinach Salad 43
Taco Salad 42
Tomato Mozzarella Salad 44
Vinegarette Dressing 44
BREADS
Apple Muffins 46
Banana Bread 46
Beer Bread 47
Blueberry Muffins 46
3 C Bread 47
Corn Sticks 47
Cranberry Nut Bread 48
Irish Soda Bread 48
Simple Irish Soda Bread 49
Pumpkin Nut Bread 49
Pepperoni Bread 50
Candlelight Popovers 50
Sour Cream Muffins 52
Strawberry Bread . . . . , ... 51
Swiss Onion Spiral Bread 51
Yogurt Bread 52

INDEX

Zucchini Bread.....................53
Zucchini Cheddar Bread.............53
Zucchini Nut Loaf..................53

POULTRY
Almond Chicken....................104
Sherried Artichoke Chicken..........105
Baked Chicken.....................104
Barbecued Chicken.................104
Barbecued Chicken.................107
Chicken-Bob.......................109
Shells with Chicken and Broccoli.......106
Chicken in Brown Gravy.............107
Chicken Cacciatore.................108
Cheese-Filled Chicken Breasts........106
Chicken Confetti...................109
Chicken Cordon Bleu................107
Chicken Cordon Bleu................108
Chicken Delicious..................110
Chicken Divan.....................111
Foolproof Fried Chicken.............110
Janet's Chicken Kiev................105
Lucie's Chicken....................108
Chicken Marinara..................110
Chicken Marsala...................111
Chicken and Peppers................111
Chicken Breast Piquant.............112
Chicken Cutlets Alla Pizzaiola.........112
Chicken in a Pot...................112
Chicken and Rice Dinner............113
Roast Chicken with Vegetables........114
Chicken Roll Up....................113
Sweet and Sour Chicken.............114
Chicken Cutlets in Wine.............115
Chicken Breast in Wine..............115
Coq Au Vin........................113
Golden Chicken Wings..............115
Turkey Croquettes..................116

SEAFOOD
Alaskan Crab Cakes.................122
Ciopino Fish Stew..................120
Lobster Shell Stock.................119
Mussels Piquant....................123
Mussels with Rice..................118
Salmon Loaf.......................125
Scalloped Scallops..................118
Scampi Alla Livronese...............124
Seafood Scampi....................121
Barbecued Shark Steak..............118
Shrimp Curry......................121
Shrimp in Garlic Butter.............121
Shrimp De Jonghe..................120
Marinated Shrimp..................125
Shrimp Milanese...................122
Shrimp Scampi.....................123

Shrimp Scampi.....................124
Shrimp Scampi.....................125
Shrimp Scampi.....................126
Tunaburgers.......................126
Tuna Cakes........................126

CAKES
Apple Cake........................128
Apple Walnut Cake.................128
Banana Cake.......................128
Banana Nut Cake...................132
No Bake Banana Split Cake...........135
Blueberry Tea Cake.................137
Carrot Cake.......................129
Carrot Pineapple Cake...............130
Cheesecake........................129
Cheesecake........................130
Cheesecake........................131
Cheesecake........................132
Rosalie's Blueberry Cheesecake.......132
Marie's Brass Rail Cheese Cake.......133
California Style Cheese Cake.........133
Chocolate Swirl Cheesecake..........136
Cream Cheese Cakes................134
Deluxe Cheesecake.................134
Fluffy and Light Cheesecake.........136
Melt-In-Your-Mouth Cheesecake.......137
Mini Cheese Cakes.................147
Peaches 'N Cream Cheese Cake.......135
Black Midnight Cake................138
Dark Chocolate Cake................138
Sour Cream Chocolate Cake..........140
Sour Cream Chocolate Frosting.......140
Chocolate Chip Crumb Cake.........139
Chocolate Chip and Nut Cake........145
Filled Coffee Cake.................139
Sour Cream Coffee Cake.............148
Streusel Coffee Cake................146
Walnut Sour Cream Coffee Cake......147
Crumb Cake.......................148
Crumb Cake.......................144
Aunt Jean's Tasty Crumb Cake........145
Blender Custard Cake...............137
Old Fashioned Granola Cake..........141
Jelly Roll.........................141
German Kuchen....................144
Lazy Crazy Cake...................142
Pistachio Cake....................143
Jewish Pound Cake.................141
Mace Pound Cake..................140
Sour Cream Pound Cake.............143
Red Velvet Cake...................142
Ricotta Cake.......................131
Rum Cake.........................146
White Cake........................142

INDEX

Zucchini Cake...................149

ETHNIC

CHINESE
Chicken with Nuts in Hoisin Sauce.....195
Chow Mein......................192
Egg Rolls with Chicken............194
Pork with Black Bean and
   Garlic Sauce..................193
Chinese Sweet and Sour Pork........192
Sweet and Sour Pork...............191
Shrimp with Lobster Sauce..........191
Tung Ting Lake Shrimp............196
Spicy Triple Delight................190
Oriental String Beans..............190

CZECHOSLOVAKIAN
Houska.........................197

FINLAND
Finnish Pancakes..................198

FRENCH
Chicken, Shrimp and Scallop
   Provencale....................198
Epiphany Cake....................199

GERMAN
Chicken Corn Soup................199
Hoppelpoppel.....................202
Kartoffelklosse...................201
Kartoffel Pfannkuchen..............201
Sauerbraten......................200
Spatzle.........................202
Wiener Schnitzel..................203

GREEK
Spana Kopeta.....................203

HAITIAN
Grillot..........................204
Riz Et Pois National...............205
Sauce Ti Malice...................204

HUNGARY
Cabbage and Haluska...............205
Palaczynta.......................206

ITALIAN
Chick Peas and Macaroni...........207
Italian Cookies....................207
Italian Fig Cookies.................206
Fettucine Alfredo..................208
Macaroni and Broccoli..............209
Italian Meat Sauce.................208
Spaghetti Carbonaro...............208
Baked Spaghetti and Cheese.........210
Ziti Al Forno.....................209

LITHUANIAN
Potato Kugel.....................210

MEXICAN
Flan............................211
Picadillo........................210

SPANISH
Beef and Rice Fiesta...............213
Flan with Cheese..................211
Paella..........................212

SWEDISH
Swedish Meatballs.................213

KID'S KORNER
Apple Crisp......................216
Betty or Barney Bread..............217
French Cheese Bread...............216
Kid's Broccoli Casserole............217
Brownies........................218
Butter Crunch....................218
Carrot Cake......................220
Kathy's Karrots...................218
Chewies.........................216
Choc-Oat Bars....................219
Chocolate Cookies.................219
Chocolate Cookie Treats............221
Chocolate Cream Pie...............219
Cathy's Clam Dip..................217
Homemade Cracker Jacks..........223
Dormir Sonado....................223
Homestyle Frank and Cheese Dinner...220
Foolproof Chocolate Fudge...........221
Fudge Cake......................222
Peanut Fudge.....................221
Gelatin Blox......................223
Ginger Snaps.....................224
Country Style Granola Snack........222
Orange Oatmeal Cookies............222
Homemade Peanut Butter...........223
Peanut Butter Rolls................226
8 Minute Light 'N Fruity Pie.........224
Popeye Salad.....................226
Pretzels.........................224
Reuben Sandwiches................225
Rice Cereal Treats.................225
Safety Rules for Youngsters..........227
Child's Summer Salad Lunch.........225
Giant Snickerdoodles...............227
Strawberry-Orange Ice..............226

VEGETABLES
Artichoke Pie..................... 56
Artichoke Rice Salad............... 56
Green Beans Caesar................ 57
Baked Broccoli.................... 57
Carol's Broccoli Casserole.......... 58
Broccoli and Cheese Puff........... 58
Rice and Cheese Broccoli Casserole.... 58
Broccoli Cheese Quiche............. 59
Broccoli, Mushroom, Swiss Quiche...... 59
Sweet N' Sour Red Cabbage......... 56

Creamed Carrots.................... 60
Curried Cauliflower Casserole 60
Golden Cheese Bake 60
Fried Eggplant 59
Stuffed Eggplant Rolls 61
Corn Fritters...................... 61
Lima Beans with Bacon 62
Misto Fritto 63
Mushrooms Bordelaise 62
Stuffed Mushrooms................. 63
Beer Batter Onion Rings 64
Potatoes Au Gratin 63
Potatoes Oreganato 64
Potato Pancakes.................... 67
Potato Pudding..................... 64
Potato Soufflé..................... 65
Rice Pilaf 65
Savory Spinach 66
Spinach Pie....................... 66
Spinach Pie....................... 67
Spinach Quiche..................... 66
Zucchini 68
Baked Zucchini..................... 68
Fried Zucchini 68
Zucchini Lasagna................... 70
Zucchini Pie 69
Italian Zucchini Quiche 69

CASSEROLES
Chinese Beef Casserole.............. 73
Beef Chow Mein Casserole........... 72
Broccoli Quiche 72
Saucy Cheese Bake 76
Cheese Casserole................... 77
Chicken and Broccoli................ 72
Chicken Casserole 74
Chicken Divan 75
Hot Chicken Salad.................. 74
Baked Chick Peas 74
Texas Chili 73
Hamburger Corn Bread Pie........... 75
Hamburger Pie 78
Quick Italian Casserole 80
Beef and Macaroni Casserole 76
Old Fashioned Macaroni and Cheese.... 78
Macaroni, Cheese and Tuna 78
Pork Chop, Onion, Rice Bake 80
Pork Chops and Potatoes 81
Rattatouille, Low Calorie 79
Cheese Sausage Casserole 81
Italian Sausage and Lentil Skillet 79
Spaghetti Pie 77
Tuna Casserole.................... 81
Elephant Stew..................... 82

MEATS
Barbecued Beef..................... 88
Beef Paprika....................... 84
French Beef Stew 85
Good Beef Stew 85
Three Hour Beef Stew 86
Winter Barbecued Roast Beef Dinner... 86
Glazed Corned Beef with Vegetables.... 87
Quick Frankfurter Potato Skillet 88
Hamburger Stroganoff 88
Ham Hawaiian...................... 89
Barbecued Lamb.................... 89
Polish Kielbasa and Sauerkraut 89
Meatballs in Buttermilk 84
Granny's Meatballs 91
Sweet and Sour Meatballs 90
Italian Meatloaf 91
Stuffed Peppers, Low Calorie.......... 90
Chops and Stuffing 95
Favorite Pork Chops 93
Oven Baked Pork Chops.............. 94
Polynesian Sweet and Sour Pork 94
Pork Roast 95
Country Style Pot Roast.............. 92
Firehouse Pot Roast 91
Mushroom Pot Roast................. 92
Savory Pot Roast.................... 92
Barbecued Ribs 93
Chinese Spareribs 93
Rosy Ribs.......................... 96
Rice Balls.......................... 99
Sausage and Peppers................. 95
Sausage and Spinach Pie.............. 97
Minute Steak Stew 98
Pepper Steak 96
Pepper Steak 98
Shortcut Cube Steak Stew 97
Steak Teriyaki 98
Veal Cordon Bleu.................... 99
Veal Scallopini Marsala 101
Veal Stew Italian Style 100
Venison Steak Providence Style........101

COOKIES
Almond Crescents ....,..152
Almond Icebox Cookies...............152
Joanne's Brownies 154
Van's Green Brownies 153
Linzer Cookies......................152
German Butter Cookie Kisses 155
Jam Butter Cookies..................156
Candy Cane Cookies 153
Chocolate Chip Cookies..............154
Chocolate Cinnamon Bars............154
Chocolate Kiss Cookies..............155

INDEX

Chocolate Lassies 155
Chocolate Peanut Butter Pile-Ups 156
Chocolatetown Chip Cookies 156
Christmas Cookies.................... 158
Christmas Cookies.................... 160
Cream Cheese Cookies 158
Merry Cheese Cakes 157
Creme De Menthe Bars 157
Fruitcake Cookies 158
Ice Box Cookies 163
Lemon Squares 160
Mexican Besitos De Meringue 159
Mexican Wedding Cakes 164
Oatmeal Cookies 161
Paluski............................. 161
Christmas Pecan Balls............... 160
Pinoli.............................. 161
Sandies 163
Seven Layer Bars 162
Shortbread 159
Spritz Cookies 164
Spritz Cookies 165
"No-Stir" Squares 162
Strufoli, Honey Balls................. 166
Tea Tessies 162
Thumbprint Cookies 163
Vanilla Cookies...................... 165
Walnut Crescents.................... 164

DESSERTS

Ambrosia 168
Apricot Salad Mold 168
Crustless Creamy Cheesecake 170
Cream Cheese Tarts 173
Quick Cherry Crisp 170
Cherry Delight...................... 171
Chocolate Mousse 172
Cold Chocolate Souffle 172
Chocolate Yummy 171
Cream Puffs........................ 174
Black Forest Crepes 169
4 Layer Dessert..................... 174
Banana Donuts...................... 174
Donut Holes........................ 176
Fruit Cocktail and Cream Dessert...... 172
Fruit Gelatin 175
Fresh Fruit Medley.................. 168
Striped Gelatin Mold 175
Hawaiian Delight.................... 176
Jewel Dessert....................... 173
Ice Box Cake 176
Meltaways.......................... 177
Meringues.......................... 178
Brandied Peaches.................... 170
Easy Fresh Peach Cobbler 177

Glazed Peach Creme 175
Apple Crumb Pie.................... 178
French Apple Pie.................... 181
Impossible French Apple Pie 180
Cheese Cake Pie 177
Cherry Cream Cheese Pie 178
Cherry Pie Supreme 179
Cream Cheese Pie................... 179
Low Calorie Fruit Pie............... 181
Impossible Pie 185
Frozen Lemon Pie................... 184
Lime Chiffon Pie 180
Pumpkin Ice Cream Pie 181
Raspberry Ribbon Pie............... 182
Strawberry Frozen Pie 183
Strawberry Ice Cream Pie 183
Raspberry Dessert 183
Rice Pudding 185
Creamy Rice Pudding............... 184
Old Fashioned Rice Pudding.......... 184
Snow Pudding with Custard Sauce 182
Sour Cream Twists 186
Strawberries Romanoff............... 185
Trifle 187
Walnut Cream Roll 186

BEVERAGES, MICROWAVE, MISCELLANEOUS

BEVERAGES

Gardner's Apple Cider Cooler 230
Blackberry Brandy 230
Champagne Punch................... 230
Coffee Liquor...................... 231
Egg Nog........................... 231
Joanne's Eggnog 231
Spiced Fruit Punch 233
Homemade Irish Cream 230
Pat's Orange Cooler................. 231
Orange Liquor 232
Plum Cordial 232
Strawberry Daiquiri 233
Summer Punch...................... 232

MICROWAVE

Apple Betty 234
1 Minute Garlic Bread............... 233
Chicken Cutlets Mozzarella........... 235
Chili.............................. 234
Chocolate Pudding.................. 235
Hamburger Medley 236
Lasagne 236
Mini Pizza......................... 234
Nachos 235
Home Style Pot Roast............... 237

MISCELLANEOUS

Applesauce......................... 237

INDEX

Barbecue Sauce .237
Ed's Barbecue Sauce 238
Miracle Frosting 240
Hot Fudge Sauce 238
House Fragrance 228
Beer Marinade for Beef. 238
Three Day Marmalade 239
Peanut Brittle. .240
Personal Pizzas. 239

Creamy Tomato Sauce Topping 240
Welsh Rabbit 239
FOR YOUR INFORMATION
The Cook's ABC's 242
Herbs and Spices 244
Kitchen Tips 246
Simple Substitutes. 249
Timetables 250
Reducing Diet .253

NOTES